Dale Lindskog

Diagnosis and Dissolution

From Augustine's Picture to Wittgenstein's Picture Theory

PETER LANG
Europäischer Verlag der Wissenschaften

Bibliographic Information published by the Deutsche Nationalbibliothek
The Deutsche Nationalbibliothek lists this publication in the Deutsche Nationalbibliografie; detailed bibliographic data is available in the internet at <http://www.d-nb.de>.

ISSN 1439-7668
ISBN 978-3-631-55732-7
US-ISBN 0-8204-8727-9

Printed in Germany 1 2 3 4 5 7

www.peterlang.de

For Candace and Katharine

Preface

In the preface to *Philosophical Investigations*, Wittgenstein remarks that his mature philosophical reflection can be seen in the right light only against the background of his old philosophy. There is evidence for this in the extent to which differences of opinion—over the correct interpretation of Wittgenstein's later work—often turn on disagreements over what are the important features of his transition from the early philosophy. But in itself this is not peculiar to the study of Wittgenstein. Like many other philosophers, his thinking is a reaction against some old way of thinking. Consequently, misunderstanding his earlier work can effect a misunderstanding of his later criticisms. This is comparable, for example, to the importance of the rationalist-empiricist debate for understanding Kant's *Critique*; and it would be an instance of the general rule that philosophical reflection does not act in a vacuum, but rather in the stream of the history of philosophy.

There is however a more subtle sense in which this is particularly true for Wittgenstein. He reminds us again and again that his intention is not to solve philosophical problems, but rather to dissolve them. Just what this amounts to could be called the *Grundgedanke* of this book, and I shall have a great deal to say about it. Yet even straightaway it is clear that this conception of philosophy must affect the relationship between his earlier and later work. That relationship must be fundamentally different from that of one theory being superseded by another. For the relationship between two such theories is that they are supposed to be in competition for the truth. Hence they *both* are supposed to be an answer or set of answers to a question or set of questions. The two theories are therefore independently intelligible. Roughly speaking, 'answers', though parasitic on the 'questions', are intelligible in isolation from other answers. However, if we are to take seriously Wittgenstein's non-theoretical characterization of his later thinking, we should suspect that it has a much more intimate relationship to his earlier work.

This book is a revision of my PhD thesis. The second chapter originates in things I wrote in 1994, when I was an MA student at York University. And a very rough draft was written in 1997. I have incurred many debts along the way. My greatest debt is to my PhD supervisor, Stuart Shanker, not only for his comments on various drafts. More importantly, he coached me through most every stage of writing, from my most inchoate and even harebrained ideas, right through to the finished product. Without the benefit of these discussions—his comments, criticisms, and encouragement—this book would be a good deal poorer than it is.

I am also greatly indebted to Peter Hacker, who supervised me in 1996, while I was a visiting student at St. John's College, Oxford. During this time I was writing very quickly, and very roughly. In sorting through my virtually unintelligible essays, he went far above the call of duty with his time and patience. And his criticisms were truly invaluable: I was saved time and again from gross errors and distortions. Without the benefit of this discussion, my book would also be much poorer than it is.

Both Gordon Baker and Evan Cameron commented on drafts, and I am indebted to them for their perceptive remarks and criticisms.

Lastly, I am indebted to Norm Gall, for his generous assistance in typesetting this document.

Dale Lindskog
July, 2006

Abbreviations

The following are abbreviations I use for some of Wittgenstein's writings. Publication details are in the bibliography.

BB *The Blue and Brown Books*

NB *Notebooks 1914–1916*

OC *On Certainty*

PG *Philosophical Grammar*

PI *Philosophical Investigations*

PR *Philosophical Remarks*

TLP *Tractatus Logico-Philosophicus*

TS 220 Unpublished typescrypt by Wittgenstein

Table of Contents

1

Introduction

> Work on philosophy is actually more of a work on oneself. On one's own conception. On the way one sees things. (And what one demands of them.)
>
> TS 213, translated in Ludwig Wittgenstein, *Philosophical Occasions*, James Klagge and Alfred Nordmann (eds.) (Hackett, 1993), pp. 161f.

1.1 Preliminaries

This work examines the later Wittgenstein's treatment of the confusions embodied in the picture theory. Wittgenstein discusses these issues in many of his later writings, and although I frequently draw from these sources, the axis around which my examination revolves is his treatment in *Philosophical Investigations*. Surely the *Investigations* is the most definitive exposition of Wittgenstein's views. Furthermore, it is in *Philosophical Investigations* that we find the most painstaking treatment of these confusions.

Based on this examination, I draw conclusions about the method of philosophy propounded and practiced by the later Wittgenstein. My interpretation of both Wittgenstein's later discussion of the picture theory in particular, and of his philosophical method in general, are in many respects at odds with influential scholarship. Indeed, the following chapters are highly polemic. In this introductory chapter I will outline that disagreement, beginning with a familiar yet puzzling feature of Wittgenstein's later philosophy.

Wittgenstein claimed that, as he practiced it, philosophy was atheoretical and undogmatic (*PI* §109, §128). Any contentious claim should be dropped for the purposes of argument, for it plays no essential role in philosophical discussion. 'If one tried to advance *theses* in philosophy, it would never be possible to debate them, because everyone would agree to them' (*PI* §128).

I argue that Wittgenstein's method is diagnostic, that his method of treating a philosophical problem consists in showing how that problem arises. His method consists in tracing the kind of thinking that leads to it being felt as a problem. For the later Wittgenstein, experience reveals that tracing the genesis of how a philosophical problem arises *is* the 'solution' to that problem. The only theories which could rightly be attributed to Wittgenstein are theories about how a philosophical problem arises, or even just how a philosophical problem often arises. Or even: how a philosophical problem arose for *somebody*, e.g., Wittgenstein himself. Yet these sorts of 'theories' are among those which Wittgenstein is most happy to drop.

My outline above can be sharpened by setting it against the background of the interpretation I will criticize; I will call it the 'anti-thetical' interpretation of Wittgenstein's method. Let me, then, detail the most important tenets and presuppositions of that anti-thetical interpretation.[1] Again, a good place to start is with a likely anti-thetical response to the aforementioned puzzle about Wittgenstein's later method.

1.2 The Anti-thesis

If Wittgenstein's 'no theory' position is to be taken seriously, it needs to be explained in the following way. Wittgenstein does indeed make philosophical claims of a sort, but they are not theoretical claims. He makes 'grammatical remarks' based on observations of word usage.

Grammatical remarks are, for a proponent of the anti-thesis, remarks about the rules *we* actually employ in our use of words. Consequently, at some level we must surely be aware of these rules. 'Grammatical remarks' are in this sense 'logical claims', and in this sense *a priori*. Wittgenstein's 'grammatical remarks' are not contentious in the same kind of way that remarks about the rules of chess are not contentious to experienced chess players. (This is true, at any rate, to the extent that he restricts his remarks to clear cases.)

How is it that philosophers nonetheless manage to entangle themselves in these rules? On the anti-thetical interpretation, the reply to this is twofold. First, compared, for example, with the rules of chess, the rules governing word usage are immensely complicated, and at best poorly tabulated. This is especially so with respect to the rules relevant to philosophical problems. Second, philosophical problems may arise if one is misled by simplistic pictures of language (or segments of language), and by certain forms of expression and analogies embedded in our language. Because of this, the philosopher, but not necessarily only the philosopher, can be lead into breaking these rules, and usually in subtle and not easily noticeable ways.

According to the anti-thesis, then, philosophical problems arise through an *inadvertent* transgression of grammatical rules, and it is this which causes confusion. An entanglement in grammatical rules manifests itself in confused questions, and often in nonsensical answers to these questions. An example of such entanglement might be the question, How is it *possible* to know another has pain? This betokens confusion, probably arising from a bad comparison with a question like, How can I know she has a penny in her pocket? Under the influence of this comparison, there may be an inclination to say that the judgment that another is in pain is necessarily inferential, and that one cannot know with certainty that another is in pain. One might even consider the unwelcome conclusion that it is unintelligible to suppose that another has pain (cf. *PR* §64).

But the psychology of philosophical puzzlement is tricky business. And anyway, these explanations are, for an adherent to the anti-thesis, somewhat peripheral to the treatment of philosophical confusion. For the antidote to such confusion is a careful description of word usage. How do we *actually* use the word 'pain' when ascribing pain to others (and to ourselves)? Such a careful description will, on this view, show that the confused questions arise from *errors* in our conception, characterization, or description of the rules governing the grammar of our language.

I do not argue that the anti-thesis has got Wittgenstein completely wrong. Rather, I will argue against certain aspects of this account of Wittgenstein's method. I agree that Wittgenstein understood philosophical problems to arise as a result of a certain kind of confusion regarding word usage. I also agree that, according to Wittgenstein, this confusion is intimately related to our looking at aspects of our use of language, our 'grammar', through naive and simplistic 'pictures'. I disagree, however, that (1) a philosophical problem is necessarily rooted in an *inadvertent* 'transgression' of grammatical rules. And I disagree that (2) the *focus* of Wittgenstein's treatment of philosophical perplexity is necessarily an examination of ordinary, i.e. non-philosophical, word usage. On the contrary, it is *philosophical* word usage, i.e., the *dogmatic* application of a 'picture', that is very often the focus of Wittgenstein's treatment of philosophical problems. I suggest that this is especially true for *Philosophical Investigations* §§1–133.

Let me draw a sharper picture of these two central features of the anti-thesis. First, why is it above all the ordinary—non-philosophical—uses of words that must be investigated? Why is ordinary word usage the key to dissolving philosophical problems? For an adherent to the anti-thesis, it is because careful investigation of non-philosophical word usage will reveal that an apparently intelligible question is based, as it were, on an unintelligible assumption, viz., an 'assumption' which is itself the product of a misuse of words. Consider again the question, How can one know that someone else is in pain? This question only arises from the 'unintelligible assumption' that I at any rate *know* that *I* have pain. In this context, it is a misuse of 'know' to say that one knows that they themselves have pain. That this 'assumption' embodies a misuse of 'know' is a conclusion established by an examination of the ordinary use of 'know'.

Instead of investigating 'the nature of pain' ('the nature of time', 'the nature of colour'), we must turn 'our whole examination around... but about the fixed point of our real need' (*PI* §108). That is to say, what we really need to investigate is the use of words in ordinary contexts. What must be accepted *ab initio*, for an adherent to the anti-thesis, is that we must bring words back from their *incorrect* use, as manifest in the expression of philosophical problems, to their *correct* use, as manifest in the practice of everyday discourse (cf. *PI* §116).

Second, consider the role the anti-thesis must allot to these misleading comparisons or analogies. What importance must the anti-thesis give to their examination? What role should their examination play in the alleviation of confusion and perplexity? The examination of misleading analogies must be seen as secondary to, or at least parasitic on, the correct tabulation of the rules governing word usage in ordinary discourse. This ranking is implied by the anti-thetical conception of a philosophical problem. For if it is largely due to such analogies or pictures that philosophical problems arise; and if philosophical problems are the direct result of an (inadvertent) mischaracterization of the rules governing word usage, the role played by these pictures or analogies should be that they (at least partially) cause us, for one reason or another, to break the 'rules of grammar'. That is to say, these pictures or analogies effect a misuse of ordinary language. By comparison, therefore, careful description of ordinary word usage should show *that* this is a misuse. Consequently, careful description of ordinary word usage should help expose the potentially pernicious character of the analogies in question. But obviously, to indict such pictures *as* misleading or erroneous in the first place depends on an investigation of the actual use of words in ordinary, non-philosophical contexts. For the picture's status *as* misleading or erroneous is contingent on their role in causing us to break the rules of language.

Admittedly, even on this anti-thetical conception, the examination of these pictures or analogies is very important. For, relative to particular contexts (of human prejudice, preconception, 'cravings for generality', etc.) they generate philosophical problems. Indeed, these pictures may continue to mislead even when careful examination of the rules governing word usage has shown the problems to be based on the transgression of this use. Over-simple 'pictures' can be insidious, and may play an unconscious, inhibiting role in our attempt to get a clear view of *various* areas of language. Moreover, they may continue to cause tension even in those areas of language to which we have given careful attention. The labyrinths of language are complicated. We are in constant danger of losing the ground we have already made, falling back into comfortable and simplistic pictures when our investigation approaches language from different angles or perspectives.

These qualifications, stated in the last paragraph (and which in and of themselves I do not disagree with), do not jeopardize my argument. My claim here is that, according to the anti-thesis, thwarting these pictures nonetheless depends on showing the extent to which they are responsible for someone misdescribing the grammar, or breaking the grammatical rules of our language. For (to repeat) to expose the picture's role in the temptation to break the ordinary rules governing the use of words presupposes an establishment of the fact that rules *have* been broken.

1.3 The Thesis

My goal is not to indict the anti-thesis as an incorrect characterization of the entirety of Wittgenstein's discussions of the problems of philosophy. To a large degree, the argument in the following chapters is only that it incorrectly characterizes Wittgenstein's treatment of the influence of Augustine's picture. I try to suspend judgment on the extent to which generalization is licit. Nor do I wish to claim or deny that no 'philosophical problem' can be dissolved in this way. (Who am I to characterize the nature of a philosophical problem, once and for all and in advance of future experience? (cf. *PI* §92)) I argue, rather, that for the problems Wittgenstein considers in §§1-133 of *Philosophical Investigations*, this method is (1) not Wittgenstein's, and (2), it tends to result in question-begging arguments against those philosophical propositions/problems treated by Wittgenstein in §§1-133.

This book examines §§1-133 in the *Investigations*, but I base the crux of my account of Wittgenstein's method on my interpretation of (roughly) §§1-64. §§1-64 are largely concerned with an examination of the influence Augustine's picture[2] has on the formation of certain philosophical problems. My interpretation of these sections forms the background to my interpretation of a cluster of Wittgenstein's remarks on the nature of philosophy (§§65-133). Since my interpretation of the sections 'on philosophy' is also at odds with the anti-thesis, unfolding my reading of these two sets of sections in tandem is not only congruent with *Philosophical Investigations*: this strategy also pays dividends in understanding. For these sections on the nature of philosophy, whatever else they are intended to illuminate, are surely commenting on the preceding sections (i.e., *PI* §§1-64). I will argue that the aforementioned (anti-thetical) conception of Wittgenstein's method—of his *strategy*—does not fit the practice in those earlier sections concerned with the influence of Augustine's picture (viz., *PI* §§1-64). Correspondingly, I also argue that it does not correctly capture the import of Wittgenstein's methodological remarks in §§65-133.

Wittgenstein's examination of Augustine's picture is not an examination *for the purposes of* exposing sundry transgressions from the everyday rules governing word usage. Nor is Wittgenstein's task to refute the presuppositions on which such transgressions are based. Nor is he engaged in showing those presuppositions to be unintelligible (whatever it might mean to call something both a 'presupposition' and 'unintelligible'). Of primary importance is a *diagnosis* of these philosophical problems, a diagnosis intended to bring to light the unconscious role that Augustine's picture can, and for Wittgenstein did play in the *description* of the use of *our* words. That role, I will argue, is not that it may cause *errors* in the description of word usage. Or at any rate, this is a very unhappy way of putting it. For the early Wittgenstein, Augustine's picture is better characterized as exercising tyranny over the *expression* of grammatical distinctions. Augustine's picture, or rather a particular application of it, *subsumes* or *assimilates* ordinary grammatical distinctions to a particular form of expression.

The early Wittgenstein's dogmatic application of Augustine's picture is better characterized as casting the rules for the use of words in a misleading *notation*. The sense in which such an assimilation 'misdescribes' grammar and hence generates 'nonsense' is highly peculiar. Suppose a philosopher says—without blinking, as it were—that numbers or colours are objects. Then someone could probably make a pretty good case for saying that, *relative* to the ordinary use of 'object', they are talking nonsense. But suppose this is a serious philosophical claim. Such a *patent* transgression of ordinary use can only amount to an *objection* to ordinary use. It is better described as an attempt to find a different expression for a class of grammatical distinctions, in terms of a comparison with the concept of an object. It is better characterized as a 'full-blown pictorial representation of our grammar... as it were illustrated turns of speech' (*PI* §295). I aspire to bring this out more clearly in the following chapters.

This exegesis has a philosophical point. It raises a difficulty for the (anti-thetical) conception of Wittgenstein's method expounded above. Let us suppose, surely correctly, that Augustine's picture is intended to be an example of one of those misleading analogies. Recall that, according to the anti-thesis, Wittgenstein's method is to describe carefully the ordinary, non-philosophical uses of words. And indicting Augustine's picture—for crimes against clarity—would be *justified* by appeal to the ordinary use of words. For Augustine's picture, *ex hypothesi*, to some extent causes errors in our conception, characterization, or description of the rules governing the grammar of our language.

Is it reasonable, on these grounds, to convict Augustine's picture of causing confusion? A simple example should goad the reader's incredulity. (We will see more intricate examples in the following chapters.) Suppose a philosopher calls both 'red' and 'Excalibur' names of 'objects', and suppose I protest both that this contradicts how *we* use the word 'object', and that this philosopher is ignoring type distinctions between colours and physical objects. If I protest in this way, do I not ignore the possibility that this philosopher is *in a sense* perfectly aware that they are using the word 'object' differently? For instance, would we expect this philosopher to look for the bearer of 'red' under the couch? Perhaps my criticism does no more than *alert* us to the fact that this philosopher is using the word 'object' in an extended sense. (Perhaps also, for this philosopher, it brings this fact into the foreground.)

Such a criticism might be sufficient to displace the picture, but appeal to ordinary usage is not necessarily relevant. For this philosopher is not necessarily obliterating any logical distinctions. This philosopher may still make room for the grammatical difference between 'Excalibur' and 'red', which ordinary language earmarks with the categories 'object' and 'colour'. This distinction might find expression in a different way. For example, this philosopher might say that "so-called 'ordinary objects' and colours are *altogether different* kinds of objects. They have a different 'logical form'."[3]

Moreover, unearthing inconsistencies or unresolved tensions in such a characterization as this need not displace the picture. For objections of this sort may be met by creating a more sophisticated form of representation, i.e., a more sophisticated superstition. That is to say, objections such as these may be met with a more sophisticated *application* of the picture. (Cf. Wittgenstein's appeal to analysis in the *Tractatus.*) It may do no more than effect a rallying cry to erect 'ever larger and more complicated structures' (*PR, Preface*). Indeed, this activity may itself begin to exercise a fascination on its own. *Indeed*, pointing out inconsistencies and gaps in such a description of our use of language may exacerbate the entrenchment of the picture. (Compare Wittgenstein's use of the private language argument. This argument *opens* his discussion of the language of sensations. He does not place 'QED' at the end of it. It is not presented as a *refutation* of a picture of sensation language. Rather, it is itself an expression of a philosophical problem.)

The issue here is not merely the rhetorical vices, or practical inefficacy of this project of "bringing words back from their metaphysical to their everyday use" (cf. *PI* §116). Whatever else underlies a tendency towards the 'metaphysical' use of words—as Wittgenstein used the term 'metaphysics' (see Chapter Five *infra*)—it is at least a reaction to a philosophical problem. According to Wittgenstein, a philosophical problem has the form: This isn't how it is, but this is how it *must* be (*PI* §112). For example, one could imagine the early Wittgenstein expostulating, "Obviously it is false to say that every word designates some*thing*, but just as surely every word must designate *some*thing". And in the *Tractatus*, this philosophical problem was met with a reaction of the form: Look! how it *must* be is how it really is! Wittgenstein postulated an 'object' as the bearer of each logically proper name; not a normal object of course, but rather that *some*thing which every genuine name must designate.

In a certain sense this form of reaction, 'How it *must* be is how it really is', is the form the reaction must take if the corresponding problem takes the above form. For if it *must* be like this then obviously it is! To criticize a reaction of this form because it fails to tally with the grammar of our language is question begging. For such a criticism can only amount to something of the form: "This isn't how it is, so clearly it doesn't *have* to be this way." This form of criticism merely contradicts the form of the reaction.[4]

The method practiced in the early sections of the *Investigations* is not to attack contraventions of ordinary word usage, but rather to examine 'musts'. According to Wittgenstein, this is the heart of a philosophical problem. That is to say, to diagnose the root of the philosophical problem is to examine the role such pictures or analogies play in the formation of 'musts' in philosophy. We ought not to say, "Look, rules are being broken, nonsense is being uttered". Rather, we should say, "Look at *why* you're saying all this; look at the analogy that informs all these twists and turns".[5] In this context, the 'fixed point of our real need' (*PI* §108) is *not* the use of words in ordinary language, but the *picture* that lies at the root of our method of representing that (*ordinary*) use of words. Accordingly, I will argue that examination of the analogies themselves plays the primary role in Wittgenstein's diagnosis of the picture theory.

The 'picture' under consideration in §§1-64 of *Philosophical Investigations* is the one Wittgenstein derives from Augustine's reflections on how he learned his native tongue. Wittgenstein's inquiry in these sections revolves around the ideas of meaning, reference, description, and ostensive definition. Although Augustine's picture of language has, if broadly construed, informed the philosophical reflections of many a thinker, I will argue that it is the picture theory in particular which is under diagnosis. I should think it is only the extent to which this is true that is worthy of debate. I hope to show that it is very true, that the *Tractatus* is very much in the forefront in these sections of the *Investigations*. Here there is a quite literal sense in which, for Wittgenstein, 'philosophy is a working on oneself'.

My first chapter is dedicated to certain aspects of the picture theory which at first are likely to seem remote from the concerns addressed in this introduction. In particular, it is dedicated to certain technical details regarding Wittgenstein's early conception of (what might be called) the 'naming relationship'. I argue and emphasize that, in the *Tractatus*, the connection or 'link' between a name and its meaning—its object—is not conceived of as fixing or establishing the combinatorial possibilities—the 'form'—of that name. Rather, the 'link' presupposes these combinatorial possibilities. This can be put slightly differently. In the *Tractatus*, an agreement of form between name and object is a necessary condition for that object being the meaning of that name. I will give a preliminary clarification of why this argument matters:

This aspect of the picture theory has implications which must be addressed by any adequate interpretation of Wittgenstein's later discussions of ostensive definition. For Wittgenstein draws an important conclusion in his discussions of ostensive definition, viz., that an ostensive definition, like any other explanation, *presupposes* a background of grammatical conventions. More specifically, a bare ostensive definition—i.e. an ostensive gesture and uttering "this is *x*"—constitutes a definition only if it is clear what position in grammar the word occupies (*PI* §§31f.). Is it a colour word, a shape word, a number word, or what?

What theory or conception of language learning is this conclusion intended to contradict? Perhaps one rooted in Augustine's picture? But if my argument in Chapter Two convinces you, you will agree that this conclusion does not contradict anything expressed or implied by Wittgenstein in the *Tractatus*. On the contrary, the *Tractatus* itself makes claims which parallel the conclusion established by Wittgenstein in his later discussions of ostensive definition. The form of a name is *presupposed* if that name is to have meaning.

This is puzzling. The picture theory is surely an example of a conception of language rooted in Augustine's picture. However, it is unclear what relevance Wittgenstein's later discussion of ostensive definition has to the picture theory. For Wittgenstein seems to be *criticizing* a foundational conception of ostensive definition, yet that criticism passes the picture theory by. This is a serious problem if the discussion of ostensive definition is designed to play a role in undermining Augustine's picture. Can we confidently claim that a natural development of Augustine's picture is that ostensive definition constitutes a complete explanation of a word?[6] The picture theory is rooted in Augustine's picture, but is not committed to the completeness of ostensive definition. Rather, in its peculiar way the picture theory denies it. If we understand this argument regarding ostensive definition to be an attack against a certain conception of meaning, it looks as though he later partially vindicated his position in the *Tractatus*, albeit in less misleading terminology. I argue in Chapter Three that this misrepresents Wittgenstein's intentions in discussing ostensive definition.

I argue that it is towards the picture theory that Wittgenstein is directing the discussion of ostensive definition. At the root of the picture theory is precisely Augustine's picture: the words of language name objects, and sentences are combinations of such names (*PI* §1). The aforementioned puzzle arises only if we insist on interpreting the discussion of ostensive definition as somehow criticizing *something*. I will argue that this examination of ostensive definition plays a diagnostic role. It is a step in the *diagnosis* (as opposed to a straightforward criticism) of certain philosophical problems in the picture theory, viz., problems regarding the naming relation and language learning. Wittgenstein's intentions are not to criticize a conception of language learning which places ostensive definition in a foundational role.

1.4 The Anti-thesis on the Autonomy of Language

My reinterpretation of Wittgenstein's intentions in the early sections of the *Investigations* ramifies into subsequent sections. The discussion of ostensive definition is followed by another theme from the *Tractatus*. Wittgenstein examines the temptation to think that '*a name ought really to signify a simple*' (*PI* §39). In the *Tractatus*, it is a metaphysical (and ineffable) truth that simple 'objects' necessarily exist. In the *Investigations*, Wittgenstein reflects on the reasoning and motivation behind this necessity: 'One would... like to say: existence cannot be attributed to an element, for if it did not *exist*, one could not even name it and so one could say nothing at all of it. But let us consider an analogous case...' (*PI* 50). Wittgenstein continues,

> Let us imagine samples of colour being preserved in Paris like the standard metre. We define: "sepia" means the colour of the standard sepia which is there kept hermetically sealed. Then [like the standard metre] it will make no sense to say of this sample either that it is this colour or that it is not.
>
> We can put it like this: This sample is an instrument of the language used in ascriptions of colour. In this language-game it is not something that is represented, but is a means of representation. And just this goes for an element in language-game (48) [a language-game for describing combinations of coloured squares on a surface akin to a chessboard] when we name it by uttering the word "R": this gives this object a role in our language-game.... And to say "If it did not *exist*, it could have no name" is to say...: if this thing did not exist, we could not use it in our language-game. What looks as if it *had* to exist, is part of the language. (ibid.)

In the *Tractatus*, the insistence that 'objects' necessarily exist is in some (ineffable) sense a requirement of, or presupposition for, the possibility of language. In §50, Wittgenstein extends language-game (48) such that the *samples* are also a presupposition or requirement (of that language-game). He is drawing a comparison between *Tractarian* objects and the samples of language-game (48).

Unlike *Tractarian* objects, however, Wittgenstein recommends that we consider these samples as part of the language (*PI* §50, cf. §16). For they are used in the teaching and perhaps also the employment of the words of this language. The individual words are taught by reference to these paradigms (*PI* §51).

Let us focus in on one feature of Wittgenstein's comparison between the necessary *existence* of these 'objects' and the sample characterized as a *presupposition* of this imagined language-game (48). Without prejudging too much at this early stage, I may safely make a few leading remarks regarding this comparison. In the *Tractatus*, objects belong to the realm of *that which is represented*. In the *Investigations*, the samples of this imaginary language-game are conceived as belonging to the *means of representation*. It is tempting to interpret the conclusion drawn in §50 (quoted above) as pinpointing one explanation for the apparent necessity of *Tractarian* objects. It lay in (mis)characterizing an element of the *means* of representation as though it were an element that is represented. 'What looks as if it *had* to exist is part of the language' (*PI* §50).

The anti-thesis extends this interpretation of §50 in the following way. The function that necessarily existing 'objects' are intended to fulfil is actually fulfilled by the role samples play in our language.[7] (For, like 'objects', samples give meaning to the words for which they act as paradigms.) That is to say, we mistake an important 'observation concerning our language-game—our *method of representation*' (ibid., my emphasis)—for a truth about reality. For an adherent to the anti-thesis, Wittgenstein generalizes this diagnosis in §104: 'We predicate of the thing what lies in our *method of representing* it. Impressed by the possibility of a comparison, we think we are perceiving a state of affairs of the highest generality' (my emphasis). We predicate of reality what really belongs to our language. We project grammar onto reality.

I will argue against this reading of Wittgenstein's use of the expression 'method of representation'. A 'method of representation' is not language as such, but rather a method of representing—even describing—some subject matter. Indeed, in this case that subject matter is itself language, or at least some aspect of it.[8] This is another reason my first chapter is dedicated to the picture theory. Let me explain:

On the anti-thetical reading, Wittgenstein charges the *Tractatus* with predicating of reality what really lies in our method of representation, i.e., in our use of words. Of course, *Tractarian* objects are not coloured squares, but imagine how this tendency to project language onto reality might manifest itself in terms of language-game (48). One might be inclined to cast features of the grammar of our colour *words* onto the colours themselves, as if they *had* the necessary properties that the practice of using these words manifests. For example, one might say that it is due to the nature of *red* (and, more generally, *colour*) that we cannot simultaneously predicate red and green of the same thing (unless, of course, we are speaking of different parts of that thing). But this is to confuse features of our means of representation with features of that which is represented.

On this (anti-thetical) reading, the conclusion at §50 seems to be part and parcel with a *leitmotif* in Wittgenstein's later philosophy, viz., his rejection of the *Tractarian* idea that the essence of language is 'responsible' to reality. On the contrary, language is 'autonomous': 'The connection between "language and reality" is made by definition of words, and these belong to grammar, so that language remains self-contained' (*PG* §55). 'Like everything metaphysical, the harmony of thought and reality is to be found in the grammar of our language' (*PG* §112).

With language-game (48), the crux of Wittgenstein's attack on necessarily existing 'objects' is his assertion that samples belong to language. Yet this discussion also pokes holes in the idea that the grammar of our language is responsible to reality. The rules governing the use of 'red' are not somehow determined by the nature of *red*. What seems to be a reflection of the necessary properties of 'objects' is rather a reflection of features of our use of samples, i.e., features of language.

For an adherent to the anti-thesis, therefore, Wittgenstein's later treatment of *Tractarian* 'objects' is a refutation grounded in a new conception of the status of grammar. This treatment of *Tractarian* objects even appears, on this reading, to be a kind of microcosm of his later method of philosophy. 'What looks as if it *had* to exist [be true], is part of the language [grammatical truth]'. This sentence and its putative generalization at §104 seem to characterize Wittgenstein's later attitude to the 'musts' so predominant in philosophy. The 'musts' of metaphysics are the result of projecting the grammar of our language onto reality. (On this canvassing of necessary truths in philosophy, Wittgenstein conferred the title 'metaphysics'.)

This refinement of the anti-thetical conception of the nature of a philosophical problem dovetails with the anti-thetical conception of Wittgenstein's method of treatment expounded earlier. The philosopher's job is to 'bring words back from their metaphysical to their everyday use' (*PI* §116). If the metaphysical use of words is the result of projecting language onto reality, the philosopher's job should consist in revealing the true nature of what are mistakenly cast as descriptions of the essence of reality. Namely, these 'necessary truths' are, correctly conceived, mangled expressions of the rules which govern the use of words in our *everyday* discourse. For my purposes, there is an equally important connection between these two aspects of the anti-thesis, i.e., between (1) the status of grammar and (2) the method of philosophy in general. Not only do these two aspects of the anti-thesis dovetail, but I begged the question against an adherent to the second aspect in criticizing the first. In short, the anti-thesis is more sophisticated than was revealed in my initial presentation of it.

Recall my argument against the first aspect expounded at the beginning of this introduction. I was sceptical about a certain interpretation of Wittgenstein's discussion of Augustine's picture. I denied that Wittgenstein's diagnosis is that Augustine's picture results in or embodies an erroneous description of ordinary word usage. Wittgenstein's earlier dogmatic application of Augustine's picture is a subsumption, or assimilation, of grammatical distinctions under a form of representation. It was for this reason, I argued, that careful description of word usage in ordinary contexts could not constitute a decisive refutation of those metaphysical pronouncements resulting from the application of the picture. That is to say, if used in indicting Augustine's picture as producing nonsense, an appeal to ordinary word usage in a sense begs the question. In the *Tractatus*, the dogmatic application of Augustine's picture embodies an *objection* to ordinary word usage. All that an appeal to ordinary word usage might establish is that the early Wittgenstein is talking nonsense *relative* to ordinary word usage. There is, however, a rejoinder to my criticism, a rejoinder which makes use of Wittgenstein's later claims about the autonomy of language:

Early in the *Investigations*, Wittgenstein criticizes certain applications of Augustine's picture. To cast the different uses of our words into a uniform mould—e.g. the form of expression '"X" signifies *X*' (cf. *PI* §§10, 13)—is merely to present a convention of grammar, even a truism, as though it were a discovery about the nature of signification: we have not so far said anything (*PI* §13). Wittgenstein concedes that,

> Of course, one can reduce the description of the use of the word "slab" to the statement that this word signifies this object. This will be done when, for example, it is merely a matter of removing the mistaken idea that the word "slab" refers to the shape of building-stone that we in fact call "block"—but the kind of '*referring*' this is, that is to say the use of these words for the rest, is already known...
>
> But assimilating the descriptions of the uses of words in this way cannot make the uses themselves any more like one another. For, as we see, they are absolutely unlike. (*PI* §10)

The rejoinder to my earlier criticism might draw inspiration from this passage in the following way. In so far as such an assimilation is incomplete, it causes inconsistencies and generates incoherent pronouncements—in short, nonsense.[9] For example, a dogmatic application of Augustine's picture might produce a piece of nonsense like

"*Red* is an 'object'", and (more serious perhaps) an inconsistency between this claim and the idea that one cannot, in principle, 'point' to it in the same sense that one can point to something that is red (see Chapter Three *infra*). To the extent that such an assimilation is consistent, worked out, it amounts only to as it were imposing a differently, perhaps less finely, calibrated grid upon the facts of our language. Consequently, no facts about our grammar are changed, but only the way in which distinctions are expressed. *Since grammar is autonomous*, nothing new has been achieved. An appeal to the autonomy of grammar grounds the backlash against 'philosophical' deviations from ordinary usage. What we must accept, *since grammar is autonomous*, is that words must be brought back to their ordinary use. For the motivation behind the metaphysical use of words is that this use reveals something about the way things *really* are (e.g. that numbers are *really* 'objects' in *some* sense).

For an adherent to the anti-thesis, the 'autonomy of grammar' lies at the *very foundation* of this philosophical method. An indispensable justification for the project of "bringing words back to their ordinary use" is the thesis that grammar is autonomous. On this conception, the metaphysician's original sin is the wrong or confused idea that grammar is responsible to reality.

There is an unanswered difficulty for a proponent of this (antithetical) conception of the errors of the 'metaphysician'. Is the problem of the status of the 'grammar' or 'logic' of our language not *itself* a topic for *philosophical* scrutiny? Or is it a *discovery* that grammar is 'autonomous' and thus, *pace* Wittgenstein, we find that philosophy does sometimes manage the odd discovery? Any adequate discussion of Wittgenstein's later method must address the *status* of his later treatment of the *Tractarian* conception of the isomorphism between (what is essential in) language and (what is essential in) reality.

I will argue that there is something subtly wrong with this reading. I do not dispute that the later Wittgenstein radically re-orients his conception of the relationship between grammar (or logic) and reality. I disagree, rather, with this reading of the argumentative strategy in these sections of the *Investigations*. I proffer an alternative reading of Wittgenstein's method, drawing from his own methodological remarks.

Although I do not pretend to be able to give a comprehensive treatment of the issue in the following chapters, I will address 'the autonomy of grammar' as it bears on Wittgenstein's later criticism of the picture theory. The picture theory is indeed committed to the claim that the essence of language is in some sense responsible to the essence of reality. And this commitment is, most would argue, closely related to the picture theory's conception of word meaning as a correspondence, or connection, between words and things, between language and reality. Many of the obscurities of the picture theory *can* be made sense of in terms of an attempt to reconcile this conception of the meaning of a word with the difficulties it raises. A related organization of certain facts about Wittgenstein's transition makes it tempting to look at the later philosophy as grounded in (1) a discovery about meaning and (2) a tracing out of the implications of this discovery. Put rather bluntly, and skipping a lot of steps, the story goes like this: The meaning of a word is not an object, but rather its use. *Therefore*, grammar is autonomous. *Therefore*, metaphysics (even of the sort practiced in the *Tractatus*) is a spurious enterprise.

I do not contest this story, if intended as a (very rough) story about the development of Wittgenstein's thought. There is, I believe, truth in it. But it neither grounds nor characterizes Wittgenstein's treatment of these problems in the *Investigations*. Rather, Wittgenstein's early perplexities about 'meaning' ("How can language be *connected* with the world?") are themselves fed by reflections on the essence of symbolism (e.g., 'name'), under the shadow of a primitive picture.[10] The conception of *meaning* in the picture theory is itself inspired, or even virtually necessitated, by Wittgenstein's dogmatic application of Augustine's picture to ordinary language. Moreover, this conception of meaning plays a primary role in Wittgenstein's conception of the relationship between 'grammar' or 'logic', and reality. The implication is that this manifestation of Wittgenstein's earlier conception of the *status* of logic, or 'grammar', is motivated by the dogmatic application of a picture of *language*.

Consequently, any appeal here to the autonomy of grammar would itself be question begging. The putative harmony between language and reality is itself a topic for philosophical scrutiny, and does not lie at the foundation of Wittgenstein's later method. Since it was a dogmatic application of Augustine's picture of language that led to the *Tractarian* conception of the status of grammar, there is clearly something awry about appealing to the 'autonomy of grammar' to undermine Augustine's picture.

In the following chapters I present an interpretation of the first 133 sections of *Philosophical Investigations.* My interpretation portrays the argumentation in these sections as more cohesive, linear, and self-contained than is normally done in commentaries on the text. I present what seems to me to be the dominant and crucial thread in the weave of argument running through these sections. For the most part, I ignore the other threads.

This approach should throw light on Wittgenstein's argumentative strategy in *Philosophical Investigations*, a strategy perhaps partly obscured by the fact that the *Investigations* is written in short sections. Wittgenstein's style might incline the reader to focus greater attention on a section or small set of sections, and thereby focus less attention on his argumentation at a more global level. My attempt to trace a theme, or a small and tightly knit set of themes, throughout a substantial chunk of *Philosophical Investigations* is purposely on guard against this inclination.

The beginning point of this approach is that *Philosophical Investigations* is a readable book. It is not, as Von Savigny correctly notes, the mere tips of icebergs in a whole underwater mountain range of manuscript sources.[11] This is not to suggest that it is never illuminating to compare the manuscript sources with their published versions in the *Investigations.* In certain instances (and most extensively in Chapter Five) I do discuss some of the more direct sources of the *Investigations.* Largely, however, much more energy is spent on the close reading of these sections: on attention to detail.

The following exposition also persistently contrasts itself with rival interpretation. This introduction has already provided an exemplification of this. This incessant interpolation certainly complicates matters, and one might judge it to be counter-productive to a close reading and perspicuous exposition of the *Investigations*. But it seemed to me that representation by way of comparison and contrast might actually be in the interests of perspicuity (cf. *PI* §133). This is certainly true for myself with respect to the present inquiry. For much of what is written here is a reaction on my part to interpretations of *Philosophical Investigations* (both 'in the small' and 'in the large') that I at one time accepted uncritically (and am here wrestling with). Perhaps this is not the reader's standpoint, but I conjecture that these same interpretations at least inform many a reader's understanding of the passages running from §§1-133.

I conclude this introduction by noting that the method of philosophy I attribute to Wittgenstein bears similarites with, and in one case, inspiration from other writers. Most importantly, and as will become increasingly evident in the following chapters, some of the argument in this book is inspired by certain writings by Gordon Baker. See 'Section 122: neglected aspects' (op. cit.) and *Wittgenstein, Frege and the Vienna Circle* (op. cit.). I am especially indebted to his discussion of Wittgenstein's use of the phrase 'method of representation'. In this and certain other cases, these debts are obvious and easy to acknowledge. Often, however, I have found that my debt to these writings is either too vague or too indirect, or even too pervasive to footnote systematically. Where this is so, I hope that this general acknowedgment is excusable.

Furthermore, there are some vague similarities between what I write here and interpretations of the later Wittgenstein that emphasize the therapeudic aspects of his philosophical method. For example, Cora Diamond makes a remark which, on my understanding, bears a striking resemblance to certain things I write in this book:

> If we read the *Tractatus* as containing metaphysical claims about reality...we shall miss entirely the character of Wittgenstein's later philosophy. We shall see it as rejecting a metaphysical account of reality, the rejection being dictated by a shift from one set of philosophical requirements to an-

> other. Whereas what I am suggesting is that the criticism of the *Tractatus* may be viewed as a criticism of the *laying down of philosophical requirements.*[12]

This notion of a 'philosophical requirement' also plays a central role in my interpretation of Wittgenstein's method, and I agree that Wittgenstein's criticism of the picture theory is indeed a criticism of the laying down of philosophical requirements. On the other hand, Diamond would undoubtedly think that I have misunderstood the *Tractatus*, perhaps even think that I have misunderstood it in such a way that I cannot but entirely miss the character of Wittgenstein's later philosophy.

For, a big part of what distinguishes the interpretation of Wittgenstein by Cora Diamond (and others who follow her lead, sometimes collectively referred to as "The New Wittgensteinians"[13]) is that she also characterizes the method of philosophy practiced by the *early* Wittgenstein as therapeudic. Indeed, many of these commentators, including Diamond, argue for substantial continuity in Wittgenstein's work, at any rate in this respect.

In contrast, my work here fits squarely within the framework of 'traditional' interpretations of the *Tractatus*. Although I do argue for a novel interpretation of certain details in Wittgenstein's *Tractatus*, and most especially the picture theory, my purpose in doing so is not to introduce a different interpretation of the early Wittgenstein's conception of philosophy. Rather, my interpretation of aspects of the *Tractatus* serves as a starting block from which I present a different conception of the later Wittgenstein's method of practicing philosophy. For myself, the 'kink' in the evolution of philosophy still occurs *after* the writing of the *Tractatus*.

I said above that I do not introduce a different interpretation of the early Wittgenstein's *conception* of philosophy. I said this because there is a sense in which my understanding of the *Tractatus* might be conceived as not being traditional, if 'traditional' means that 'we read the *Tractatus* as *containing* metaphysical claims about reality'. Indeed, if this is our understanding of the *Tractatus*, Diamond is probably correct that 'we shall entirely miss the character of Wittgenstein's later philosophy';[14] we will certainly miss the character of his criticism of the picture theory. But it is one thing for a book to *contain* metaphysical claims about reality, and another thing for it to be *conceived of* (even by its author) as containing metaphysical claims about reality. I believe that Wittgenstein did at times conceive it thus, as Hacker has convincingly argued.[15] But I argue that the Wittgenstein of *Philosophical Investigations* conceived of the metaphysics of the *Tractatus* as having its foundation, as Diamond puts it, in the laying down of philosophical requirements.

David Finkelstein is another example of a writer who emphasizes the therapeudic aspects of Wittgenstein's work. In the context of Wittgenstein's discussions about following a rule, Finkelstein makes the following remark, which also bears a striking similarity to what I write in this book:

> Typically, Wittgenstein's response to platonism is not, "What you're saying is *false*," but rather, "What you say is all right, only there's nothing queer or magical about it." Wittgenstein doesn't deny that when I grasp the sense of a rule, the steps that I'm supposed to take are, in some sense, already present to my mind... The platonist's problem is not that he wants to say that the steps are present, but that he imagines that *in* saying this, he's remarking on a mind-boggling fact.[16]

I suggest in the following chapters that Wittgenstein's response to the picture theory is very similar to Finkelstein's description of his response to the platonist. Indeed, the above quotation captures pretty well what I mean by 'dissolution'. But I also show that it is a big part of Wittgenstein's approach that he investigates—*diagnoses*—the motivations for *thinking* that there is something 'queer or magical about it'. Indeed, I argue that diagnosis and dissolution are (for lack of a better phrase) *internally* related.

For these reasons and others, the similarities between my work and the writings of many of the 'New Wittgensteinians' are often, in my estimation, more superficial than in the case of Baker's work, which directly influenced the writing of this book. The similarity arises because I (indirectly, via the notions of diagnosis and dissolution) also give quite a bit of prominence to the therapeudic aspects of the later Wittgenstein's method.

As with Baker's writings, I also do not directly confront these writers on their interpretations of the later Wittgenstein, but rather note similarities and differences where they occur to me. To do otherwise would fall outside the scope of this book as it is presently organized; for the organization of this book is akin to a dialectic, and decomposes into two parts. On the one hand, it is a detailed polemic against a particular interpretation of Wittgenstein's method, an interpretation best characterized by the collaborative, exegetical works on Wittgenstein written by Baker and Hacker. On the other hand, I present and contrast my opposing interpretation of Wittgenstein, which is itself very tightly interwoven with that polemic. As with Baker's writings, I hope these introductory remarks go some way to make up for the lack of a detailed consideration of these writings.

Notes

1. As I clarify further on, I understand, by 'the anti-thetical conception of Wittgenstein's method', not only a position which attributes this method to Wittgenstein. Moreover, a proponent of the interpretation is also a proponent of this method. See, e.g., P. M. S. Hacker, *Insight and Illusion* (Clarendon Press, 1986), rev. edn, ch. 6; H. J. Glock, 'Section 128: no theses in philosophy' in Arrington and Glock, *Philosophical Investigations: Text and Context* (Blackwell, 1991); Paul Johnston, *Wittgenstein and Moral Philosophy* (Routledge, 1989), ch. 1; G. P. Baker's and P. M. S. Hacker's essay, 'Philosophy', in *Understanding and Meaning* (Blackwell, 1980).
2. By 'Augustine's picture' I refer, following Wittgenstein, to the idea that all words name objects, and that sentences are combinations of names (PI §1). See Chapter Three.
3. Here I have begged a question against the anti-thesis. For to characterize a grammatical distinction as a kind of ontological distinction is, in a sense, to obliterate a grammatical distinction. I will address this in a rudimentary way later in this introduction. I give it extensive treatment in Chapter Four.
4. Moreover, to claim something like, "it does not have to be this way, for you can look at it differently", is by itself no better (cf. G. Baker, 'Section 122: neglected aspects'). Such a method also, in abstraction from any diagnosis, merely contradicts. I.e., the proposal of the possibility of an alternative picture says: not: must-p. The proposal that the picture is incorrect says: not-p, from which it obviously follows that: not: must-p. Of course, to accept that one can look at it differently does amount to getting rid of the 'must', as does the acceptance of the 'incorrectness' of the picture (athough in this latter case we perhaps replace one 'must'

with another). And it is perhaps easier to persuade someone that something can be looked at differently than that it must be looked at differently. My point is only that the proposal of the possibility of an alternative picture stands on the same level, with respect to the 'must', as indicting the picture for incorrectness or unintelligibility. They both immediately contradict the 'must', and hence neither constitute an argument.

5. It is interesting to note that, at least in sections §§1-133, Wittgenstein does not use the word 'nonsense' as a term of philosophical appraisal. Not even in §40, as I explain in detail in Chapter Three. Rather, the kinds of words he tends to use are words like 'misleading', and 'useful'.
6. As argued by Baker, G. P., and Hacker, P. M. S., *Understanding and Meaning* (Blackwell, 1980), p. 160.
7. Ibid., pp. 201ff.
8. This issue has already been broached by G. Baker in 'Section 122: neglected aspects', in Arrington and Glock (op. cit.). More discussion can be found in Chapter Four of this book.
9. See Hacker, P. M. S., *Insight and Illusion* (Clarendon Press, 1986), pp. 193ff. for a defence of this account of Wittgenstein's conception of metaphysics.
10. This general issue, of the role reflections on symbolism play in the *Tractatus*, has been addressed in Gordon Baker's *Wittgenstein, Frege, and the Vienna Circle* (Blackwell, 1988). Baker focuses on Wittgenstein's early reflections on the essential bi-polarity of the elementary proposition.
11. E. Von Savigny, 'No Chapter "On Philosophy" in *Philosophical Investigations*' (Metaphilosophy, Vol. 22, No. 4, Oct. 1991), p. 308.
12. Cora Diamond, *The Realistic Spirit: Wittgenstein, Philosophy, and the Mind* (MIT Press, 1991), p. 20
13. For a representative sample these writers, see *The New Wittgenstein*, Alice Crary and Rupert Read (eds.) (Routledge, 2000).
14. Diamond (op. cit.), my emphasis.
15. Hacker, P. M. S., 'Was he trying to whistle it?', in Crary and Read (op. cit.).
16. Finkelstein, David H., 'Wittgenstein on rules and platonism', in Crary and Read (op. cit.), p. 68.

2

Logic Must Take Care of Itself

> The obscurity obviously resides in the question: what does the logical identity of sign and thing signified really consist in? And this question is . . . a main aspect of the whole philosophical problem.
>
> (*NB* p. 3)

2.1 Definitions and Thesis

In the *Tractatus*, the essence of language mirrors the essence of reality. Our language is arbitrary only to the extent that it is a *possible* mode of signification (*TLP* 3.341, 3.3421). In this chapter I discuss how this 'logical identity of sign and thing signified' finds formulation in the picture theory. Is it the 'link', or 'connection', between a name and its object that *fixes* which syntactically possible combinations (with other names) that name can enter into? I argue that this is backwards. Rather, the possibility of a name standing for an object *presupposes* that there is an identity between the form of a name and the form of its object. This chapter is dedicated to arguing and clarifying this interpretation. In later chapters I discuss in detail the importance this interpretation has for understanding parts of the *Investigations*.

I need to define two terms more precisely: (1) 'link' and (2) 'isomorphism'. First, by 'link', or sometimes 'connecting link', I designate this connection between the object and name, i.e., the fact that the name stands for the object. My use of the term 'isomorphism' requires some setting up. First, a preliminary on Wittgenstein's use of the terms *Tatsache* and *Sachverhalt*:

A state-of-affairs (*Sachverhalt*) is a combination of objects. There are, as it were, two kinds of states-of-affairs: those that exist, and those that do not exist. A 'fact' (*Tatsache*) is not a possibility, but rather an actuality, and is also a more general notion than 'state-of-affairs'. There are both positive and negative facts (*TLP* 2.06). A positive fact is the existence of states-of-affairs (*TLP* 2), and not necessarily the existence of only a single state-of-affairs. Conversely, a negative fact is the non-existence of states-of-affairs (*TLP* 2.06). (So if a state-of-affairs does not exist, that itself is a fact.) In the final analysis, therefore, positive facts would be represented in the propositional calculus by sentences of the form: '*p*', '*p* & *q*', '*p* & *q* & *r*' etc. Negative facts would be represented by sentences of the form: '-*p*', '-*p* & -*q*', '-*p* & -*q* & -*r*' etc.

Of course, there are also sentences such as '*p* & -*q*'. According to Wittgenstein's definitions, if this sentence is true, that which is represented by it would seemingly have to be an amalgamation of a positive and negative fact. Unfortunately, I discern no explicit discussion in the *Tractatus* of what these (and similar) amalgams are to be called. So I will assume that a fact, beyond being either positive or negative, can be such an amalgam. Facts are, then, the existence and/or non-existence of states-of-affairs. Therefore, facts are representable by propositions of any sort in a propositional calculus containing only '&' and '-' as logical connectives. Some examples are '*p*', '-*p*', ' -(*p* & *q*)', '-*p* & *q*' and so on. A state-of-affairs can be represented only by propositions of the form '*p*'. An articulated proposition is a picture of reality (*infra*). I will usually only consider pictures in so far as they picture a state-of-affairs. This simplifies matters considerably and nothing in the argument turns on it.

I will use the term 'isomorphism' to refer to a certain sort of commonality: a commonality between the 'form' of an element (in an elementary proposition) and the 'form' of the object (in a state-of-affairs) which that element is linked with. Wittgenstein defined the 'form' of a

(*Tractarian*) object as its possible modes of combination with other (*Tractarian*) objects, i.e., the states-of-affairs into which the object *can* enter (*TLP* 2.0141).

The minimal elements of a picture also have a 'form'. However, there are two importantly (and subtly) different senses in which one can say that something is an element of a fact that pictures. Disentangling these two different senses is a task requiring a fair amount of discussion. But roughly, the difference between these two senses turns on what we are considering the element to be an element *of*. Is it an element of the *picture*, or of the *fact* that constitutes that picture? I will call an element of the *picture* a 'name'. An element of the *fact* that constitutes that picture I will call a 'constituent'. (When I do not wish to beg any questions regarding the correct reading of Wittgenstein's '*Element*', I will use the term 'element'.)

Wittgenstein does not make this distinction himself, but it is legitimate. And it is not altogether obvious which sense he has in mind for the term '*Element*'. Is it to be understood as I defined 'constituent', or as I defined 'name'? I will argue that it is to be understood as I defined 'name'.

Corresponding to this distinction between a name and a constituent, there are two senses in which one can say that an element has a form. Wittgenstein defined pictorial form as the possibility of the *de facto* determinate (*infra*) combination that the *Elemente* enter into (*TLP* 2.15). I will argue that a 'possible combination' is a combination that is possible for the *names*. It is not to be understood as a combination which is possible for the constituents.

This reduces to the claim that this combination is one that is possible for each name. Presumably this possibility is one among several possibilities. (At any rate, nothing speaks against this possibility being one among several possibilities. I ignore, as it were, the possibility that there is only one possibility.) So we may define the 'form' of the *name* as the mode(s) of combination (with other names) into which that name *can* enter: the picture(s) of which the name *can* be an element. Let us not trouble here about what this possibility consists in. At this stage, it is sufficient that the form of a name corresponds to the form of the object it stands for.

While for the *constituent*, I will argue below that it is illuminating to conceive of its 'form' as the mode(s) of combination (with other constituents) into which that constituent *may* enter: the picture(s) of which that constituent *may* be an element. The form of the element qua constituent is, in a sense, identical with the form of that same element qua name. (What a name *can* do corresponds with what a constituent *may* do.) Though identical in this sense, they are defined differently. For one is defined in terms of permissibility ('form-of-a-constituent') while the other is defined in terms of possibility ('form-of-a-name'). Here again we will not worry about what determines permissibility. And again like the name, the form of a constituent corresponds to the form of its object.

The argument in this chapter will rely heavily on the distinction between 'name' and 'constituent'. Attention must also be paid when I use 'element', i.e., as an English translation for Wittgenstein's *Element,* yet without any assumptions about how this term is to be construed (i.e., whether it is construed as 'constituent' or 'name'). Much of the discussion in this chapter will not make sense unless one pays attention to which one I use at any given time.

In logic, according to Wittgenstein, all that is possible is also permitted (see *TLP* 5.4733). That is, all that is legitimate, or permissible in logic *amounts* to all that is possible in logic. Logic takes care of itself. I exploit my distinction between 'name' and 'constituent' in an attempt to throw light on how this claim about possibility and permissibility finds formulation in the picture theory.

Let us ignore the 'name', and focus on the object and (pictorial) 'constituent'. In the picture theory there is a logical identity between a pictorial constituent and the object it stands for. The form of the pictorial constituent mirrors the form of its object. This 'mirroring' consists in the fact that the combinatorial permissibilities of the pictorial constituent correspond to the combinatorial possibilities of its object. I wish to designate this 'mirroring' between the normative feature of the pictorial constituent, and the metaphysical aspect of the object, with the term 'isomorphism': they are 'isomorphic' with respect to each other.[1]

I can now state my thesis in this chapter. I argue that the 'isomorphism' between an element of a picture and its object is *not* the result of the 'link' between an element and its object. The 'logical identity' between an element and its object is not the result of having that pictorial element go proxy for that object (however that might be achieved). Rather, I shall argue that the *possibility* of effecting a connecting link presupposes that a pictorial element and the object to which it is linked are isomorphic. The consequence of this interpretation is that the word 'constituent' is an incorrect characterization of Wittgenstein's employment of the word '*Element*'. Rather, 'name' correctly characterizes Wittgenstein's use of '*Element*'.

I wish to briefly remind the reader of the role I intend this chapter to play in subsequent chapters. I will appeal to it when discussing those passages in the *Investigations* that are concerned with ostensive definition. The interpretation I argue against in this chapter, viz., that the link fixes isomorphism, bears a striking resemblance to the position apparently *criticized*, perhaps even refuted, by Wittgenstein at §§28-31:

> Now one can ostensively define a proper name, the name of a colour, the name of a material, a numeral, the name of a point of the compass and so on. The definition of the number two, "That is called 'two'"—pointing to two nuts—is perfectly exact.—But how can two be defined like that? The person one gives the definition to doesn't know what one wants to call "two" ... (*PI* §28)
>
> Perhaps you say: two can only be ostensively defined in *this* way: "This *number* is called 'two'" .... One already has to know (or be able to do) something in order to be capable of asking a thing's name (*PI* §30)
>
> This explanation again only tells him the use of the piece because, as we might say, the place for it was already prepared. *Or even*: we shall *only say* that it tells him the use, *if*

> the place is already prepared (*PI* §31, my emphasis; cf. *TLP* 5.4733 regarding this last sentence)

If the interpretation of the picture theory which I criticize in this chapter were correct, these conclusions about the nature of ostensive definition would be a criticism of the picture theory. I discuss this in some detail in subsequent chapters, and I draw consequences from it in interpreting the strategical role played by the above sections in the *Investigations*. For the present, however, I hope that as we examine the picture theory the reader will bear this connection in mind.

2.2 The Picture Theory

The picture theory is a theory about the pictorial nature of the proposition. The distinction and relationship between the 'link' and 'isomorphism' operates both at the level of the picture, and at the level of the picture's elements. At the level of the picture, it can be roughly understood as a distinction between sense and syntax. In other words, it is roughly a distinction between meaningfulness and well-formedness. An elementary proposition is meaningful, or has sense (the latter being Wittgenstein's technical term), if all its elements stand for objects, i.e., if all its elements are meaningful. An elementary proposition is well-formed if all its elements are combined in such a way that it represents a possible configuration of the objects.

We get a vague idea of Wittgenstein's conception of the relationship between meaningfulness and well-formedness from a criticism he makes of Frege:

> It must in a certain sense be impossible for us to go wrong in logic. This is already partly expressed by saying: Logic must take care of itself .... Frege says: Every well-formed sentence must make sense; and I say: Every possible sentence is well-formed, and if it does not make sense that can only come of our not having *given* any meaning to certain

> of its parts. Even when we believe we have done so. (*NB* p. 2, cf. *TLP* 5.4733)[2]

At the very least, it is clear from this passage that a 'possible sentence'—a propositional sign—lacks sense because certain (perhaps all) of its parts have not been assigned meaning. Yet whence the 'only' in the above passage? Wittgenstein says that this can *only* come of our not having given any meaning to the parts of the propositional sign. What is this explanation of 'not making sense' being contrasted with? What account of 'not making sense' is Wittgenstein banishing?

Wittgenstein is denying that a propositional sign might lack sense because it is ill-formed. 'Every possible sentence is well-formed'. Thus if something is *not* well-formed then it is not *possibly* a sentence. So Wittgenstein is suggesting that, in order for an expression to be a *candidate* for sentence-hood, it must be the case that that expression is well-formed. In order for an expression to be a 'possible sentence', it must be the case that its parts are combined in an appropriate way. As James Conant notes,

> The critical difference between Frege's formulation and the one which the *Tractatus* endorses is that the former implicitly distinguishes between those propositions that are legitimately constructed and those that are not, while the latter rejects the idea that there is such a thing as a logically illegitimately constructed proposition.[3]

Wittgenstein's criticism of Frege may then be reformulated in the following way. If a combination of signs is not well-formed, then it is not as though it *represents* in an ill-formed or illogical way, and *consequently* makes no sense. Rather, if it is ill-formed it just does not represent. And so it is on account of the fact that it does not *represent* that it does not make sense (as opposed to because it 'represents illogically'). '[I]f it does not make sense that can *only* come of our not having *given* any meaning to certain of its parts' (*NB*, p. 2, my emphasis on 'only').

Why is this? *What is it* that makes it 'as impossible to represent in language anything that 'contradicts logic' as it is in geometry ... to give the co-ordinates of a point that does not exist' (*TLP* 3.032)? Much light can be thrown on this question if we investigate this disagreement with Frege as it finds its formulation in the picture theory.

The general form of the proposition, Wittgenstein tells us, is 'This is how things stand' (*TLP* 4.5). A proposition is a model of reality used to say "*this* is how things are" (or, "*this* is how things *aren't*."). If the proposition is elementary, it asserts the existence of a state-of-affairs. The elementary proposition is a picture of the state-of-affairs (*TLP* 3.21, 4.01, 4.011). With an elementary proposition, the elements of a picture correspond to the atomic components of what it pictures. These elements are called 'elements' and 'objects' respectively (*TLP* 3.2-3.22).

A picture is a picture of a state-of-affairs. Its status as a picture does not presuppose the existence of that state-of-affairs; it presupposes the existence of the objects which make up that state-of-affairs.

A necessary condition for something being a picture is that it is a fact (*TLP* 2.141). But being a fact is clearly insufficient for picture-hood. Of course, lots of facts are not pictures. If a fact is to be a picture we must use it to picture something. If the picture represents a state-of-affairs, its elements must stand in a 'pictorial relationship' with the elements of what it pictures (*TLP* 2.1513). This pictorial relationship consists in the elements of the picture having a 'link' to the elements of the (perhaps non-existent) state-of-affairs (*TLP* 2.1514). The particular configuration of objects which the picture does represent depends upon the 'structure' of the picture, viz., the particular configuration of pictorial elements. Wittgenstein defines the 'structure' of the picture as consisting in the determinate way which the elements of the picture are related to one another (*TLP* 2.15). Given a correlation of signs with objects—given the links—'the fact that the elements [*Elemente*] of a picture are related to one another in a determinate way represents that things are related to one another in the same way' (ibid.).

This is a good place to address potential confusion. What did Wittgenstein mean by a 'determinate' relation? For the picture, it is the *determinate* way in which its elements are combined which constitutes the structure of that picture. The use of the word 'determinate' evidently indicates that there is nothing undetermined about this relation between pictorial elements. Moreover, the text seems to treat this idea as a corollary of the claim that a picture is a fact (see *TLP* 2.14-2.141, 3.14). But this is problematic, for a fact need not, according to Wittgenstein, be determinate. I noted earlier that a fact is the sort of thing that can be represented by a proposition of *any* sort. Even a disjunction, since *p* v *q* is equivilent to -(-*p* & -*q*). But that which is represented by a disjunction is not a determinate relation, nor a determinate set of relations between objects.

Let me clarify this puzzle with an example. Suppose I use the fact that my book is above this table to represent the state-of-affairs that I am sitting in this chair. Further suppose that, in the state-of-affairs, it is the objects *I*, (*am*) *sitting in*, and *chair* that fit into one another in a 'determinate' way. (Wittgenstein would never have allowed such things to count as objects, but he too is short on examples.) In this example it is entirely irrelevant, for representational purposes, whether the book is touching the table or not. I stipulate that what matters is only whether the book is above the table. Whether or not the book is touching the table is not a feature of the structure of the picture, even though it is a feature of the fact which constitutes that picture. This 'irrelevancy', and the structure of the *picture* (although not the structure of the fact which constitutes the picture) pass one another by.

It is not an irrelevant feature of the *picture*. Rather, that it is irrelevant in this sense is tantamount to its not constituting an aspect of the structure of the picture at all. The problem, however, is that although it is irrelevant to the picture whether the book sits directly on top of the table, or rather hovers mid-air three inches above it, it *follows* from either of these 'irrelevancies' that the book is above the table. Yet we cannot infer from this that the fact *I-am-sitting-in-this-chair* can also be analyzed into a disjunction of possibilities. *Ex hypothesi* it is a state-of-affairs, and there are no indeterminate states-of-affairs.[4] Nonetheless, Wittgenstein treats the claim that pictorial elements stand in a 'determinate' relation as a corollary of the idea that pictures are facts. Yet facts are potentially indeterminate, for they might be analyzable.

This puzzle arises, therefore, because the fact which constitutes the picture (which itself constitutes a representation of a state-of-affairs) need not itself be an (existent) state-of-affairs. It is sufficient for the picture to be a fact of any sort. (Absolute simplicity, as this applies to objects, is not a requirement of the elements of the fact which constitutes an elementary proposition.[5]) The *pictorial* elements never need to be simple 'objects'.

The problem vanishes with the realization that the concept of simplicity, as this concept functions with respect to the *picture*, turns not on the simplicity (or lack of simplicity) in the fact which constitutes that picture. 'Simplicity' with respect to the picture is a function of what that picture represents (*TLP* 3.2f.). A simple sign is simple by virtue of its *representational* status. In my example the signs are indeed simple, for they represent simple objects. (This foreshadows my argument later in this chapter that the structure of a picture cannot be reduced to the structure of the fact which constitutes that picture.)

2.3 Structure and Form

Integral to a correct understanding of the picture theory is Wittgenstein's notion of 'structure'. Commentators have claimed that, by structure, Wittgenstein merely meant the determinate way in which the *constituents* of a picture are related to one another.[6] This, together with its consequences, is the anti-thetical interpretation in this chapter. On this reading, the structure of a picture amounts to the structure of the fact which constitutes that picture. And the structure of a fact is constituted by the determinate relation between its elements. So for the anti-thesis, the structure of a picture is just the fact which that picture is. Hence, on this conception, structure is conceived in abstraction from the picture's function as a representation of a state-of-affairs.

Although incorrect, this reading is perfectly natural. The anti-thesis portrays pictorial 'structure' as formally analogous to Wittgenstein's use of 'structure' with respect to the state-of-affairs. For 'the determinate way in which objects are connected in a state of affairs is the structure of the state of affairs' (*TLP* 2.032). For an adherent to the anti-thesis, if a fact is to be a picture of something it must, in addition to having a structure, *also* stand in a pictorial relationship with what it pictures. That is to say, its elements must also be correlated with objects: each element must be linked with an object.

I argue that this is mistaken. Wittgenstein's notion of pictorial structure encompasses the picture's pictorial relationship to reality. It cannot be conceived of in abstraction from the connecting links between the elements of the picture and their objects. The structure of the picture cannot be reduced to the structure of the fact which constitutes that picture.

This is not a minor terminological issue. Misinterpreting Wittgenstein's use of 'structure' distorts our understanding of Wittgenstein's conception of isomorphism. The anti-thetical reading of 'structure' leads to the idea that it is the 'link' that fixes the 'isomorphism' between language and reality. More generally, the anti-thesis leads to the idea that it is *because* language is connected with reality that it is isomorphic—'in harmony'—with it. That is to say, this reading leads to the idea that what a sign *means* determines the syntactic rules which govern the use of that sign.

In the following two sections I will, respectively, (1) point out some preliminary difficulties with this interpretation of 'structure' and (2) trace out the consequences of this anti-thetical reading.

2.4 Some Problems with the Anti-thesis

Let us examine more closely what Wittgenstein says on this:

> The fact that the elements of a picture are related to one another in a determinate way represents that things are related to one another in the same way.
>
> Let us call this connexion of its elements the structure of the picture ... (*TLP* 2.15)

This passage defines structure as the determinate relationship between the elements of the picture. On the anti-thetical reading, we can ignore that this determinate relationship between elements is a *representation* of a state-of-affairs. That is, we may ignore it in our characterization of what 'structure' consists in: of course we do not deny that the picture is a representation. Rather, we ignore the pictorial status of the picture. That 'a picture... includes the pictorial relationship, which makes it into a picture' (*TLP* 2.1513), does not enter into the definition of pictorial structure. I will show below that this amounts to conceiving Wittgenstein's *Elemente* as I defined 'constituents' at the beginning of this chapter.

If we understand 'structure' as consisting solely in the determinate relationship between the constituents of the picturing fact, what are we to make of 'pictorial form'? Wittgenstein defines pictorial form as the possibility of structure (*TLP* 2.15). So for a picture to have a particular structure, this structure must be a possible one. On the face of it this seems obvious enough. For instance, it is possible for the elements of a spatial picture to stand in a spatial relationship but not, e.g., to stand in a relationship of higher and lower pitch. As noted (see endnote 6), this seems to be the way in which Peter Hacker conceives of pictorial form. As an example of pictorial form he cites the 3-dimensionality of a diorama. It is the 3-dimensionality of the diorama that renders it possible for the elements of the diorama to enter into different 3-dimensional spatial configurations (i.e., different structures). It is also 3-dimensionality which circumscribes the possibilities of structure. For the fact that the diorama is 3-dimensional is what makes it (obviously) impossible for the elements of the diorama to stand in 2-dimensional geometrical configurations, or stand in different configurations of musical notes.

This is not to say that the pictorial form—the 3-dimensionality—of the diorama renders it impossible for the diorama to represent configurations other than spatial objects in three dimensions. Nor does this conception of 'structure' suggest that situations in 3-dimensional space can only be represented by the same (i.e., 3-dimensional spatial situations). Rather, the *3-dimensionality* of the diorama can only *depict* in three dimensions (this is a pleonasm). Furthermore, 3-dimensionality is not even an essential feature of the use of the diorama to picture. For we need not exploit the 3-dimensional features of it. Yet if this were the case, the diorama's pictorial form (as conceived by the anti-thesis) would not (in this case) consist in its 3-dimensionality.

Suppose a picture has a pictorial form (conceived as the anti-thesis does) *in common with* what it pictures. (Also, take for granted that the picture and what it pictures have the same number of elements.) Clearly, it is just as *impossible* for us to represent an 'impossible state-of-affairs' as it is impossible for the 'impossible state-of-affairs' to exist itself. If the fact that you are sitting in your chair is used to represent my sitting in my chair, it will be *impossible* for one to configure the constituents of the picture in such a way that they represent my chair sitting in me. (So that we may preserve the example, let us concede here that no sense can be made of a chair sitting.)

But this example is certainly not paradigmatic. Of course, the sentences of our ordinary language do not need to have a pictorial form (understood in this sense) *in common with* what they represent. For we use printed or spoken words to express virtually any sense whatsoever. (Analogously, the diorama's representational capabilities are not thus restricted, though a particular use of the diorama to *picture* is thus restricted.)

We need not use a temporal relationship to model another temporal relationship, or a spatial relationship to model another spatial relationship, etc. Yet according to Wittgenstein, all the propositions of language are 'pictures' of what they depict (*TLP* 4.011). How are we to guarantee that the structure of our picture does not represent an 'impossible state-of-affairs', i.e., a combination into which the objects cannot enter? On the anti-thetical reading, the natural answer would seem to be that 'What any picture, of whatever form, must have in common with reality in order to be able to depict it—correctly or incorrectly—in any way at all, is *logical* form, i.e., the form of reality' (*TLP* 2.18, my emphasis). One might argue that it need not *share* a pictorial form with what it pictures (though it must *have* one), it need only share logical form.

The initial problem is that Wittgenstein explicitly contradicts this reading. In the *Tractatus* a picture that shares logical form with what it pictures *ipso facto* shares pictorial form with what it pictures. A picture must have pictorial form in common with what it pictures in order to be able to depict it in the way it does (*TLP* 2.17). The closest example of a picture which shares only logical form with what it depicts is what Wittgenstein calls a 'logical picture'. Yet even a logical picture is not a picture *lacking* a pictorial form in common with what it pictures. Rather, it is a picture whose pictorial form *is* logical form (*TLP* 2.18).

Anthony Kenny gives an account which, *prima facie*, reconciles the anti-thesis with Wittgenstein's definitions:

> Wittgenstein seems to have thought that for A to be a picture of B, A must be not altogether like B . . . and not altogether unlike B . . . What makes A like B, what it has in common with B, is . . . called by Wittgenstein 'pictorial form' . . . .
>
> Pictures can be more or less abstract, more or less like what they picture: their pictorial form can be more or less rich. But there is a minimum which must be common between reality and picture if the picture is to be able to portray even incorrectly: this minimum, Wittgenstein says, is logical form.[7]

According to Kenny, then, logical form is the minimum amount of pictorial form a picture can share with the fact it depicts in order to be able to depict it. Logical form is, as it were, just a *little bit* of pictorial form. It follows trivially from this that, if a picture has logical form in common with what it depicts, then it *ipso facto* has pictorial form. It also follows trivially that the picture has this pictorial form in common with what it depicts.

Even without digging too deeply, there are a couple of minor problems with Kenny's reading. First, Kenny's interpretation does little to explain the following conjunction of claims from the *Tractatus*. (1) 'a picture whose pictorial form is logical form is called a *logical picture*' (*TLP* 2.181); *and* (2) 'a *logical picture* of facts is a thought' (*TLP* 3, my emphasis).[8] On Kenny's reading, there is nothing *a priori* absurd in the idea of creating a picture (which is not necessarily a *thought*) that shares *nothing* but logical form with what it depicts. Why, on this reading, would it be impossible to create a sensibly perceptible picture which shares only logical form? Why does this sort of picture have to be a 'thought'?

One might just reply dogmatically that any sensibly perceptible picture—i.e., any picture which is not merely a thought, not merely a logical picture—does in fact share something over and above bare logical form. But it is unclear to me why this should be so, or on what grounds it might be demonstrated. For if logical form is a minimal quantity of pictorial form, and if pictures can, as Kenny says, be more or less abstract, why are the—and presumably only the—*most* abstract of pictures incapable of being sensibly perceptible?

Second, Kenny's reading is not smoothly reconciled with 2.182: 'Every picture is *also* a logical picture'. Wittgenstein's emphasis on 'also' is surely meant to earmark an important and/or non-obvious point. It would be odd to emphasize 'also' if the claim at 2.182 was as trivial as Kenny's interpretation implies. On Kenny's interpretation, it is a trivial consequence because (1) logical form is a little bit of pictorial form, a minimal commonality between picture and fact; and (2) a logical picture shares only logical form with what it depicts. 2.182 would then amount to the claim that what has *more* than, or the same as, this minimum commonality, also has this minimum commonality. This is comparable to asserting that, if the minimum quantity of water one can have in a pitcher is *n*, then every pitcher which contains a quantity of water greater than or equal to *n also* has—at least—the quantity *n*! Hacker's interpretation also fits the anti-thetical reading of structure. He (rightly) interprets 'pictorial form' as identical with the possibility of structure. We have noted that the example of pictorial form Hacker proffers is the 3-dimensionality of a diorama. This does explain three important features of Wittgenstein's conception of pictorial form. It explains (1) Wittgenstein's identification of pictorial form with the possibility of structure. For it is indeed the 3-dimensionality of the diorama which underlies the possibility of depictions done in three dimensions. (Again, as opposed to the 3-dimensionality of the diorama underlying the possibility of depicting 3-dimensional situations. Pictorial form, on this interpretation, circumscribes the possibilities of the depiction, not the depicted.) It succeeds in accounting for (2) how it is that a picture must have both logical and pictorial form. For logical form is what different pictorial forms (capable of representing the same state-of-affairs) have in common with one another. And it explains (3) what a fact and picture having *logical* form in common consists in. Logical form is identical with the form of that represented. If we are discussing the representation of a state-of-affairs, logical form is identical with the combinatorial possibilities of the objects in the state-of-affairs.

Yet how can this interpretation be reconciled with sections 2.161 and 2.17 of the *Tractatus*? In those sections Wittgenstein clearly claims that *pictorial* form and the form of the state-of-affairs depicted must be identical. The picture must *share* its pictorial form with what it pictures. Hacker fails to assimilate Wittgenstein's contention that a picture must have pictorial form *in common with* what it depicts (*TLP* 2.17). On Hacker's interpretation, it is understandable why a picture must have a pictorial form in order to represent. Yet it is completely mysterious why the picture must have pictorial (as opposed to logical) form in common with what it depicts (in order to be able to represent). All the picture need have in common with what it depicts is logical form. That is, each element of the picture must be isomorphic with the object with which it stands in a connecting link.

Let us bypass these difficulties and focus on the consequences of this reading of 'structure'.

2.5 Consequences of the Anti-thesis

I noted in the previous section that, on the anti-thetical reading of 'structure', pictures, for instance sentences or dioramas, do not need to share pictorial form (viz. combinatorial *possibilities*, e.g. 3-dimensionality) with what they represent. We use the spoken or written word to represent anything we want. So perhaps, as Hacker implies, and as Kenny virtually suggests, they merely need to have logical form in common. But what is this logical form? It must, somehow, be distinguishable from the pictorial form: the combinatorial *possibilities* of the constituents. (For example, suppose musical notes were 'objects'. Then it would be a combinatorial possibility that we can align two musical notes in a sequential relation, as opposed to a spatial relation.)

There is only one account of logical form compatible with this reading of pictorial form. Since a picture and what it pictures need not share pictorial form (qua combinatorial possibilities), *something* must foreclose the possibility of representing 'impossible states-of-affairs'. That is to say, in some sense of 'form', the form of the pictorial elements must be isomorphic with the form of their objects. Well, the form of an object is its combinatorial possibilities, and I explained in section 2.1 that pictorial *constituents* too have a kind of form over and above their combinatorial possibilities, viz., their combinatorial *permissibilities*. (An impermissible combination of pictorial constituents would be a possible combination which, as it were, represents an 'impossible state-of-affairs'.) On this reading, it is only logical form that a picture must have in common with what it pictures. Thus logical form must surely be the combinatorial permissibilities of the constituents of the picture.

Suppose 'aRb' is such a picture: 'a' goes proxy for *a*, 'b' goes proxy for *b*, and 'R' goes proxy for *R*. Let us further suppose that while *aRb* is a state-of-affairs, *abR* is an 'impossible state-of-affairs'. Such a (determinate) combination of objects is contrary to their forms. They *cannot* enter into such a combination. It will accordingly be *impermissible* (in this notation) to combine the signs 'a', 'b', and 'R' into a fact with the structure 'abR'. Of course, it is *possible* for the constituents to be combined in this manner. (I just did it.) Logical form, on this reading, cannot consist in what is possible for the constituents. It must consist in what is permissible for them.

How, then, is this logical form set up? Or better: by virtue of what are the rules of logical syntax (in this notation) to be governed? If logical form circumscribes what is *permissible* for the pictorial constituents, what is the standard by which we judge what is and what is not permissible? There are no alternatives here: clearly the objects would have to play this role. For it is the form of the objects that logical form must mirror. It must be *by virtue of* these constituents standing for objects that logical form fixes what combinations these signs may and may not enter into. Conclusion: 'isomorphism' is the result of the 'connecting link'. This is the crux of the anti-thesis in this chapter.

To summarize, I supposed the structure of the picture to consist merely in the determinate relation between the constituents of the picture (i.e., elements conceived in abstraction from that picture's pictorial relation). On this reading of structure, Wittgenstein's definitions entailed that pictorial form amounts to what is *possible* for these constituents. This, together with the fact that we use the written or spoken word to represent most anything we want, entails that the picturing fact need not share its pictorial form with what it pictures. They must have something in common, something that forecloses the possibility of representing 'impossible states-of-affairs'. Let's call it 'logical form'. However, this reading of logical form makes sense only if logical form circumscribes combinatorial permissibilities, not combinatorial possibilities. That it is impossible to represent an 'impossible state-of-affairs' must be due to the fact that it is impermissible to combine the constituents of the picture such that, if they represented despite this, they would represent a configuration that is not possible for the objects. If logical form circumscribes permissibilities, then we need a standard by which to judge what is and what is not permissible. This must be the picture's pictorial relationship to reality. In the next section I refute the reading of 'structure' from which I have derived these consequences.

2.6 The Refutation

What is *possible* for the constituents does not necessarily coincide with what is *permissible* for them: here at any rate, all that is possible is not necessarily permitted. Recall that Wittgenstein defines pictorial form as the possibility of pictorial structure (*TLP* 2.15). He also defines pictorial form in another way, viz., as the possibility that the objects linked with the pictorial elements are structured as the picture is structured (*TLP* 2.151). From these two definitions of pictorial form it follows that, what the anti-thetical reading calls an impermissible combination of pictorial constituents, Wittgenstein calls an impossible combination of pictorial elements. Yet the anti-thetical reading identifies pictorial elements with pictorial constituents. Clearly a problem is going to arise.

In fact a contradiction arises. Let the structure of a picture be the determinate relationship between constituents. A picture stands in a representing relation to reality, i.e., to be a picture is to have the constituents of this picture standing in a connecting link with the objects of what it pictures (*TLP* 2.13, 2.131). A picture is also a fact, so it can be defined as follows. A picture $=_{def}$ a fact that has its elements going proxy for the objects of a state-of-affairs. On this reading of 'structure' it follows that: the *structure* of a picture $=_{def}$ the determinate way in which the constituents of that picturing fact are related to one another—taking it for granted, of course, that those constituents are 'linked' with, i.e., stand in a representing relationship to the objects of a state-of-affairs. Since *pictorial form* $=_{def}$ the possibility of *structure* (*TLP* 2.151), and given our definition of 'structure', we may also make the following definition of 'pictorial form': *pictorial form* $=_{def}$ the *possibility of* the determinate way in which the ('linked') constituents of a fact are related to one another.

Since Wittgenstein also defines pictorial form in a different way, as $=_{def}$ to the possibility that the objects of a state-of-affairs are combined with one another as are the 'linked' constituents of the picture (*TLP* 2.15), we are entitled to make the following cumbersome assertion of identity. The very possibility of the determinate way in which the constituents of the picture are related to one another $=_{def}$ the possibility that the objects of the state-of-affairs are combined with one another as are the constituents of the picture. And this amounts to saying that the possibility of *structure* with regard to a picture $=_{def}$ the possibility that the objects of that state-of-affairs which is depicted stand in the same relationship as the constituents of that fact which depicts it.

So if it is *not* possible for the objects of that which is depicted to stand in the same relationship as the constituents of the picture, it follows that it is *not* possible for that picture to have a structure.

This is an odd conclusion to reach if we understand the 'structure' of a picture to consist *merely* in the way in which the elements of that picture are related to *one another*, i.e., if that relationship is conceived in abstraction from the links between the elements and the objects which they stand for. It is odd, that is, if we do not see the concept of pictorial structure as in any way tied up with what that picture represents. It is perplexing why Wittgenstein contends that the *structure* of the picture is responsible to reality.

One might suggest the following explanation for this oddity. Let us define: (i) 'possible structure of a picture' $=_{def}$ 'possible configuration of the constituents of that fact which depicts'; (ii) 'possible structure of that which is depicted' $=_{def}$ 'possible configuration for the objects of that state-of-affairs which is represented by the picture'. The explanation might then run: suppose the structure of the picture is a possible one, i.e., suppose we have some fact the elements of which we have linked to objects. Further suppose that the corresponding structure in reality is impossible. Then, so this explanation might run, the picture cannot represent the 'impossible state-of-affairs' it purports to represent. In short, 'attempts' to represent 'impossible states-of-affairs' are not representations at all. Illogical representations are not representations at all.

What Wittgenstein really meant by 'impossible' with respect to pictorial structure is just: not in accordance with the logical form of reality.

First, we are still left in the lurch regarding *why* the picture does not manage to represent the 'impossible state-of-affairs' it 'attempts' to. What is the problem with having the constituents stand for certain objects, and then configuring these constituents into a fact which conflicts with the combinatorial possibilities of the referents of these constituents? It seems to fulfil the requirements for picture-hood, so what is it that disqualifies this from being a representation, and hence a representation of an 'impossible state-of-affairs'?

A second, and perhaps more serious objection is that this explanation (viz. the explanation given in the paragraph before the previous one) is gibberish within the confines of Wittgenstein's definitions. If a possible structure of the picture corresponds to an 'impossible state-of-affairs', it follows from Wittgenstein's definitions that the picture *has no structure.* Wittgenstein's definitions imply it in the following way.

Suppose a possible pictorial structure corresponds to an 'impossible state-of-affairs'. It is then possible for me to structure a picture that, if *per impossibile* it could, would depict in a way that is impossible for that which is depicted to be structured. Yet, by definition, 'the possibility of a picture *having* structure' (= 'pictorial form') *is* the possibility that the objects of that which is depicted are combined in the same way as the elements of the picture. So if we identify the structure of a picture merely as the way its constituents are related to one another, we get the following identity: the possibility of a picture *having structure* $=_{def}$ the possibility that the *structure* of that which is depicted is the same as the *structure* of the picture. But it is incoherent to say that the very *possibility* of pictorial structure depends on whether or not a possible pictorial structure coincides with a state-of-affairs. For if it is *not* possible for the referents of the constituents to be structured as the constituents themselves *are* structured, then it is not possible for the picture to *have* a structure. We could, under certain conditions, argue from the claim that the so-called 'picture' does have a structure, to the claim that it has no structure. (More precisely, we could assume that a 'picture' has a structure, and conclude from this (*inter alia*) that it is impossible for it to have a structure, and hence that it does not.) Contradiction.

Of course, it must be noted that this contradiction amounts to a refutation of the anti-thesis only on the assumption that Wittgenstein consistently inter-defined the words under consideration here. I argue presently that they should be interpreted so as to be consistent.

2.7 The Thesis: the connecting link presupposes isomorphism

The contradiction arose because we ignored the fact that the structure of a *picture* is a determinate relationship between names. Unlike the possibility of structure in the state-of-affairs, the possibility of a picture having structure is dependent on the possibility of what that picture represents. (We might say here that 'structure' cannot even be understood merely syntactically.) What a picture represents is a matter of (1) the way in which those elements of the picture are related to one another, and (2) what objects those elements of the picture stand for. So the possibility of pictorial structure is dependent on two things: (i) the possibility that the elements of the picture stand in the determinate relation that they do; and (ii) the possibility of there being a link between those pictorial elements and the objects of that which is pictured. And it is (ii) which really differentiates a picture from a mere fact. It is plausible that we will find our distinctive requirement for pictorial structure here.

We have seen so far that the constituents of our so-called 'picture' (as it were our fact trying to be a picture) can stand in a determinate relation to one another and *not* have a structure (not really constitute a picture). One could say that it has a structure conceived merely as a fact,[9] but does not have a structure conceived as a picture. This is because we 'attempt' to represent a configuration that is not possible for the objects which are designated by the pictorial constituents. That is to say, if the so-called 'picture' could depict despite this, it would depict an 'impossible state-of-affairs'. This entails that our 'picture' can fulfil the first requirement (1), viz., that the elements do stand in a determinate relation to one another, without having a structure. Consequently, it cannot then fulfil our second requirement (2), viz., that there are links between its elements and the objects designated by those elements. For otherwise, according to Wittgenstein's definitions it would *be* a picture. But it cannot be a picture, because it does not have a structure.[10] It is potentially misleading (though correct) to say—as Wittgenstein does—that a picture must have pictorial form *in common* with reality. For to not have pictorial form in common is for the picture not to have pictorial form *simpliciter*. To talk of having pictorial form 'in common with' reality makes it sound as though a picture might have pictorial form which was not in common with what it pictures. By the lights of the *Tractatus*, this does not make sense. To be a picture is *ipso facto* to have a pictorial form. This follows form (1) the fact that to be a picture is to be a picture *of* something; and (2) that if a picture does not have pictorial form 'in common with what it pictures', then it does not picture (cf. *TLP* 2.17).[11] This does, incidentally, partly characterize the difference between the conception of 'structure' I advocate, and the one I have been criticizing.

If our would-be picture satisfies requirement (1) for picture-hood, then it cannot satisfy requirement (2). It seems inevitable, then, that the reason our so-called picture does not have a structure—the reason our 'picture' is not really a picture—is that it is impossible for there to be links between the elements of the 'picture' and the objects of that which is 'pictured'. The explanation for this is surely that, in order for it to be possible to set up such links, it must be the case that the combinatorial possibilities of the elements of the picture are isomorphic with the combinatorial possibilities of the objects of that which is pictured. These elements would not be *Elemente* if they did not conform in this way, since a possible structure is a structure that is possible for *meaningful* elements.

If a combination of signs 'does not make sense that can only come of our not having *given* any meaning to certain of its parts' (*NB* p. 23). The set of combinatorial possibilities for a pictorial element is not something that falls out of or results from that element having or being given meaning. Rather, these combinatorial possibilities of a pictorial element are a presupposition to the possibility of that element having a meaning. Conceived in this way, it follows that 'isomorphism' is not the consequence of, but rather presupposed by, the 'link' between the pictorial element and object. At the level of the picture, this amounts to saying that logico-pictorial form is presupposed by the pictorial relationship.

I urge the reader to try to set aside their bewilderment regarding *why* such a positively bizarre issue should have concerned—indeed even have occurred to—the early Wittgenstein. I address this '*why*' in the following chapter. For now, I do contend *that* this is the correct reading. For the elements of the picture to be 'isomorphic' with their referents is, roughly speaking, for that picture to be syntactically well-formed. For the pictorial elements to stand in a connecting link with the objects is for the elements to have 'meaning'; and for all the pictorial elements to stand in a connecting link with their respective objects is, roughly speaking, what constitutes that picture's 'content', or 'sense'. And if a propositional sign is to be used to express a sense, then it must be well-formed.

We still have one problem left: how precisely does pictorial form differ from logical form? We have seen that it cannot be the 3-dimensionality of the diorama that constitutes its pictorial form. For this would entail that the picture need not have pictorial form in common with what it represents, which is explicitly denied by Wittgenstein (*TLP* 2.17). Further, this is what led to the contradiction, so it must be inconsistent with other assertions in the text.

I *conjecture* that Wittgenstein had something close to the following in mind. The picture has pictorial form in common with the fact it depicts. This is because its pictorial form consists entirely in the *concrete instantiation* of logical form. The actual combinatorial possibilities of the constituents in the picture instantiate logical form. Two pictures representing the same state-of-affairs may differ in their combinatorial possibilities precisely because those combinatorial possibilities are identical when considered *abstractly*. For example, let us say the combinatorial possibilities of 'a' and 'b' are: 'ab' and 'ba'. Also assume that for 'c' and 'd' they are: '${}^{c}d$' and 'd^{c}'. There is obviously a feature shared between these two notations, yet to combine 'c' and 'd' in this diagonal manner is *different* than combining 'a' and 'b' horizontally. The difference consists (merely) in that one is diagonal and the other is horizontal. Another (though flawed) example might be the spoken sentence versus the written one, if we may suppose generally (and wrongly) that the *only* difference between them was that one was spoken and one written. Logical form is not, as Kenny suggests, a maximally abstract sort of pictorial form. Rather, it is pictorial form *considered* abstractly. It constitutes that *feature* shared by alternate (but compatible) pictorial forms. Logical form is not something distinct from pictorial form. Every picture is *also* a logical picture (*TLP* 2.182). Logical form is what one is left with if one abstracts from the way in which it is instantiated in any particular case.[12] The next section examines Wittgenstein's explicit treatment of propositions starting at 3.1 in the *Tractatus*.

2.8 The Proposition

I distinguished two aspects of Wittgenstein's concept of a picture: form and content. A picture is both well-formed and meaningful. I emphasized further that 'well-formed-ness' is in a certain sense prior to 'meaningful-ness', i.e., that certain syntactic conditions must be satisfied in order for a picture to have sense. A proposition is a picture (*TLP* 4.021), so if it is important, this priority of syntax over sense should somehow apply to Wittgenstein's discussion of the proposition.

Not only does it apply, but furthermore, the issue is discussed explicitly in a number of places. In particular, it finds expression in Wittgenstein's distinction between (1) the propositional sign and (2) the proposition. Wittgenstein's characterization of the distinction between the proposition and propositional sign not only reinforces my interpretation that the 'link' presupposes 'isomorphism'. More importantly, it shows to what extent Wittgenstein was at pains to emphasize it, and hence that it is not merely some remote implication I am drawing from the definitions in the text.

I will argue that, roughly at least, what we ordinarily mean by the distinction between (i) being well-formed, and (ii) having 'content' or 'sense', corresponds, in the *proposition*, to Wittgenstein's technical distinction between (i_1) syntax and (ii_1) sense. With respect to a *name* occuring as an element in the elementary proposition, I will argue that the distinction between (i) and (ii) corresponds to Wittgenstein's technical distinction between (i_2) syntax and (ii_2) meaning.

A proposition is a picture, and an elementary proposition is a proposition, so an elementary proposition is also a picture. Like a picture, an elementary proposition has elements; here Wittgenstein actually calls them 'names' [*Namen*] (*TLP* 3.202). These names stand for objects (*TLP* 3.22). Wittgenstein also introduces the notion of an (elementary) 'propositional sign', and calls *its* elements "simple signs" [„*einfache Zeichen*"] (*TLP* 3.201).[13] Wittgenstein's explanation of this distinction in the elementary proposition, between names and simple signs, is precisely analogous to the distinction I drew earlier in this chapter between (1) the elements of the picture qua *names* of objects and (2) the *constituents* whose concatenation constitutes the fact which depicts. And the distinction between a propositional sign and a proposition is precisely analogous to the distinction between a fact which is used to picture and a picture.

In the *Tractatus*, both propositions and proper parts of propositions fall under the more general heading 'symbols'. Moreover, propositional signs and (not necessarily simple) proper parts of propositional signs fall under the general heading 'signs' (*TLP* 3.31-2). Like the rest of this chapter, for the sake of simplicity I confine my examination in this section to the elementary proposition. Since an elementary proposition is also a proposition, the distinction between sign [*Zeichen*] and symbol [*Symbol*] should apply to it *mutatis mutandis*.

'In a proposition a thought finds expression that can be perceived by the senses' (*TLP* 3.1). And in the proposition a 'sign is what can be perceived of a symbol' (*TLP* 3.32). Among other—less simple—types of things, a name is a proper part of an elementary proposition. Correspondingly, a "simple sign" is a proper part of an elementary propositional sign. So discussion of symbols and signs should apply to the names and "simple signs" of the elementary proposition.

Wittgenstein makes a number of points regarding signs and symbols: The sign is entirely arbitrary, for a common sign can be used to express different symbols (*TLP* 3.322). 'In the proposition, 'Green is green'—where the first word is the proper name of a person and the last an adjective—these words do not merely have different meanings: they are *different symbols*' (*TLP* 3.323). To recognize the form that a name has—the aspect of the symbol that mirrors the form of its referent—the sign must be taken together with its logico-syntactic employment (*TLP* 3.327). But paying attention to the logico-syntactic employment of a sign is something different from paying attention to the *meaning* of a sign. The meaning of a simple sign is, in the case of the elementary proposition(al sign), the object with which it stands in a connecting link. The syntax of a sign is not *what* it signifies, but *how* it signifies:

> In logical syntax the meaning of a sign should never play a role. It must be possible to establish logical syntax without mentioning the *meaning* of a sign: *only* the description of the expressions may be presupposed. (*TLP* 3.33)

The rules of logical syntax must go without saying, once we know how each individual sign signifies (*TLP* 3.334). This is noteworthy. It must be possible to establish logical syntax without mentioning the meaning of sign. But if so, the logical syntax of a simple sign is established without reference to the meaning that simple sign has qua name. Therefore, unlike the permissibilities of the constituent discussed earlier in this chapter, the criterion by reference to which we *establish* our logical syntax cannot be an appeal to the meaning (the object).

Despite this, the meaning of a symbol is not *irrelevant* to the syntax of that symbol. For 'In order to recognize a symbol by its sign we must observe how it is used with a sense' (*TLP* 3.326)— i.e., how it is used in meaningful propositions. A simple sign is responsible to its meaning, yet we do not *appeal* to its meaning to justify its logical syntax. This fits my interpretation like a glove: in order to be *able* to use a simple sign with *a* meaning, it must be the case that its logical syntax is fixed.

Wittgenstein marks a distinction between the essential and accidental features of the proposition (*not* the propositional sign[14]). (*TLP* 3.34). This is precisely analogous to the distinction, in the picture theory, between pictorial and logical form. Not only are the actual signs we use arbitrary, but our syntax itself is also to *a certain extent* arbitrary (*TLP* 3.3421). In the same way that syntax is arbitrary, pictorial form is also arbitrary. For it is not that a picture must have pictorial form in common with reality, in order to be able to depict it *no matter what.* Rather, pictorial form is essential for the picture to depict *in the way it does* (*TLP* 2.17).

This point is subtle. The picture can *only* represent 'in the way it does', i.e., it cannot represent in any other way than 'in the way it does'. The 'way it does' represent is essential to its identity, to its being the picture that it is. Hence pictorial form is not arbitrary in the slightest relative to the picture that has that pictorial form. A picture's pictorial form is constitutive of that picture. The extent to which a particular pictorial form is arbitrary is, rather, the extent to which the state-of-affairs represented with that picture can be represented by other pictures with a different pictorial form. What is essential to *any* proposition whatever is that it have logical form in common with reality, i.e., logical form in common with the fact it pictures:

> What any picture, of whatever form, must have in common with reality, in order to depict it—correctly or incorrectly—*in any way at all,* is logical form, i.e. the form of reality. (*TLP* 2.18)
>
> Every picture is *at the same time* a logical one. (On the other hand, not every picture is, for example, a spatial one.) (*TLP* 2.182)

Just as a picture must have pictorial form, so a proposition must have a syntax. Both are to some extent arbitrary. However, what any syntax, if it is to be a *possible* mode of signifying, must have in common with reality is that it cannot allow for the production of representations that 'contradict logic'. It must share a common form with what it depicts (see *TLP* 3.03-3.032):

> A proposition possesses essential and accidental features. Accidental features are those that result from *the particular way* in which the propositional sign is produced. Essential features are those without which the proposition *could not express its sense.* (*TLP* 3.34, my emphasis)

It 'could not express its sense'[15] because the possibility of so doing presupposes these essential features. These essential features constitute the *possibility* of the proposition expressing its sense. Hence, that a proposition has sense (and there are no other sorts of propositions) *presupposes* those essential features (cf. for the sake of interest *NB* pp. 15, 108).

Wittgenstein's discussion of sign and symbol, together with his conception of structure in the picture theory clearly indicate that he was intent on emphasizing that syntax is somehow prior to sense. It is presented as though it was among the most significant discoveries in the *Tractatus*. Indeed, we can easily see why it should be considered important. For it plays a most central role in the early Wittgenstein's account of how a proposition can be false yet meaningful. It is the fruit of Wittgenstein's struggle to provide an explanation of that 'obscurity that *obviously* resides in the question' that opened this chapter. A quotation from the *Notebooks* is particularly illuminating here.

> The proposition is a measure of the world.
>
> This is the picture of a process and is wrong [i.e. the proposition is false]. In that case how can it still be a picture of that process?
>
> "a" *can* go proxy for a and "b" *can* go proxy for b when "a" stands in the relation "R" to "b": this is what that potential internal relation that we are looking for consists in. (*NB* p. 41)

In the next chapter I begin to take up why this was felt to be such a problem for the early Wittgenstein, and what drove him to the picture theory's peculiar solution to that problem.

Notes

1. This term, 'isomorphism', is introduced by P. M. S. Hacker in an exposition of the picture theory, and his use of the term is closely related to mine. See *Insight and Illusion, Revised Edn.* (Clarendon, Oxford, 1986), p. 58ff. If there are differences, I can't pinpoint them. If I have appropriated it, I hope my definition makes clear any divergence of use between the two.
2. James Conant has discussed the implications of Wittgenstein's disagreement with Frege here. See 'Elucidation and nonsense in Frege and early Wittgenstein', in *The New Wittgenstein*, Alice Crary and Rupert Read (eds.) (Routledge, 2000). Conant's concern is with how this disagreement with Frege throws light on Wittgenstein's conception of the propositions of the *Tractatus* itself. My concern here is only with how this disagreement finds formulation in the picture theory.
3. Ibid., p. 176.
4. And even a fact can only be indeterminate in the sense that, e.g., $p \vee q$ is indeterminate. I.e., it is *determinately* indeterminate (cf. *TLP* 3.251).
5. In a sense, a good example of an (indeterminately) indeterminate relation between elements would be a complex. This however is potentially misleading; for the *representation*—description—of a complex is not indeterminate. If it is an incomplete description of a complex (e.g., 'this book is above the table') it reduces to a disjunction of possibilities (e.g., 'this book is touching the top of the table' *or* 'this book hovers ...' and so on (*ad infinitum*?)). This would amount to a *determinately* indeterminate relation between the elements of the state-of-affairs (as opposed to a complex). I.e., a determinately indeterminate relation is essentially represented with *multiple* elementary propositions.
6. For instance, this seems to be Hacker's conception (op. cit., p. 59). For he cites as an example of 'pictorial form' the 3-dimensionality of the diorama. This has nothing to do with what that picture represents, for what it represents presumably need not be 3-dimensional. Hence the possibilities (i.e., possible structure(s)) which this 3-dimensionality circumscribes need not have anything to do with what the diorama represents.
7. Anthony Kenny, *Wittgenstein* (Harvard, 1973), p. 57.
8. It is difficult to conceive of what Wittgenstein had in mind when he envisaged a picture whose pictorial form *was* logical form. As will become clear in the next section, I understand logical form to be the common *feature*, that different pictorial forms share, allowing them all the possibility of representing the same situation. We get a hint as to what he might be on about when he says that 'A picture whose pictorial form is logical form is called a logical picture' (*TLP* 2.181), and then goes on to define a 'logical picture' as a 'thought' (*TLP* 3). A 'thought' is what different sentences which express the same sense have in common. This is all quite natural, but it becomes mysterious when Wittgenstein identifies a 'thought' with a 'logical picture'; for this seems to give 'thought' some sort of substantive existence—probably in the mind. One is inclined then to understand the thought as a picture having all the essential, formal properties of a regular picture (sentence), but lacking any of the conventional properties. That is, it has in *substantive* form what is merely the shared feature different but compatible pictorial forms share. How this is so is, indeed, mysterious. For an illuminating discussion of this, see A. J. P. Kenny's

'Wittgenstein's Early Philosophy of Mind', in I. Block (ed.), *Perspectives on the Philosophy of Wittgenstein* (Blackwell, 1981).

9. Although even this is ultimately problematic. For as was noted in the first section, an element of a picture *is* an element only by virtue of the fact that it stands for a simple object. Excepting this, however, we can for the moment say that our 'picture' has a structure when conceived merely as a fact.
10. There is no such thing as a picture without a structure. For 'if a fact is to be a picture, it must have something in common with what it depicts' (*TLP* 2.16). 'What a picture must have in common with reality is ... pictorial form' (*TLP* 2.17). And the fact that a picture has pictorial form presupposes that it has a (possible) structure.
11. We have shown in this case that it is impossible for this picture to have a structure. This is identical with saying that it does not have a pictorial form (i.e. 'pictorial form' $=_{def}$ 'possibility of structure'). If it does not have pictorial form then, as we see from 2.16 and 2.17, it cannot be a picture.
12. I recognize, however, that on this reading there is a *sense* in which a picture does not have pictorial form in common with what it pictures. For the only thing that 'has' a particular concrete instantiation of logical form is that particular concrete instantiation. But there is also a sense in which the picture does have pictorial form in common with what it represents. For, as it were, the combinatorial possibilities are the *same*, even if they are not *identical*.
13. It is significant that Wittgenstein employs the same verb form (*vertreten*) to express the relationship between (1) the elements of a *picture* and their respective objects; and (2) the relationship between *names* of a *proposition* and their respective objects. For he does not call the elements of a propositional sign names, but, as noted, "simple signs". This is a further indication that an element [*Elemente*] of a *picture* is not (as we presumed in a previous section) to be conceived of in abstraction from its 'connecting link' with its object.
14. I say 'not the propositional sign' because this can lead to a mistaken interpretation. One might think that the unessential features of the propositional sign are determined by the method of projection (see *TLP* 3.1-3.13). It would be the *method* by which we project the propositional sign that determines which aspects of it are essential (i.e., are part of the *proposition*). This seems to me to be a conflation of (1) the propositional sign qua fact and (2) the various facts about a complex containing the elements which (in a different sense) constitute the propositional sign; for what is essential, in this sense, is determined by the *determinate* relationship between the elements of the propositional *sign* (including elements that name relations). And this determinate relationship, being a feature of the propositional sign, is prior to any method of projection (except, to be sure, in so far as what constitutes an element of the propositional sign, which is indeed a function of its potential representational status). It seems to me that 'method of projection' is the process of as it were putting the signs that *go proxy* for the objects into the place where they would be if the proposition is true, as it were filling the place in logical space. It is noteworthy that in an appendix to *Philosophical Grammar* Wittgenstein criticizes his earlier conception of 'method of projection' on the grounds that it mistakenly compared a *method* of projection with projection *lines* (*PR* p. 212f.).
15. I have been ignoring the term 'sense' [*Sinn*]. The sense of a picture is what it represents (*TLP* 2.221). Propositions represent facts, which are the existence and non-existence of states-of-affairs (*p* and not-*q* for instance). The sense of an elementary proposition would seem then to be the existence of a state-of-affairs. But this cannot be so, for if a proposition has a sense this would presuppose the existence of the state-of-affairs, and then the proposition could not be false. Wittgenstein clarifies matters: 'The sense of a proposition is its agreement and disagreement with the possibilities of the existence and non-existence of states-of-affairs' (*TLP*

4.2). The sense of an elementary proposition should then be its agreement with the possibility of the existence of a state-of-affairs. It *agrees* with the structure of that state-of-affairs *if* it did exist.

3

Augustine's Language: Bild and Idee

> Frazer's account of the magical . . . views of mankind is unsatisfactory: it makes these views look like *errors*.
> I now believe that it would be right to begin my book with remarks about metaphysics as a kind of magic.
> But doing this I must not make a case for magic nor may I make fun of it.
> The depth of magic should be preserved.—
> Indeed, here the elimination of magic has itself the character of magic.
>
> Ludwig Wittgenstein, *Philosophical Occasions*, James Klagge and Alfred Nordmann, Alfred (eds.) (Hacket, Indianapolis, 1993), pp. 116, 119.

3.1 Preliminaries

Philosophical Investigations opens with Augustine's description of how he came to learn his native tongue. From this description Wittgenstein gleans a 'particular picture of the essence of human language' (*PI* §1). This picture is that the words of a language name objects, and that sentences are combinations of such names. The 'picture' is then distinguished from the 'idea': 'Every word has a meaning. This meaning is correlated with the word. It is the object for which the word stands.' (ibid.).

The picture and the idea are related too: it is 'In this picture of language [that] we finds the roots of the . . . idea' (ibid.). This relationship is reiterated, perhaps by way of emphasis: 'That philosophical conception of meaning [i.e. the 'idea'] has its place in a primitive conception of the way language functions [i.e. the 'picture']' (*PI* §2).[1] What exactly is this relationship between a conception of *meaning* and a conception of the functioning of *language*? It has been suggested by Baker and Hacker that the 'idea' is a development of the picture, that Wittgenstein is filling the picture out and tracing some natural consequences of this *Urbild* (as they call Augustine's picture). For, they argue, the picture by itself is too bare for the purposes of introducing a discussion of meaning. They claim that 'If Wittgenstein's subsequent discussion is to be related to his opening presentation of Augustine's picture, then we cannot say that this picture includes nothing apart from the initial pair of theses'.[2] The (warranted) assumption here is that Wittgenstein's subsequent discussion *is* related to his opening presentation of Augustine's picture. So Baker's and Hacker's conclusion is: we cannot say the picture includes nothing apart from the initial pair of theses that (1) words name objects and (2) sentences are combinations of such words.

Baker's and Hacker's conclusion is less compelling once we observe that they consider only one *kind* of relationship between (1) the opening presentation of Augustine's picture and (2) subsequent discussion. For perhaps there are alternatives to viewing discussion subsequent to §1 of *Philosophical Investigations* as a direct *criticism* of Augustine's picture, or even as a direct criticism of some development of Augustine's picture. In my view, subsequent discussion is a *diagnosis* of the philosophical problems arising from a dogmatic application of Augustine's picture to our description of the functioning of language. It is for this reason, I will argue, that the picture does not include more than this initial pair of theses. I suggest that to properly understand the discussion subsequent to the first section, we must keep the 'picture' and the 'idea' separate, i.e., we must *not* attribute more to the picture than Wittgenstein explicitly attributes.

With respect to discussion surrounding the concept of ostensive definition in the first thirty-six sections of the *Investigations*, I argue in this chapter that it is a diagnosis that Wittgenstein is primarily engaged in. In the following chapter, Chapter Four, I extend my interpretation of Wittgenstein's method to encompass the first fifty-five sections of *Philosophical Investigations*. Jointly, the present and following chapter contain my sustained argument that, in the first fifty-five sections of the *Investigations*, Wittgenstein is engaged in a diagnosis of how dogmatic adherence to the 'picture' can *result* in the 'idea'. That is to say, I will argue that Wittgenstein's diagnosis consists in showing how dogmatic adherence to Augustine's conception of the functioning of *words* can lead to a referential conception of *meaning*. If I am correct, it is clearly misguided to pack into Augustine's picture *ab initio* the theses and implications of that 'theory' of meaning Wittgenstein calls the 'idea'. On my view, the *whole point* of his examination is to clarify the relationship between Augustine's picture and 'that philosophical conception of meaning'.

One caveat is necessary lest this thesis appear overly dogmatic. It is not that the word 'criticism' is of *no* use when interpreting these sections of the *Investigations*. For, firstly, there are many of Wittgenstein's remarks that are directed at the inappropriateness of this picture to areas of our language (*PI* §§1, 3, 16, 27). Nonetheless, there is no license to infer that what is legitimately characterized as inappropriate is also legitimately characterized as mistaken. Indeed, according to Wittgenstein, the question is not whether this picture is right or wrong. Rather, the question is: 'Is this representation useful or not?' (*PI* §3).[3] Second, suppose for the moment that Wittgenstein is engaged in a diagnosis of philosophical problems connected with language learning and (relatedly) ostensive definition; and suppose the diagnosis is that those problems rest on the *dogmatic* application of Augustine's picture. This too is a critical discussion of the *application* of this picture.

However, Baker's and Hacker's reading of the general strategy in the *Investigations* presents the introduction of Augustine's picture as merely preliminary. Moreover, the picture's genesis into a more developed set of theses would also be preliminary. On their reading, both would be preliminary to Wittgenstein's real project of criticizing these more developed doctrines which constitute natural developments of the original picture. But I want to argue that, properly understood, Wittgenstein's 'criticism' of these more developed doctrines turns essentially on the *relationship* between Augustine's picture and its 'natural consequences'. A clear understanding of this relationship is the key feature of Wittgenstein's method of treating those philosophical problems arising out of Augustine's picture. Indeed, this relationship is the central theme in §§1-55.

Bearing my caveat in mind, let us get back to Wittgenstein's distinction between the picture and the idea. Baker and Hacker suggest that the picture itself is what informs philosophical reflection on language, and that the idea is a development one is inclined to make of the picture. Quite right, but according to Baker and Hacker, the real object of Wittgenstein's subsequent criticism is a theory of meaning they call the 'Augustinian picture'. Thus they (quite deliberately) include, in what they distinguish as the 'Augustinian picture', claims over and above Wittgenstein's description of 'Augustine's picture'. They include theses and implications over and above the claims that (1) all words are names of objects, and (2) all sentences are combinations of such names. As we will see, Baker and Hacker include theses and implications which are justifiably attributable only to the 'idea'.

I am not the first to scrutinize Baker's and Hacker's 'Augustinian picture'. Merril Ring takes them to task for sublimating this important distinction (between the picture and 'idea') and for including, in the Augustinian picture, theses and implications that Wittgenstein himself does not explicitly attach to Augustine's picture. Although Ring is correct that Wittgenstein's intention *is* to mark an important distinction between the 'picture' and 'idea', he fails to adequately address Baker's and Hacker's argument for extending the picture as they do. That is, Ring fails to address Baker's and Hacker's rationale for incorporating into the picture at least those 'consequences' which Wittgenstein seems to flesh out in the first thirty-two sections. And perhaps for this reason, Ring fails to expound on the rather radical consequences of his essentially correct observation about §1 of *Philosophical Investigations.* Ring queries:

> Why do Baker and Hacker refuse to accept Wittgenstein's own detailing of what he wants to call Augustine's picture of language? Their complaint arises immediately upon citing Wittgenstein's first mention of the picture .... [According to Baker and Hacker t]he expansion is necessary (and Wittgenstein intended it) because without it there is no possibility of the picture being the root of a theory of meaning and ultimately of an entire *Weltanschauung.* The initial response to that claim is brief: Why not? Baker and Hacker offer not one single reason for making such a claim ...
>
> Seeds do turn into plants without the plant being all along present in the seed. There is simply no reason to believe that, with the addition of a little something, the primitive idea that words name things cannot lead on to the more sophisticated idea[s] ... [4]

I too wish to reject Baker's and Hacker's argument. But reasonable rejection of their argument is not so simple as Ring suggests in the above passage. According to Ring, Baker's and Hacker's justification for extending the picture is: without such an expansion, there is no possibility of the picture being the root of a theory of meaning. It is true that they say such an extension 'is necessary to assess the extent to which this picture informs theories of meaning which Wittgenstein was criticizing'.[5] However, this remark has a persuasive argumentative context, and it is only part of their reasoning. The assumption here is that, following the introduction of Augustine's picture, Wittgenstein goes on to criticize theories of meaning. (Ring does not contradict this assumption.) Consequently, if Augustine's picture does not inform these theories of meaning, criticism of these theories would not constitute criticism of the picture. When this assumption is brought out into the open, Baker's and Hacker's argument is strong. The argument is that without such an expansion, it is impossible to *relate* subsequent discussion back to the opening presentation of Augustine's picture.

Consider an example that will occupy us in detail later in this chapter. How are we to relate Wittgenstein's discussion of ostensive definition back to Augustine's picture? Are we not compelled to interpret the introduction of that picture as preliminary? That is, must we not interpret the introduction as preliminary to, and a simplified 'picture' of, some theory committed to a set of philosophical claims about ostensive definition? Suppose Augustine's picture does not somehow lead to the idea that ostensive definition (considered in isolation) is a complete, and the most fundamental, explanation of word meaning; or in any event, lead to an idea comparable in that it is undermined by Wittgenstein's conclusions regarding ostensive definition.[6] How are we to relate Wittgenstein's arguments regarding the linguistic presuppositions of ostensive definition back to Augustine's picture?

Judiciously, neither Baker and Hacker nor Ring suggest that the picture entails these claims about ostensive definition. On the face of it, a plausible account is that the picture gleaned from Augustine's description is merely a kind of introduction to the real culprit: the 'idea' (*PI* §1). For the idea seems to be a much better candidate for a thesis committed to the completeness of ostensive definition. The 'idea' is an idea about word meaning. The meaning of a word is identical with the object which that word stands for. Presumably an ostensive definition is intended to acquaint one with the object. Therefore, an ostensive definition acquaints one with the meaning. And perhaps, in some vague way, the picture informs the idea.

Baker and Hacker have a persuasive argument. Suppose Augustine's picture does not somehow (i.e., as a consequence or natural development) encompass a commitment to the thesis identifying meaning and bearer (which itself, as noted, seems to include a commitment to the completeness of ostensive definition). If so, we shall have no licence to take those later arguments regarding ostensive definition as *criticisms* designed to play a role in undermining the picture. So the issue is not whether the 'picture' can be said to be the root of the 'idea' without conflating the two. The worry is that subsequent discussion would pass the picture by.

Ring is correct: seeds do turn into plants. But not just any seed turns into just any plant (even with the addition of a little something). In the absence of an *articulated* relationship between the picture and the idea, subsequent discussion (i.e., the alleged criticism of the 'idea'), conceived as a criticism of the picture, would be irrelevant. Baker's and Hacker's resolution of this dilemma is to see Wittgenstein's introduction of Augustine's picture merely as a simplified version of a set of more developed doctrines, as the kind of thing that can be taken in at a glance.

If we ignore *this* argument, however, Ring is correct that Baker's and Hacker's extension of Augustine's picture of language appears to lack rationale. It certainly seems to be at odds with Wittgenstein's explicit demarcation. My goal in this and the following chapter is to relate subsequent discussion back to the *picture*, and in so doing I abandon Baker's and Hacker's commitment to interpreting subsequent discussion as (strictly speaking) *criticism*. The present chapter will argue for such an abandonment with respect to certain central themes in the first thirty-six sections of *Philosophical Investigations*.

At a certain level of generality, both Baker's and Hacker's reading and Ring's reading are akin. They share a conception of the relation between the opening of the picture and subsequent discussion. On either reading, the purpose of introducing the picture would be largely fulfilled by its further development. Once the picture has been developed we can get on to criticizing the developed theories of meaning. But again, suppose the *distinction* between the picture and the idea is itself important for Wittgenstein's argumentative purposes.

Let us look more closely at the opening presentation of the picture. The 'picture' is characterized as a claim about the way words essentially function: they name objects. Wittgenstein's initial reaction to the picture is that, taken literally, it is just plain wrong. For it is incomplete (*PI* §1). Not all words are names (e.g. 'or' and 'perhaps' [7]), *a fortiori* not all words name objects. 'Red' is the name of a colour, not of an object; 'two' is the name of a number, not of an object; 'Wittgenstein' is the name of a person, but is it the name of an object? Even to say that all *names* are names of objects is a mistake demonstrated by an acknowledgment of the existence of words such as 'red', 'two', and perhaps even 'Wittgenstein'. It would seem that Augustine's description of the workings of language is based only on a consideration of certain parts of our language: 'If you describe . . . language in this way you are . . . thinking primarily of nouns like "table", "chair", "bread", and of peoples names' (*PI* §1).

Two questions need addressing here. First, why does Wittgenstein bring such an exceedingly naive error to our attention? What does it have to do with philosophy? Second, is Wittgenstein's initial criticism of Augustine's picture an indictment of unintelligibility? Indeed, *is* Augustine's picture of the workings of language in some sense 'logically impossible', or unintelligible? In what sense could it be? Let us consider the second question first.

Nothing is more obviously false then the claim that *no* word could be the name of an object, for our language contains hoards of them ('pillar'). Is it perhaps unimaginable that (counterfactually speaking) *all* words, as Augustine seems to imply, should be names of objects? Well, I do not see any reason to say this. Moreover, neither does Wittgenstein, for he urges us to imagine just such a language. This language is

> meant to serve for communication between a builder A and an assistant B. A is building with building-stones: there are blocks, pillars, slabs and beams. B has to pass the stones, and that in the order in which A needs them. For this purpose they use a language consisting of the words "block", "pillar", "slab", "beam". A calls them out;—B brings the stone which he has learnt to bring at such-and-such a call.—Conceive this as a complete primitive language. (*PI* §2)

The description given by Augustine is, according to Wittgenstein, a perfectly possible account of *a* language.[8] And if one can 'imagine that the language of §2 was the *whole* language of A and B'—'even the whole language of a tribe' (*PI* §6)—then why not the only language ever spoken? There is nothing absurd about conceiving of a language which fits Augustine's description.

On the other hand, it is also *obviously* mistaken as a characterization of *our* language which, as it turns out, is spoken. Wittgenstein is at pains to emphasize that a *literal reading* of Augustine's description of *our* language merely constitutes a rather obvious *error* (see *PI* §§2–4).

It is clear that the intention in the *Investigations* is to criticize this conception of language—in some sense of 'criticize'. Augustine's picture is at the roots of a conception of meaning which surrounds the workings of language in a haze (*PI* §5). But surely he is not interested in criticizing something which, upon the slightest reflection, nobody believes anyway. Thus we come around to the first question raised above, viz., of what relevance is Wittgenstein's discussion to philosophy? What is his motive for emphasizing the intelligibility (and erroneousness) of a literal reading of this 'primitive conception' of the workings of language?

Perhaps Wittgenstein is criticizing, as unintelligible, the idea that all words *must* be names of objects. For Augustine's picture is characterized as a picture of the *essence* of language. But how is this categorical claim about words to be understood? Is it to be compared, e.g., with the claim that all human beings must be brunette? This latter claim is certainly absurd. But just as certainly, there seems to be nothing especially philosophical about this sort of absurdity. For if presented with the assertion (and not, say, the command) that all human beings must be brunette, what might one's incomprehension consist in? Surely it would consist merely in that this assertion is incompatible with the *obvious* fact that some people are not brunette. There is nothing 'philosophical' about this: it is merely that we cannot imagine how somebody could, under normal circumstances, possibly maintain that all people must be, and hence are, brunette.

This raises a number of concerns regarding the first four sections of the *Investigations*. And it raises concerns about our interpretive strategy when examining the following sections. If Augustine's description (and the picture gleaned from it) are conceived merely as preliminaries for the purpose of introducing 'that philosophical concept of meaning', what is the point of reiterating the distinction in §2 and harping on the fact that, taken literally, this picture is both intelligible and furthermore a very crude mistake? Taken literally, what is unintelligible is not the *picture*, but rather how anyone could reasonably claim that this picture constitutes the 'essence of human language'! Whatever the answers are to these questions, if Wittgenstein really is at pains to emphasise the distinction, a de-emphasis (falling just short of obliteration) such as Baker's and Hacker's could throw Wittgenstein's whole argumentative strategy out of kilter.

Wittgenstein also suggests a process by which the primitive language of §2 might be taught. He calls this process 'ostensive teaching of words', and distinguishes it from ostensive definition proper. '[F]or', Wittgenstein supposes, 'the child cannot yet *ask* what the name is' (*PI* §6). Baker and Hacker argue that a primary aim in Wittgenstein's examination of ostensive definition is to establish it as being on a par with other explanations of meaning, and thereby dethrone its putative foundational role. This foundational role is allotted to it by the so-called Augustinian conception of language learning.[9] And Wittgenstein's argument, according to Baker and Hacker, is that the Augustinian picture is contradicted by Wittgenstein's discovery that ostensive definition presupposes the grammatical category of the word being defined. Just like other sorts of explanation of meaning, ostensive definition also operates against a background of linguistic conventions. Thus it cannot constitute an, as it were, non-normative (foundational) explanation of meaning.

Wittgenstein's argument allegedly undermines the idea that ostensive definitions are the foundation of word explanation. The reasoning is as follows. Suppose I define 'blue' by pointing to a blue book. To ensure that this explanation will bring about an understanding in the learner, it better be clear to that learner that I am explaining a colour word. Otherwise it would be but a lucky accident if the learner did not understand 'blue' to mean the same as 'book', or 'this book' etc. Hence ostensive teaching is, in this setting, only efficacious taken together with a particular training.

On Baker's and Hacker's reading, part of Wittgenstein's 'criticism' of the Augustinian picture is that it is based on a misconception about ostensive definition. It is natural to extend this reading to explain Wittgenstein's reason for introducing, in §6, a distinction between ostensive definition and ostensive teaching of words. This distinction is motivated by Wittgenstein's conception of the real foundations of language learning. Ostensive definition is by itself insufficient to effect a transition in the learner from someone lacking *concepts* to someone grasping—understanding—a concept (or concepts). For an ostensive definition itself has normative preconditions, and hence presupposes stage setting (cf. *PI* §30).[10] The foundation of language learning lies, rather, in training (at any rate, for creatures not born with an innate capacity for language use). Baker's and Hacker's interpretation of these sections is the anti-thesis in this chapter. Let me summarize:

An adherent to the anti-thesis is committed to the following points. Augustine's picture is merely a preliminary schema for the relatively complicated theory of meaning which, for convenience, we may call 'the Augustinian picture'. This theory of meaning is committed to the completeness of ostensive definition. Ostensive definition is the foundation of language learning. The first §36 or so sections of the *Investigations* contain Wittgenstein's criticism of this conception of language learning, and also his alternative. The criticism is that, in the requisite sense, ostensive definition is not 'complete'. On the contrary, as much as other sorts of word explanation, ostensive definition operates against the background of linguistic conventions. Wittgenstein's alternative to this theory is that the foundations of language learning lie in training.

On the anti-thetical reading, Wittgenstein is engaged in a refutation of a theory of meaning committed to the completeness of ostensive definition.[11] I begin attacking the anti-thesis on precisely this point, though obliquely, by referring back to the *Tractatus*. I will argue that the completeness of ostensive definition is not a commitment that finds expression in the *Tractatus*. Moreover, it is certainly a conception of language learning that rests very uncomfortably alongside the *Tractarian* conception of the relationship between meaningfulness and well-formedness argued in the previous chapter. I contend that, on the contrary, an argument *against* this conception of the role of ostensive definition is implicit in the *Tractatus*. I argue for this in the next section (3.2). In section 3.3, I argue that it is indeed the *Tractarian* conception of language learning which is under consideration in the *Investigations*. I argue that Wittgenstein is diagnosing the philosophical problems about language learning implicit in the *Tractatus*. He shows how a dogmatic application of Augustine's picture can *lead to* something close to the Augustinian picture of language learning, i.e., to the notion that ostensive definition is *part* of the foundations of language learning. However, the author of the *Tractatus* was in fact cognizant of the philosophical problems bound up with a foundational conception of ostensive definition. In the *Investigations*, Wittgenstein's treatment of certain philosophical problems about language learning consists in tracing their roots to a dogmatic application of Augustine's primitive picture of language learning.

3.2 Elucidations and Language Learning

Concern with philosophical problems connected with language learning looms large in the *Investigations*. In the *Tractatus*, however, language learning seems almost entirely unexamined. Certainly Wittgenstein's thoughts on the issue are left almost entirely unarticulated, except for one obscure remark on so-called elucidatory propositions:

> The meanings of primitive signs can be explained by elucidations. Elucidations are propositions which contain the primitive signs. They can, therefore, only be understood when the meanings of these signs are already known. (*TLP* 3.263)

This passage is notoriously difficult to interpret, and there is no consensus on Wittgenstein's meaning. It has been suggested that 'elucidations' are ostensive definitions *simpliciter*, or that perhaps they are just the elementary propositions of the *Tractatus*. More plausibly, Peter Hacker has suggested that 'elucidations' are actually a kind of confused composite of the two.[12]

The first suggestion is extremely unlikely. It would be difficult to construe 'elucidation' as referring to an ostensive definition conceived *as* a definition. Wittgenstein says straight out that they are propositions. The second alternative is actually correct, although unilluminating without *considerable* elaboration (*infra.*). For if an elucidation is *merely* an elementary proposition, why does Wittgenstein distinguish elucidations from mere propositions? Why does he introduce a new term? Moreover, the function of a proposition is not to explain the meaning of its constituent expressions. On the contrary, it would seem that a proposition is used as a vehicle of communication only in so far as an understanding of its constituent words is presupposed. I will come back to this point after careful consideration.

For various reasons which Hacker has brought to our attention, and which will come to light as this section progresses, Wittgenstein's later discussions of ostensive definition somehow bear on his early conception of language learning. Consequently, interpretations of (1) 'elucidations' and (2) Wittgenstein's later discussions regarding ostensive definition ought to influence one another. My interpretation is not different in this respect: I also believe that this relationship is intimate. But I want to consider Hacker's reading of 'elucidations' before proffering my own. Hacker's reading is the most complicated of our three alternatives: elucidations are, according to Hacker, an amalgam of ostensive definitions and elementary propositions, and they are expressions of the form 'this is A'. Elucidations are the confused precipitate of a failure to correctly distinguish between 'This is A' qua proposition and 'This is A' qua ostensive definition. (For example, one may use the sentence 'This is red' to state that a certain object is coloured red, but one may also use the same sentence to define the colour red.) Unlike the second alternative, viz. that 'elucidations' are elementary propositions simply, it is a virtue of Hacker's interpretation that it attempts to account for the *explanatory* role which Wittgenstein allots to 'elucidations'. It also has the virtue, unlike the first alternative, of attempting to accommodate the fact that

Wittgenstein's elucidations are supposed to be propositions of some sort. What is more, Hacker aspires to do justice to the textual evidence indicating that 'elucidations' are somehow connected with ostension. (We will look at some of this evidence below.) I wish to investigate carefully the way in which Hacker's interpretation of elucidations might inform our understanding of the thrust of Wittgenstein's later discussion of ostensive definition. Part of my project in this section is to show how it might lead us to see Wittgenstein's later discussions of ostensive definition as, in general, criticism of a theory of language learning, and in particular, as criticism of a theory which allots ostensive definition the foundational role.

However, my project is complicated by the fact that Hacker's interpretation is itself subject to interpretation. I will argue, however, that regardless of how we fill out Hacker's reading of elucidations, that reading still erroneously commits the *Tractatus* to a conception of language learning which allots ostensive definition the foundational role. In the interests of clarity I will bracket off my examination of Hacker's reading from the main body of this section. My interpretation of Wittgenstein's 'elucidations' follows this digression.

* * *

I discern three ways of understanding Hacker's interpretation of elucidations. However, I cannot discern which he has in mind. Exactly what *sort* of confusion, between 'This is A' qua definition and 'This is A' qua proposition, does Wittgenstein fall victim to? Notice that, if someone utters the *proposition* 'This is red', while pointing to a red sweater, then what they are pointing at is the sweater. Yet if someone is attempting to explain the meaning of the word 'red' by pointing to a red sweater and uttering the same sentence, then (perhaps in a different sense of 'pointing') they are pointing to the *colour* of the sweater. In order to pinpoint the sort of confusion which Hacker alleges the early Wittgenstein is guilty of, we must clarify what, in a *Tractarian* elucidation, the 'This', in 'This is A', is supposed to be designating. Is it (1) *both A* and that which *A* is predicated of; (2) just that which *A* is predicated of; or is it (3) just *A*. I consider each in turn.

(1) The most literal way of conceiving Hacker's interpretation produces patent incoherence. Elucidations are an impossible hybrid of two different uses of the form of expression 'This is A'. On this conception, we attribute to Wittgenstein the absurdity that elucidations—expressions of the form 'This is A'—somehow conflate two different objects as the focus of the ostensive gesture which accompanies the expression.

For instance, if 'this', in the *proposition* 'this is A', stands for *B* (where *A* is not identical with *B*), the elucidation would somehow conflate *A* and *B*. For the 'this' in the *definition* 'this is A', together with an ostensive gesture, designates *A*. This conception, it seems to me, is just too obviously confused. These two applications of 'this is A' are as it were *too* incompatible. It is highly doubtful that Wittgenstein fell victim to such a blatant muddle, and also highly doubtful that this is Hacker's interpretation of Wittgenstein's muddle, so I will leave it aside.

(2) One could conceive of the 'this' in 'this is A' as intended to point out—direct attention towards—something *other than A*. I shall distinguish this construal from (3) below thus: 'this ← is A' (think of the arrow as pointing to something other than *A*, viz., that which *A* is predicated of). The first question one may ask is, How is it that this construal does any more explanatory work then the claim that 'elucidations' are just elementary propositions? These elucidatory propositions are supposed to play an explanatory role in teaching language. How is it that this sort of proposition should play any more of an explanatory role than some proposition lacking an ostensive gesture, e.g. the proposition 'My jacket is red'? 'This ← is A' is none other than a proposition in which one name has been replaced with the conglomerate of 'this' and an ostensive gesture. To which constituent of the proposition does the ostensive gesture serve as an explanation of meaning?

It seems absurd to suppose that it explains the meaning of 'this'. For 'this', in abstraction from the pointing gesture, is not a name. A name can be substituted for 'this' plus an ostensive gesture, but not for 'this' by itself. We must include the gesture as a constituent of the name, and consequently that gesture cannot function to explain the meaning of that name (i.e., 'this' and the gesture). It would have to explain itself.

But one might retort: this elucidation could perhaps be distinguished from an ordinary proposition in that it explains what 'this' (without the gesture) stands for at the time of its use. 'This' would be taken, albeit confusedly, for a kind of name (cf. *PI* §38). To be sure, we would not fix the use of 'this' for future use, but perhaps it could at any rate effect an understanding of what I mean at the present moment (cf. *PI* §274). Every name could be replaced with a 'this' (or a 'that') combined with a pointing gesture. Understanding would here be a kind of momentary process.

This conception certainly gives us a bizarre idea of learning and understanding the meaning of words. It is not merely that every name *could* be replaced with a 'this' and the accompanying ostensive gesture. If I am to understand such a proposition, the names in effect *must* be so replaced. The only sort of names there could be would be 'names' that functioned precisely as 'this' actually does function. For presumably a name with a meaning that has been fixed conventionally (i.e., something that might replace 'this' *and* the gesture) could only have been given meaning by means of an elucidation. Yet on this reading of 'elucidation', such a convention could not be set up. For on this reading, an elucidation (e.g., 'this is A') only fixes the meaning of 'this' (or a 'name' that functions precisely like 'this') at the time of its utterance. The meaning of 'A' is presupposed. This entails that all elementary propositions, in so far as they are *taught*, operate in essence like 'this is this', 'this is that', 'that is this' etc., each accompanied by a (perhaps mental) pointing gesture.

It is possible that, in the *Tractatus*, Wittgenstein thought names must *always* be accompanied by (mental) ostensive gestures. I don't know. Yet even supposing so, these (mental) ostensive gestures cannot serve to *differentiate* elucidations (i.e. propositions with an explanatory role) from non-explanatory elementary propositions, since as we have just seen, they are not different on this reading. *Every* name must be accompanied by a (perhaps mental) ostensive gesture. Yet differentiation was our original goal.

(3) Hacker's reading is subject to yet another construal, indeed the most interesting. The focus of the ostensive gesture is directed only toward that which 'A' names: '*A* is "A"'. I shall distinguish this conception from (2) above thus: 'this → is A' (here the arrow is pointing at *A*). In support of this reading we might appeal to a parenthetical remark made in *The Blue Book*. Under consideration is the ostensive definition 'this is tove' accompanied by pointing at a pencil:

> Instead of "this is tove" I could here have said "this is called 'tove'". I point this out to remove, once and for all, the idea that the words of the ostensive definition predicate something of the defined; the confusion between the sentence "this is red", attributing the colour red to something, and the ostensive definition "this is called 'red'". (*BB* p. 2)[13]

The initial difficulty here is that, by the *Tractatus'* standards, a 'proposition' of the form 'this → is A' is not a proposition at all. If the ostensive gesture—the focus of 'this'— serves to point out the *A*, such a 'proposition' is not a concatenation of name*s*. There is just 'A'. Yet Wittgenstein explicitly defines an elucidation as a proposition. This reading is probably wrong, for otherwise Wittgenstein would be guilty of a fairly elementary inconsistency in his definitions: since elucidations are propositions, and propositions are concatenations of names, it should follow that elucidations are concatenations of names. But on this reading, elucidations are not concatenations of names.

Regardless, it has interesting implications for our understanding of Wittgenstein's later discussions of ostensive definition, so let us work it out. On this conception, how is an elucidation to be differentiated from an (ostensive) definition? One possibility is that elucidations are ostensive definitions conceived (confusedly) as propositions describing the meaning of 'A'. That is to say, the information conveyed by the definition/proposition is that the use of 'A', in the expression 'This → is A', is to refer to *this* (*A*). It 'predicates of the defined' the property of *meaning this*. The definition/proposition asserts that the meaning of 'A' is *A*—it describes what 'A' means. One might take this to be the upshot of the previously quoted passage from the *Blue Book*: 'the words of the ostensive definition predicate something of the defined'. There are two ways in which this interpretation might be seen to bear on Wittgenstein's later discussions of ostensive definition:

(i) The early Wittgenstein allots ostensive definition, or rather something very much akin to ostensive definition, a foundational role in language learning. An elucidation is presumably meant to teach someone *how to use* the word 'A', by somehow getting the learner to see *what* is being talked about. 'This → is A' does not provide an example (or set of examples) for the correct use of a name. That is to say, it does not provide an example of that name in *concatenation* with other names in accord with its 'form'. Consequently, the utterance of an elucidation is, in this sense, independent of the form of the name. For the utterance is independent of that name's use in (proper) propositions (i.e., concatenations of names). Hence, if the elucidation is to play an explanatory role in teaching form *and* content, it must be that it teaches the *form* of a name *by virtue of* getting the learner to see what the name 'A' *means*. Once you know *what* a word stands for, you know its whole use (*PI* §264).[14] Wittgenstein's remark at *Philosophical Investigations* §264 is not alluding to an *error*, but rather to a *superstition*. For, of course, if I know that *this* word stands for, e.g., *this colour* (or *this sensation*), I do indeed know its whole use. It is used to designate this colour (or this sensation). The contentious issue here is rather what 'knowing what this word stands for' actually encompasses.[15] As Wittgenstein notes just prior to my above quote from the *Blue Book,* 'If the definition explains the meaning of a word, surely it can't be essential that you should have heard the word before. It is the ostensive definition's business to *give* it a meaning' (*BB* p. 2).

At this point I wish to bring in Hacker's first piece of important textual evidence linking elucidations to ostensive definition: *Philosophical Remarks*, §6 ('Exhibit A' as it were). We are indebted to Hacker for observing that the words and even their order in the second sentence of §6 corresponds *very* closely to the third sentence of 3.263 of the *Tractatus*.[16]

> If I explain the meaning of a word 'A' to someone by pointing to something and saying 'this is A', then this expression may be meant in two different ways. Either it is itself a proposition already, in which case it can only be understood once the meaning of 'A' is known, i.e. I must now leave it to chance whether he takes it as I meant it or not. Or the sentence is a definition. Suppose I have said to someone 'A is ill', but he doesn't know who I mean by 'A', and I now point at a man, saying 'This is A'. Here the expression is a definition, but this can only be understood if he has already gathered what kind of object it is through his understanding of the grammar of the proposition 'A is ill'. But this means that any kind of explanation of language presupposes a language already. (*PR* §6)

If we have now arrived, with this third interpretation of 'This is A', at the correct conception of Wittgenstein's elucidations, then §6 of *Philosophical Remarks* is a powerful argument *against* the *Tractatus'* conception of the foundations of language learning. And against the background of this interpretation of 'elucidations', it is natural to read the above passage from *Philosophical Remarks* as a criticism of the idea that ostensive definition operates in isolation from a background of linguistic conventions (and perhaps eventually leading to Wittgenstein's alleged criticism in *Philosophical Investigations*, of the idea that ostensive teaching of words operates in abstraction from training).

If Wittgenstein's elucidations are as (3) characterizes them, then this passage is a criticism of the *Tractarian* conception of language learning. For the argument in *Philosophical Remarks* is that the ostensive explanation of the name 'A' can only be understood if we *presuppose* the grammar/form of 'A'. Furthermore, allotting a foundational role to ostensive definition seems to be a natural extension of Augustine's conception.[17] Consequently (one might argue), one rationale for Wittgenstein's introduction, in the *Investigations*, of Augustine's description of language learning is to criticize his early conception of language learning: to criticize the idea that 'elucidations' form the foundation of language learning. That criticism would consist in demonstrating that an ostensive definition *presupposes* the grammatical category of the word defined. And this criticism will by implication apply to the *Tractatus*.

Notice first that this reading of 'elucidations' is virtually inconsistent with the interpretation of the picture theory argued in the previous chapter. I argued in the previous chapter that the connecting link presupposes isomorphism, and this idea actually coheres quite nicely with what Wittgenstein says about ostensive definition in §6 of *Philosophical Remarks*. For in the *Tractatus*, Wittgenstein was committed to the idea that the possibility of assigning meaning to a name presupposes that that name is well-formed. The doctrine of elucidations expounded in (3) implies the exact opposite. This tension might suggest an alternate way of filling out (3). That is to say, it might suggest a different way of relating (this reading of) *Tractarian* elucidations to Wittgenstein's later observations about ostensive definition:

(ii) Elucidations really serve only to supply content to form. The *Tractatus* is mute on the problem of teaching form. Or perhaps Wittgenstein suspected form could not be taught at all, and hence is innate. In so far as teaching is possible at all, it consists only in explaining the *content* of the simple signs in a pre-given skeleton of language. §6 of *Philosophical Remarks* would then, in effect, amount to a vindication of the *Tractarian* conception of language learning. (Unlike (i), (ii) is consonant with my argument in the previous chapter.)

This second (ii) expansion of (3) does not embody a different reading of elucidations *per se*. The only difference is that we are supposing that Wittgenstein does not, in the *Tractatus*, attempt to overcome the problem of teaching 'form'. Perhaps he deems the problem unsolvable. Be this as it may, this clearly is the implication drawn in *Philosophical Remarks*: 'But this means that any kind of explanation of language presupposes a language already. And in a certain sense, the *use* of language is something that cannot be taught ... ' (my emphasis).[18] It would be natural here to interpret the *Investigations* as *resolving* this philosophical problem regarding language learning by appeal to the fact that *training* constitutes the (contingent) foundation for language learning (cf. *PI* §6, §9, §86).[19] An appeal to training would, therefore, be the *explanation* of the intractable problem of how language could possibly be learnt. We shall have occasion to discuss this reading of the *Investigations* later in the chapter.

A short digression: I have to be careful here not to trivialize the anti-thesis. An adherent to the anti-thesis need not suggest that Wittgenstein regards an appeal to training as part of a (philosophical?) theory of language learning. The suggestion could be something more plausible like the following.

Wittgenstein's discussion of rule-following shows us that there is a deep internal relation between the concepts of rule-governed action, practice, and regularity. Wittgenstein's emphasis on training is intended to point out a *possible*, even likely, though probably exaggerated genetic foundation for rule-governed action. And he presents this 'important possibility' as an alternative to the view that language learning consists in a lot of mental hypothesizing about the meaning of and the rules for the use of words.

I do not disagree with this interpretation, and in fact I think it is correct. My disagreement is rather with the way the anti-thesis presents Wittgenstein's rejection of the Augustinian conception of language learning. According to the anti-thesis, Wittgenstein's arguments are intended as refutations of *conclusions* about the nature of language learning. For example, a refutation of the conclusion that ostensive definition is the foundation of language learning, or that language learning relies heavily of mental hypothesizing.

On my view, Wittgenstein does not refute conclusions, at least he does not in his discussion of Augustine's picture. I mean by this that he does not argue for the falsity of statements. Rather, he rejects arguments. Wittgenstein's 'conclusions' are, at their weakest, of the form: *not proven*. And at their strongest: *not justifiable*.

But let us return to 'elucidations'. To a greater or lesser extent, all these interpretations (of Hacker's interpretation) of *Tractatus* 3.263 jar with some of Wittgenstein's remarks. I was more interested in emphasizing the way in which these conceptions might inform one's interpretation of *Philosophical Investigations.* These conceptions (excluding (1), which I concluded was incoherent) pigeon-hole the *Tractatus* into the claim that something very akin to an ostensive definition plays a foundational role in language learning. This is so even in (3), (ii). There ostensive definition plays a foundational role in so far as language learning is possible at all. For ostensive definitions are what give content to a pre-given, innate, skeleton of language, and that is all that language *learning* consists in. Consequently, they all contribute to the conviction that Wittgenstein's discussion of ostensive definition in the *Investigations*, whatever else it accomplishes, is intended to refute the *Tractarian* conception of language learning.—Either by Wittgenstein's appeal to the presuppositions of ostensive definition (to refute the idea that ostensive definitions are adequate to teach form), or by his appeal to training (to contribute to refuting the claim that the learning of 'form' is impossible). It is on this point that I end my digression on Hacker's interpretation of 'elucidations'.

⋆ ⋆ ⋆

I will now present my interpretation of 'elucidations'. Hacker notes that two pieces of *ex post facto* evidence link ostension to elucidations. We have considered briefly Exhibit A: §6 of *Philosophical Remarks* (quoted above). The other is a discussion by Waismann regarding language learning (Exhibit B). Waismann, who worked closely with and was deeply influenced by Wittgenstein, makes the following remark about explanations of meaning.

> There are two ways of giving a sign meaning: I. By means of *ostension* .... In this case we explain the use of a word in statements by constructing various propositions by means of that word and each time pointing to the fact in question. In that way we become aware of the meaning of the word. (Ostension really consists in two acts—in an external action,

> pointing to various facts, and a thought-operation, namely learning what they have in common.) 2. By means of *definition*...[20]

I too wish to exploit this evidence, but for a different interpretation. Notice that Waismann says that what is pointed to is a *fact*. The act of ostension is apparently not directed towards a *thing*. Yet in expressions of the form 'this is A', that which is 'pointed to' is not a fact but rather *this*, a thing (i.e. *A*, or something other than *A*, depending on which use of this form of expression we have in mind). In the proposition 'this ← is A' a pointing gesture serves to fix what thing it is that *A* is predicated of. In the ostensive definition 'this → is A', a pointing gesture serves to point out the *A*. In neither case is a *fact* pointed to.

What sort of ostension could Waismann have in mind here? Let us look again at Exhibit A. I re-quote the pertinent part:

> If I explain the meaning of a word 'A' to someone by pointing to something and saying 'this is A', then this expression may be meant in two different ways. Either it is itself a proposition already, in which case it can only be understood once the meaning of 'A' is known, i.e. I must now leave it to chance whether he takes it as I meant or not. Or the sentence is a definition... (*PR* §6)

Recall that the second sentence above corresponds very closely to the third sentence of 3.263 of the *Tractatus*. Moreover, Exhibit A shares a striking structural similarity with the passage from Waismann. Both passages note two forms of explanation of meaning: one by means of propositions, and one by means of definitions. It is plausible that both these passages are concerned with *Tractarian* elucidations. Yet what construal of 'this is A' is consistent with, on the one hand an elucidation being a proposition, and on the other hand being employed with the intention to explain the meaning of *A*? (Very significantly, in *Philosophical Remarks* Wittgenstein conceives *both* the definition *and* the proposition to function as an explanation of the meaning of *A*. For he says 'If I *explain the meaning of a word to someone by . . .*'. And this is so despite the fact that in the proposition, *A* is not the focus of the ostensive gesture!)

It turns out (2) above, viz., that an elucidation is of the form 'this ← is A', is closest to the mark. To be sure, as I stated it above it does not serve an explanatory role. But that is because, on the one hand, I took it for granted that, since the ostensive gesture was directed to something other than *A*, the use of this form of expression qua explanation must be to explain that something which is other than 'A'. That is, I took it for granted that however this expression was to serve as an explanation, *what* was being explained was not 'A', but rather what 'A' is predicated of. For *A* is not what is being pointed at.

On the other hand, I also did not consider the case where it is a *series* of expressions of this form that are intended to explain meaning. But both these oversights of mine are actually operating in Wittgenstein's conception of 'elucidation'. *Prima facie* paradoxically, 'this ← is A' is supposed to teach the meaning of 'A'. But not all alone, and not at all because of the ostensive gesture. The meaning of 'A' is taught by *example*, like this: "What is 'red'? Well, *this* (jacket), for example, is red, so is this wagon, and this tomato."

Both Waismann and Wittgenstein are referring to *propositions* like 'this (e.g., the table) is *red*', 'this (e.g., the chair) is *red*', 'this (the jacket) is *red*'. And the intention is to effect an understanding of *red*. Ostensive teaching of words is, on this conception, essentially an act of uttering *various* propositions. And learning the meaning of 'red' (or 'A') is a matter of finding—or guessing? (cf. *PI* §32)—the common *thing* in all these facts. We 'explain the use of a word in statements by constructing *various* propositions by means of that word and each time pointing to the fact in question.'[21]

The form of expression 'this is A' is a red herring here. It is not essential (unless, perhaps, the learner did not know the meaning of *any* word) for an elucidation to take the form 'this is A'. For the word being explained is not the focus of the ostensive gesture. If the learner understood 'table', 'chair' and 'jacket', then the teacher could dispense with 'this' altogether. Even if the various propositions did employ that form (viz., 'this is A'), they would invariably have different objects as the focus of the gesture. Only by using 'this' to designate *different* objects, and hence by pointing out *different* facts, could one get the learner to see the *common* thing (the colour red, or *A*) in those various facts (cf. *PI* §72).

On my interpretation of elucidations, then, §6 of *Philosophical Remarks* is not a criticism of the *Tractatus*. Moreover, nothing in the *Tractatus* nor *Philosophical Remarks* commits the author to postulating an innate knowledge of logical form or grammar. In the last chapter I argued that, in the *Tractatus*, having a name go proxy for an object presupposes its form, i.e., its use in propositions. With elucidations, the *meaning* of a name is gathered (somehow!) by attending to that name in *use*, i.e., in concatenation with other names. (Cf. *PR* §6, my emphasis: 'I must now leave it to *chance* whether he takes it as I meant or not'.)

What are we to make of *Philosophical Remarks* §6 if it is not a criticism of Wittgenstein's 'elucidations'? Well, Wittgenstein says of an ostensive definition that it 'can only be understood if he has *already* gathered what *kind* [cf. the 'form' of *Tractarian* objects] of object it is through his understanding of the grammar of the proposition' (ibid., my emphasis). That, on my reading, sounds like something he might have said in the *Tractatus*. Wittgenstein's remark in §6 sounds like an oblique vindication of his earlier conception of the relationship between meaningfulness and well-formedness.[22] The confused conclusion which Wittgenstein feels forced to draw from the argument of §6 of *Philosophical Remarks* is also a striking example of a sound argument which, when viewed from the perspective of the superstition which has its roots in Augustine's picture, does not serve to undermine the superstition but rather gets assimilated (cf. *PR* §4 and §54; §25 and §32). I suggest it is exactly that.

My interpretation of 'elucidations' sits uncomfortably with the antithetical interpretation of Wittgenstein's later discussion regarding ostensive definition. Precisely how are we to view this theme in the *Investigations* 'by contrast with and against the background of [Wittgenstein's] old way of thinking' (*PI Preface*)? In particular, what are we to make of those arguments regarding the presuppositions of an ostensive definition? Is it not implausible that they should be intended as *criticisms* directed towards undermining Augustine's picture? For it is impossible to regard them as criticisms of the *Tractatus*.

It seems to me that there is some pressure here to abandon the idea that the discussion of ostensive definition in the *Investigations* is intended as a straightforward criticism of some formulation of Augustine's picture. However, an adherent to the anti-thesis might find this unconvincing. An adherent to the anti-thesis might remonstrate with the following argument.

"Your interpretation of elucidations in this chapter is irrelevant to the issue at hand. Who is to say that in *Philosophical Investigations*, Wittgenstein is not refuting some other theory that *is* committed to the completeness of ostensive definition? Augustine's picture of language outlined in §1 does not have any clearly defined set of consequences.[23] An unconscious commitment to this picture of language can manifest itself in a variety of ways. There is no reason to insist that these manifestations of Augustine's picture be consistent with one another. It would be wrong to attempt to extract any necessary consequences from the picture. So even if the picture theory does not allot a foundational role to ostensive definition, to do so is still *prima facie* a natural application of Augustine's picture. Wittgenstein's discussion of ostensive definition is not directly criticizing the picture theory at all. The discussion of the normative presuppositions of ostensive definition is directed at a different—perhaps less sophisticated—formulation of Augustine's picture (there are surely many); and the picture theory was formulated so as to accommodate this (dimly perceived) issue regarding the presuppositions of ostensive definition."

I do not want to reject this remonstrance entirely. Wittgenstein's claim that an ostensive definition has normative presuppositions obviously contradicts any account that implies or assumes it does not. Thus these remarks certainly *can* be used as a criticism of such a conception of language learning. Although this does not warrant concluding anything about *Wittgenstein's* intended use, such a conclusion is a possibility which

I am open to. Wittgenstein's arguments could be operating simultaneously on more than one level.[24]

On the other hand, I do reject the idea that this was Wittgenstein's central concern in these passages on ostensive definition. Consider the implications of the anti-thesis: this 'criticism' is only relevant if directed at a formulation of Augustine's picture less sophisticated than the picture theory. The picture theory embodies no such doctrine about the foundations of language learning. Indeed, the early Wittgenstein was, in a sense, very aware of this difficulty. Thus from the perspective of the *Tractatus*, Wittgenstein's later remarks on ostensive definition are not to the point.

Yet Augustine's picture of language and language learning *precisely* parallels (in form) the picture theory: The words of language name objects, and sentences are combinations of names. Moreover, Augustine's account of language learning bears a striking resemblance to Waismann's and the account propounded in the *Tractatus*. For Augustine learns his language by hearing 'words *repeatedly used* in their *proper* places in *various sentences*'. From this he '*gradually* learnt to understand what *objects* they *signified*' (*PI* §1, my emphasis). The similarity between this statement from Augustine and Waismann's account of ostension virtually slaps one in the face. Finally, the picture theory certainly embodies a commitment to the 'idea', i.e., an identification of meaning and bearer (*TLP* 3.203).

In general, therefore, §1 of *Philosophical Investigations* is a characterization *par excellence* of the conception, in the picture theory, of (1) what words signify, (2) how words have meaning, (3) the nature of a proposition, *and* (4) the nature of language learning. And the primary issue immediately following this sketch in §1 of the *Investigations* is the normative preconditions of ostensive definition. Is it reasonable to maintain that this primary issue turns out to be, qua criticism, *completely* irrelevant to Wittgenstein's youthful formulation of Augustine's picture?

This reading is not demonstrably false, but it is unclear to me what it has going for it so far. (Whether it makes good sense of sections subsequent to §1 remains to be discussed.) Has it any justification beyond a dogmatic commitment to construing the thrust of Wittgenstein's discussion of the normative foundations of ostensive definition as somehow criticizing *something*? I suggest that much sense can be made of this discussion of ostensive definition in the *Investigations*, and its relation to the 'picture' and 'idea' outlined in §1, if we refrain from construing Wittgenstein's discussion of ostensive definition as a straightforward *criticism* of anything. Rather, I suggest that the discussion of ostensive definition is a step in the *diagnosis* of how dogmatic adherence to Augustine's picture can lead to the *Tractarian* conception of language learning. I begin my positive argument for this thesis by an examination of alternative possible motives behind Wittgenstein's introduction of 'ostensive teaching of words' at §6 of the *Investigations*.

3.3 Teaching, Training and Ostension

In §2 of the *Investigations*, Wittgenstein introduces a language for which Augustine's description of the workings of language is supposed to be correct. This language consists of the words 'block', 'pillar', 'slab' and 'beam'. §6 is a development of the language-game (though not the language) described at §2. In §6, Wittgenstein gives us a plausible example of how the children might be taught this language. He calls it 'ostensive teaching of words', and 'An important part of the training will consist in the teacher's pointing to the objects, directing the child's attention to them, and at the same time uttering a word ...' (*PI* §6).

Does Wittgenstein also intend his description of the *teaching* of this language to be an example for which Augustine's description is correct? Not strictly speaking, for Augustine does not describe the *teaching* of language at all. Rather, young Augustine merely 'picks up' an understanding of what the words signify. He observes words repeatedly used in their proper places (*PI* §1, cf. *TLP* 3.263, *PR* §6). But perhaps, if Augustine were to describe the active teaching of his first language, that teaching would be merely an attempt to facilitate this guesswork. This is comparable to the early Wittgenstein's conception of language learning.

This is not at all the way Wittgenstein imagines the learning of language-game (6). He seems intent on purging his description of any normative elements, e.g. guessing or asking for clarification. For he distinguishes the 'ostensive teaching of words' in this language-game from ostensive definition proper, imagining that 'the child cannot as yet *ask* what the name is' (*PI* §6). Furthermore, his use of the word 'training' also seems altogether foreign to Augustine's description, where the child is actively seeking out (or guessing) the meaning of the various words.

Is Wittgenstein making assumptions about the nature of language learning? Is he claiming that training is the foundation of first-language learning? If so, this is surely not a philosophical proposition, for it is perfectly *imaginable* that a child should come to be able to use a word correctly merely from one ostensive definition, i.e., merely as a result of one ostensive gesture and an utterance of the form 'this is ... '.

I suggest that, rather than making claims about language learning, Wittgenstein is making stipulations about the language learning in this *imagined* language-game. He is stipulating that the children are not sufficiently developed conceptually to *wonder* what sort of word is being explained. It is for this reason that he refrains from calling this teaching 'ostensive definition'. For this is a phrase carrying with it a certain amount of philosophical baggage. 'Ostensive teaching' is introduced purposely so as not to presuppose the normativity underlying his earlier *conception* of ostensive definition proper. Otherwise *Philosophical Investigations* would straight away beg the question against Wittgenstein's earlier arguments. In *Philosophical Remarks*, Wittgenstein contends that an ostensive definition only *teaches* the meaning in so far as the learner knows the grammar of the word defined (*PR* §6). And, as I have argued, a very similar argument is operating in the *Tractatus*.

Wittgenstein's language-game stipulates the exact opposite. Grammatical categories are unknown to the child. Although an ostensive definition is not always a response to a request for explanation, the earlier Wittgenstein contended that ostensive definition—qua *teaching*—presupposes the ability to *guess* the meaning. That is, in order for an ostensive definition to be an *explanation* the learner must be able to guess the grammatical category. And this presupposes the ability to ask, even if only 'in thought'. That is to say, it makes no sense to guess about something if it makes no sense to wonder about it. Thus it is only fair for the later Wittgenstein to distinguish this activity with the phrase 'ostensive teaching of words'. Ostensive teaching of words is, as it were, ostensive definition 'from scratch'.

Not only is Wittgenstein careful with the concept of ostensive definition. Further, he couches his characterization of the 'effects' of this 'training' in non-cognitive terms (i.e., in *PI* §6 'associative connection' ['*assoziative Verbindung*'], 'effect' ['*bewirkt*']). This suggests that, at this point, Wittgenstein wants to leave it open whether the 'effect' of this 'teaching' is even to be called 'understanding'.[25]

Since the presuppositions of this language-game are stipulations, the question is not whether the language learner *in fact* brings her active participation to bear on the learning situation. The whole scenario comes out of Wittgenstein's head, so the question makes no sense. Rather, the issue Wittgenstein wants to address is why someone (e.g., the early Wittgenstein) might say that the learner *must* bring her active participation to bear on the learning situation. That is to say, the question is whether Wittgenstein actually succeeds in describing a situation which we should feel comfortable *calling* 'language learning'. Surely he believes he does succeed, but he has a philosophical prejudice to overcome first. I will show how it is this philosophical prejudice that he is diagnosing.

Predictably, Wittgenstein develops the language described at §2 (*PI* §8, cf. *BB* p. 79ff.). Besides object words, this development includes colour words, number words, 'there' and 'this'. Wittgenstein also introduces samples into the activity of employing the colour words. (I will ignore 'there', 'this' and samples in this chapter. I give them attention in Chapter Four.) What will the ostensive teaching be like with the introduction of new kinds of words, viz., colour and number words? Surely it will be *different* for different *kinds* of words:

> When a child learns this language, it has to learn the series of 'numerals' a, b, c, ... by heart. And it has to learn their use.—Will this training include ostensive teaching of the words?—Well, people will, for example, point to slabs and

> count: "a, b, c slabs".—Something more like the ostensive teaching of the words "block", "pillar", etc. would be the ostensive teaching of numerals that serve not to count but to refer to groups of objects that can be taken in at a glance. Children do learn the use of the first five or six cardinal numerals in this way. (*PI* §9)

Wittgenstein is imagining differences in the teaching of the major types of words in this language-game. But what sort of differences is he intending to highlight? Since these are imagined differences, Wittgenstein cannot let too much ride on his detailing of what these differences consist in. (Wittgenstein is not doing speculative developmental psychology.) Is he, then, merely saying that the teaching of one sort of word will differ in some way or other from the teaching of another sort of word? Clearly this is letting too little ride on these imagined differences: to claim merely that the teaching will be different in *some* way or other fails even to distinguish these major categories of words. For the training will also differ for different words of the *same* sort. For example, the teaching of 'slab' will be different from the word 'block'. If I want to teach you the use of a new word, 'post', it will likely be counter-productive to point at a block.[26] Or is he perhaps saying that, with different sorts of words, the difference in training will be *very* different?

The natural answer is that the teaching of altogether different sorts of word will itself be of an altogether different sort. The difference will not consist merely in a difference in *what* is pointed at. Indeed, this might not differ at all, for I might explain 'red' or 'block' by pointing at a red block.

Although natural, this answer is a problematic reading of Wittgenstein's intentions. What is the rationale for saying that altogether different *sorts* of words require altogether different *sorts* of training? If Wittgenstein is not engaged in some kind of speculative learning theory, or *justifying* this claim by appeal to our intuitions (although such an appeal is not altogether irrelevant), surely the only rationale is that they are different sorts of words. Yet that they are different sorts of *words* is precisely what the difference in training is intended to illustrate (see *PI* §9). It is important to remember that, according to the picture Wittgenstein is scrutinizing, these are not altogether different sorts of *words*. Rather, they are the same sort of word (names), which designate altogether different sorts of *things* (shapes, colours, numbers). Is Wittgenstein's argument going round in a circle?

No. The rationale for the emphasis on a difference in training corresponds to the rationale for the introduction of the more complicated language. This more complicated language contains words that are not names of ordinary objects. Hence it is a language that does not conform to a literal reading of the picture harvested from Augustine's description of language learning. The ostensive teaching of the words of this more complicated language will not, *whatever* it happens to consist in, fit the case described in §6, viz., just pointing to ordinary objects and uttering words. For if the teaching did uniformly fit this case, there could be no discernable difference between the teaching of 'slab' and the teaching of 'red'. Both might be taught by pointing at a red slab and uttering a sentence of the form, "This is *x*". Thus the learner would have to *guess* what 'kind of thing' is being pointed at. But *ex hypothesi* the learner cannot guess!

Wittgenstein is developing his diagnosis of this philosophical problem about language learning. More precisely, he is proffering a simplified story of how this philosophical problem might arise. It does not seem problematic to apply Augustine's picture to language-game (6). Why not 'reduce the description of the use of the word "slab" to the statement that this word signifies this object' (*PI* §10)? For the *difference* between the training in the use of 'pillar' and 'slab' consists in a difference of the object pointed to. And *that* difference is inherent in the ostensive *gesture* itself. The situation becomes problematic with the more complicated language. If the ostensive teaching of words in §6 is what teaching of the language in §8 consists in, how is a learner of the language in §8 supposed to tell what sort of word is being explained with the ostensive gesture?

In order to see the *philosophical* problem which Wittgenstein is diagnosing here, it is illuminating to consider its non-philosophical analogue:

Suppose I were to expand the language described at §2 (i.e., the language which is taught in the language-game described in §6) to incorporate the word 'brick'. An ostensive teaching of 'brick' (i.e., "that is a brick") will probably not be taken for a colour word. For there are no words in this language comparable to our colour words. Moreover, the ostensive teaching of 'brick' will very likely not be confused with an ostensive teaching of 'slab' because the difference in the teaching is entirely captured by what is pointed at. But when the ostensive teaching of 'brick', as typified by the ostensive teaching in §6, is applied to the more developed language-game at §8, it will likely be more easily confused with (say) a colour word. For there may in fact be similarities between the ostensive teaching of a colour word, and the ostensive teaching of an object word. Both words might be taught by reference to the same object, e.g., a brick of such-and-such a colour. If a teacher employs the method of teaching typified in the simpler language in §6, to the more complicated language in §8, it will probably cause a certain amount of confusion.

This is not (yet) a philosophical problem. If we stop here it looks like Wittgenstein has unearthed an empirical problem about language learning. It may even appear as though he has given us a solution to the problem, viz., a discovery about the way language is taught, i.e., that different sorts of words require different sorts of training.

We need to dig deeper to show that Wittgenstein is not engaged in speculative learning theory here. To be sure, aside from the fact that these language-games are invented, the claims made in the last paragraph are all empirical: claims about what might, might not, probably will, or probably will not happen. But these are not the claims of primary interest to Wittgenstein. How do we get from such empirical claims to metaphysical claims about ostensive definition or ostensive teaching?

By some subtle linguistic legislation, resulting from a dogmatic application of Augustine's picture to language-game §6. As it were a little *magic*, or a kind of conjuring trick—an illusion of equivocation:

The language of §2 is a language which fits (a literal reading of) Augustine's picture of the essence of human language. The ostensive teaching in §6 was Wittgenstein's imaginary description of the teaching in that language. In this description of ostensive teaching, the essential thing distinguishing the various ostensive teachings ('block', 'pillar', 'slab', 'beam') is that something different is pointed at (viz. a block, pillar, slab, or beam). Excluding of course the names, everything else could remain constant. There might be no difference in the form which the utterance or the training takes. It is even imaginable that the bare ostensive teaching is all that teaching *simpliciter* consists in for the language consisting only of the names of building stones.

Now imagine someone dogmatically applying this *concept* of ostensive teaching to the language-game of §8. Let us distinguish the concept of ostensive teaching typified in §6 by quoting it: "ostensive teaching". "Ostensive teaching" is *only* an ostensive gesture and the utterance 'this is . . . .'. That is to say, "ostensive teaching" is what is left over from ostensive teaching if we abstract contextual factors revealing what sort of word the teacher intends to explain. In Wittgenstein's example this would be the training. The ostensive teaching of 'brick' *might* be misinterpreted. For example, the learner might take the ostensive teaching of 'brick' for an explanation of a colour word. But it makes no sense to say the "ostensive teaching" might be misinterpreted in this way. For the "ostensive teaching" does not *distinguish* between pointing to the object and pointing to its colour. It is, as it were, *essentially* ambiguous. Considered relative to the language described at §8, the "ostensive teaching" (i.e. *as typified in* §6) *must* be ambiguous. It is *impossible* to tell what sort of word is being explained. This is an extremely important difference between language-games (2) and (8). In language-game (2), "ostensive teaching" is as unambiguous as ostensive teaching might be in either language-game (2) or (8).

To repeat, this is not to say that the ostensive teaching of 'brick' *will* be misinterpreted (cf. *PI* §28). That would be an empirical matter, to be determined, e.g., by whether the learner goes on to use 'brick' properly. But it is to say that, in and of itself, the "ostensive teaching" does not serve to fix the meaning of 'brick'. In and of itself, it is no explanation at all for the words of language-game (8). How *can* "ostensive teaching" constitute an explanation of meaning if it does not distinguish between pointing to the brick and pointing to the colour of the brick? One feels forced to say that "ostensive teaching" is not, *in and of itself*, 'teaching'. (This is a remark on how one might, under the influence of Augustine's picture, be inclined to use the words 'ostensive teaching' and 'teaching'.) If the "ostensive teaching" serves to effect an understanding in the learner, this will either be a happy accident (*PR* §6), or a function of something *external* to the "ostensive teaching".

I illustrated this philosophical problem by proposing 'brick' as an example of a new word for the languages of *both* §2 and §8. I could have illustrated the same point—about the application of the ostensive teaching of §6 to the language of §8—with the example 'red'. However, I was trying not to obscure the issue. Relative to the language in §8, it is not that "ostensive teaching" is unambiguous if it serves to define a regular object word, but is (essentially) ambiguous when it serves to define a colour or number word. "Ostensive teaching" of any sort of word will be ambiguous considered relative to the language in §8. "Ostensive teaching" is unambiguous in the simple language game at §2 because distinctions of type (e.g. blocks and slabs) are differentiated entirely by virtue of the pointing gesture. "Ostensive teaching" inherently differentiates explanations of the names of the various building-stones.

But in the more complicated language in §8, *every* "ostensive teaching" is essentially ambiguous, even explanations of the names for building-stones. For nothing in the ostensive definition differentiates between pointing to the shape as opposed to the colour. When we apply the paradigm of ostensive definition, i.e. the one I described in incorporating 'brick' into the language in §2, to the language in §8 (which *inter alia* has words like 'block' and 'pillar'), it appears inadequate *in toto* (even for words like 'block' and 'pillar').

Viewed from the perspective of a more complicated language, an ostensive definition akin to the ostensive teaching typified in §6 can create an illusion of what I want to call 'essential ambiguity'. The ambiguity is 'essential' because the concept of teaching typified in §6 is imposed on the more complicated language-game at §8. A dogmatic application of Augustine's picture transforms a plausible *empirical* claim into a metaphysical claim. The empirical claim is that,

> the ostensive definition explains the use—the meaning—of the word when the overall role of the word in language is clear. Thus if I know that someone means to explain a colour-word to me the ostensive definition "That is called 'sepia'" will help me to understand the word .... This explanation ... only tells him the use ... because ... the place for it was already prepared. (*PI* § 30-31)

Conjured out of this empirical claim is the metaphysical, or even *grammatical* claim that 'we shall only say that it *tells* him the use, if the place is already prepared.' (*PI* §31, my emphasis).

I want to emphasize this transformation in the use of 'ostensive definition'. I will single out a pair of sentences from this quoted material: '[1] This explanation again only tells the use ... *because*, as we might say, the place for it was already prepared. Or even: [2] we shall *only say* that it tells him the use, if the place is already prepared' (my emphasis). Herein lies the conjuring trick. The first has the form of an empirical claim. The second has the form of a grammatical remark, i.e., a claim about how we are going to use 'ostensive definition'. The first is the plausible statement that if someone understands an ostensive definition, and goes on to use the word correctly, this is likely due to the fact that they already have an understanding of that sort of word which is being explained. They are familiar with the concept.

The second is a 'must' claim: it is *impossible* that someone should understand a word *merely* as a result of its "ostensive definition". This 'must' claim amounts to a commitment to employing the expression 'ostensive definition' only for the kind of ostensive definition typified in §6. If I ostensively define a word without the specification of category, and the person to whom I give the definition goes on to use this correctly, this can *only* have come about if the learner already knew—understood, had the concept of—the sort of thing being defined, and guessed (from context perhaps) that this was what was under consideration. And even here something *external* to the *teaching* (where 'teaching' = "ostensive definition") brought about this understanding, viz., the guessing, or the context. And if the learner did not already have a mastery of the concept, then something external—we know not what—brought about that understanding.

Let us step back for perspective. This strand of the discussion from §§1-31 in the *Investigations* is a diagnosis of *Wittgenstein's* (former) philosophical problem regarding the possibility of learning/teaching a language. It started with a picture of the nature of our language that, taken literally, is obviously incorrect ('words uniformly name objects'). It was, however, an imaginable language (*PI* §3). Furthermore, the conception of language learning natural to that picture was an entirely intelligible account of language learning (*PI* §6). Assuming natural dispositions to look in the direction of the gesture, demonstrative teaching is an entirely plausible, though probably simplified, account of how the language at §2 might actually be learned. Although perhaps a simplification, this account captures *differences* in the teaching of the different words. For differences in training, between the teaching of 'block' and 'slab', will mostly amount to differences in what is pointed to. That is what the *difference* in teaching will mostly amount to.

The problem arises, however, with the introduction of the more complicated language (*PI* §8). The ostensive teaching that went along quite well with the language at §2 seems potentially ambiguous for the language in §8. If one is dogmatic about the idea that teaching consists in the kind of ostensive definitions which are appropriate to ordinary objects, then it becomes obscure what an ostensive definition of 'red' is. How is it differentiated from a definition of a word which stands for the thing which is red? And this issue now arises for an ostensive definition of *any* word in this language. If one insists that §6 characterizes what teaching the meaning of words is, not only will the ostensive teaching be potentially ambiguous. It will be essentially *inadequate*. But if *that* is what teaching *is*, then *teaching* is essentially inadequate. Or better, there is not, in a certain sense, really any *teaching* at all (*PR* §6). Or perhaps even better, we object to the ordinary application of the word 'teaching'. Teaching is *really* like how

> Someone coming into a strange country will sometimes learn the language of the inhabitants from ostensive definitions that they give him; and he will often have to *guess* the meaning of these definitions . . . as if the child came into a strange country and did not understand the language of the country; that is, as if the child could already *think*, only not yet speak. (*PI* §32)

Wittgenstein diagnoses that this philosophical problem about language learning is rooted in Augustine's picture of language learning (ibid.). Augustine's picture of language learning is applied to a language which we should not say it literally applied. This is an example of a dogmatic application of a primitive picture, and the pair of sentences I singled out from §31 is an excellent characterization of the kind of transformation in the use of words this dogmatic application can engender.

Such a dogmatic application is due in part, Wittgenstein suggests, to the possibilities of transformation that actually exist in the forms of expression in our language. Perhaps under the influence of the picture (perhaps not), we impose an *appearance* of uniformity on the differences between, e.g., colour words and object words (*PI* §§22, 24; *BB* §6). Colour, number, and object words are names. The possibility in our language of distinguishing the meaning of 'red' from that of 'slab' in terms of the former '*referring to*', '*standing for*', '*meaning*' a colour (as opposed to a shape) might incline us to think they all operate in the same way. They all name 'something'. This can lead to the idea that ostensive definitions are inadequate for teaching. For the application of Augustine's picture of the functioning of words might bring in its wake the application of Augustine's picture of language learning. If 'red' is a name of something (viz., a colour), we should be able to give that something some kind of ostensive definition.

The problem begins by applying Augustine's picture of the functioning of words to the more complicated language. Relative to the employment of 'name' in §2, this is an *extension* of the application of 'name'. Wittgenstein did not, however, likewise extend the application of 'ostension'. While he extended 'name' and 'thing designated by a name' for the characterization of the language, he did not consistently extend the application of 'thing designated' with respect to what is pointed to in the ostensive definition. So the 'impossibility' of teaching arose from extending the employment of 'name', yet not consistently extending 'ostensive definition' (or perhaps less technically, *pointing*).

"Well", one might say, "there you have it: Wittgenstein has revealed the inconsistent use of words underlying the application of Augustine's picture to a language which it does not, literally speaking, fit. And thereby, he has refuted a conception of language learning which allots "ostensive definition" a foundational role."

Not necessarily. For if the unintelligibility of teaching arose from not consistently extending 'ostensive definition', why not just extend it? After all, Augustine's picture is a picture of the *essence* of human language.

Wittgenstein investigates just such an extension further on in the *Investigations*. Viewing these different sorts of words as if they all operate in the same way leads to the conclusion that an ostensive definition of a word is always ambiguous (and hence some guesswork is essential on the part of the learner). This might be something one would be prepared to live with. (I have argued that the author of the *Tractatus* was committed to it.) But it is absurd to suppose further that, for the person *giving* the ostensive definition, the focus of the gesture is likewise ambiguous. Certainly *I* know that I mean *red* ('mean' in the sense of the German *meinen* as opposed to *bedeuten*) when I give the definition 'this is red'. I do not clarify my explanation to *myself* by giving a category specification. Still, my meaning the colour as opposed to the shape is not something that can be discerned from the bare ostensive gesture and the words. Yet the essential ambiguity of the bare ostensive definition that the learner is faced with cannot, surely, also apply to the teacher. Accounting for this,

Wittgenstein suggests, partially motivates the inclination to postulate an act of meaning, perhaps conceived as a mental process or activity.

> And we do here what we do in a host of similar cases: because we cannot specify any *one* bodily action which we call pointing to the shape (as opposed, for example, to the colour), we say that a *spiritual* [*g e i s t i g e*] activity corresponds to these words. (*PI* §36)

This inclination is here characterized as the result of an attempt to purify the concept of ostensive definition. Such a purification appears necessary in the face of the apparently essential inadequacy of the paradigm case of ostensive definitions of ordinary objects. It seems futile to attempt to single out any one bodily action as distinguishing pointing to the shape from pointing to the colour (*PI* §33f.). The application of Augustine's picture to colour and number words gives all these word types a uniform appearance. One might feel impelled to impose a similar order upon our conception of the ostensive definitions of these words. Saying that the *real* pointing is something like a mental activity is an attempt to overcome the difficulty of what understanding language consists in, in the face of this unconscious assimilation to Augustine's picture. (Indeed, it is this mental activity of 'pointing' to the shape or colour that the teacher is trying to effect in the learner.)

Although we are still left, it seems, with a lot of necessary guesswork on behalf of a learner (and in this sense teaching is still inadequate) we have, at any rate, managed to mark the *distinction* between explaining 'red' and 'round' within the parameters of Augustine's picture. So even though the learner must guess, there is something to guess about. The learner must necessarily *interpret* the ostensive definition, but there is at least something to interpret correctly or incorrectly. It appears that, at any rate, one can give *oneself* an unambiguous "ostensive definition" (cf. *PI* §274).

It is illuminating to once again relate this back to elucidations in the *Tractatus*. That elucidations are essentially *various* meshes nicely with the inclination to say that no one *bodily* action is going to differentiate between pointing to the shape and pointing to the colour. Guesswork on behalf of the learner is essential, and can only (and perhaps not entirely) be overcome by getting the learner to see the common constituent of various states-of-affairs. This bears a noteworthy resemblance to Augustine's account of how he came to learn language.

If my account in this chapter of this theme in §§1-36 of *Philosophical Investigations* is correct, then it is indeed the word 'diagnosis' that best captures the main contour lines.[27]

Notes

1. Merril Ring has previously drawn attention to the importance of this distinction in §1. As I will argue later in this chapter, it seems to me that careful attention to the distinction between 'picture' and 'idea' has more radical consequences than Ring is inclined to draw. See 'Baker and Hacker on Section One of the *Philosophical Investigations*' (*Philosophical Investigations* 8: 3 July 1985), pp. 259-75.
2. Baker, G. P. and Hacker, P. M. S., *Wittgenstein: Understanding and Meaning* (Basil Blackwell, 1980), pp. 33f.
3. My translation here differs slightly from Anscombe's. I render '*brauchbar*' as 'useful', which is more literal. And Anscombe translates '*Darstellung*' as 'description'. This is fine of itself. Yet elsewhere in *Philosophical Investigations*, '*Darstellung*' is consistently translated as 'representation' (e.g. §§50, 280, 435, p. 198). It is worth making explicit these correspondences. Moreover, '*Darstellung*' (and its cognates) generally have a less restricted application than 'description'. For it would be perfectly legitimate to characterize a painting, e.g., as a '*Darstellung*', but this is seldom true of the word 'description'.
4. Baker and Hacker (op. cit.) pp. 266f.
5. Ibid., p. 36.
6. Ibid., pp. 37f.
7. Cf. Waismann, 1969, p. 94
8. One might object here that the imaginary language at §2 does not fit Augustine's description because it fails to accommodate the claim that sentences are combinations of names. And there are no sentences in this language that contain more than one word. This is true, but little turns on it. The imaginary language could be easily modified by including such commands as "block slab pillar beam". This order would be obeyed if B brought a block, slab, pillar and beam (in no particular order). So a call like "slab" would then, given my minor modification of the language game, be a kind of degenerate combination of names.
9. Baker and Hacker (op. cit.) p. 207.
10. Cf. ibid., p. 87.
11. As argued by Baker and Hacker, ibid.
12. For a brief exposition of the first two interpretations, and a less brief argument in favour of this third interpretation, see Hacker, *Insight and Illusion* (Clarendon Press, 1986), pp. 76ff.

13. As I shall argue presently, the confusion which Wittgenstein is calling attention to here is not an 'elucidation'. The confusion is, however, importantly connected with the *Tractatus'* conception of the naming relation. I discuss this in the next chapter.
14. It was indeed true, in the *Tractatus*, that 'Once you knew what a word stands for you knew its whole use'. But this was because it was *impossible* for a word to stand for an object unless its use was fixed. This must be differentiated from the claim that knowing what a name stands for *fixes* its use. See Chapter Two.
15. Cf. P. M. S. Hacker, *Wittgenstein: Meaning and Mind* (Blackwell, 1990), Exg. §264.
16. Hacker (op. cit.) p. 78.
17. Baker and Hacker (op. cit.) pp. 35ff.
18. On the other hand, it is not obvious on this reading why Wittgenstein would *qualify* his remark about learning the use of language: it is *in a sense* that the use of language cannot be taught. For, on this reading of elucidation, the 'use' of language cannot be taught *simpliciter*, not merely 'in a certain sense'. Explanations of meaning serve only to give content to form. This glitch will assume importance following this digression, when we come to my interpretation of elucidations.
19. Cf. P. M. S. Hacker, *Wittgenstein: Meaning and Mind* (Blackwell, 1990), p. 89.
20. Waismann, 1979, p. 246.
21. Ibid., my emphasis.
22. It is noteworthy that the conclusion Wittgenstein draws from his argument in §6 of *Philosophical Remarks* is that 'in a certain sense, the use of language is something that cannot be *taught*' (my emphasis). He is not saying that everybody is born with an innate language; rather he is forging an external connection between learning and teaching. The learner must just pick up the meaning of words by attending to their use (cf. *PI* §1 'as I heard words repeatedly used in their proper places in various sentences, I gradually learnt to understand what objects they signified . . .'). It is a matter of *chance* whether the person takes the expression as it is intended (*PR* §6).
23. See Baker and Hacker (op. cit.) p. 34f.
24. The case here could be very much analogous to the relationship Wittgenstein discerned between the *Tractatus* and Ogden and Richard's *The Meaning of Meaning* (Kegan Paul, 1923). In a letter to Ogden he wrote, 'I think I ought to confess to you frankly that I believe you have not *caught the problems* which—for instance—I was at in my book (whether or not I have given the correct solution)' (Monk, p. 214). Perhaps Wittgenstein considered his discussion of the presuppositions of ostensive definition to be relevant to a theory which "had not caught the problems" about ostensive definition which the *Tractatus* did.
25. Indeed, even as deep into the *Investigations* as §146, Wittgenstein is undogmatic about what we should and should not call 'understanding': 'Suppose I now ask: "Has he understood the system when he continues the series to the hundredth place?" Or—if I should not speak of 'understanding' in connection with our primitive language-game: He has got the system, if he continues the series correctly so far . . . '. I am indebted to Stuart Shanker for pointing out the mechanist undertones in these early sections.
26. At any rate, *something* must differentiate the teaching of 'pillar' from 'block'. Of course, it *could* be the case that, for some strange reason, pointing to a block, in addition to or instead of resulting in the ability to use the word 'block', managed to result in the ability to use the word 'pillar' (or even 'red'). That is, we can easily imagine this happening, even though it would be altogether mysterious *why* this happened. Undoubtedly, *why* this happened needs explaining, but an appeal to a difference in the teaching is ruled out. *Ex hypothesi* there is no difference. And since there is no difference between the 'training' or 'teaching' of these two words it would, *qua* teaching, be entirely unrelated to what is learned. It would be doubtful

whether we should *call* this activity 'teaching' or 'training'. I am indebted to Peter Hacker for this point.

27. Warren Goldfarb's essay, 'I want you to bring me a slab' (*Synthese*, Vol 56, 1983), makes remarks similar, at least in a general way, to my depiction here of the character of these early sections of *Philosophical Investigations.* For example, consider the following remark from his essay:

> The "decisive moves in the conjuring trick" ... do not amount to specific theses held by this or that philosopher; they are made without notice at a point in the course of philosophizing far earlier than the development of a particular position. Thus I see the opening of the *Investigations* as crucially concerned with exhibiting such an early stage and with evoking its character (p. 266ff.).

I agree with this, and I think it is important. However, it seems to me that here Goldfarb has not quite grasped, in a substantial way, the diagnostic role these earlier sections are intended to play in subsequent sections of the *Investigations.* For Goldfarb's characterization is subject to the same criticism as Ring makes of Baker and Hacker (*supra.*). That is to say, Goldfarb does not pay heed to Wittgenstein's explicit distinction between Augustine's picture and 'that philosophical conception of meaning' which identifies meaning and bearer (ibid., p. 267). As I have emphasized, and will continue to flesh out in subsequent chapters, the point of introducing these roots is, crucially, to detail the way in which they inform the development of philosophical problems and conceptions, and most especially that particular conception of meaning which Baker and Hacker (and Goldfarb) pack into Augustine's picture.

4

Objects and Necessary Existence

> Why is philosophy so complicated? It ought, after all, to be *completely* simple.—Philosophy unties the knots in our thinking, which we have tangled up in an absurd way; but to do that, it must make movements which are just as complicated as the knots. Although the *result* of philosophy is simple, its methods for arriving there cannot be so. The complexity of philosophy is not in its matter, but in our tangled understanding.
>
> (*PR* §2)

4.1 Canonical Samples and Sempiternal Objects

In the previous chapter, we looked at Wittgenstein's treatment of a philosophical problem regarding language learning. In a certain sense, language learning seems to be impossible. For 'any kind of explanation of a language presupposes a language already. And in a certain sense, the use of language . . . cannot be taught' (*PR* §6). I characterized Wittgenstein's approach to this problem as primarily diagnostic. Generally speaking, Wittgenstein traces transformations in the employment of words, and also discerns the temptations motivating those transformations. At bottom it is Augustine's picture, when conceived as a picture of the essence of language, that lies at the root of these philosophical problems.

Wittgenstein imagines a dogmatic application of Augustine's picture to a simple language which, *prima facie*, it does not fit (viz., in *PI* §8). This application of Augustine's picture seems to necessitate the postulation of *something* in order to mark even a distinction between, e.g., meaning the shape as opposed to meaning the colour. For, one might say, surely *I* know I mean the shape, and not the colour. A mental pointing mechanism appears to fulfil this role.

Wittgenstein's method is to inquire into the genesis of this philosophical problem about language learning. To some extent, this diagnosis probably simplifies matters. Surely Wittgenstein's imagined account does not completely capture all and only the reasoning underlying the formulation of the picture theory and the conception of elucidations at 3.263 of the *Tractatus*. On the other hand, undoubtedly something closely resembling this underpins the thinking that led to those doctrines. Perhaps one could say that this imagined genesis is a perspicuous *fable* of the motivations underlying these aspects of the picture theory. Even so it is not without value, for among the most important steps in the dissolution of a philosophical problem is, I suggest, a depiction of the *character* of the confusion surrounding a philosophical problem.

To repeat, it is due to a transformation in the employment of 'name' that every ostensive definition appears 'essentially ambiguous'. The reaction to this philosophical problem about ostensive definition is itself a transformation—this time a transformation in the employment of 'pointing'. These transformations are good microcosms of the kind of thing Wittgenstein is indicating with his distinction, in §1, between the picture and the 'idea'. (In this chapter I will distinguish *the* 'idea', that the meaning of a word is the object to which it refers, by always putting single quotes around it.) That is, they are good examples of how a 'purified' use of words (i.e., 'name', 'pointing') can have its roots in a primitive picture (Augustine's picture). However, neither of these transformations are *the* 'idea' presented at the opening of the *Investigations*. Except for its introduction in §1, nothing so far has been said about the temptation to *identify* the meaning of a name with the object to which it refers. Rather, the issue so far has been the inclination to uniformly view the *explanation of* meaning as performed by an ostensive definition, where the concept of ostensive definition is conceived under the paradigm of ostensive explanations of ordinary object words. Augustine's picture is partially defined by the claim that all words name objects. Neither the claim that all words name 'objects', nor even the claim that all words are explained by pointing to 'objects', is equivalent with the claim that the meaning of a word is identical with the object to which it refers. It is this latter claim that Wittgenstein calls the 'idea' (*PI* §1). In what relation do these claims about names and their explanation stand to the 'idea'? In the previous chapter, I suggested that the distinction between Augustine's picture and the 'idea' is important for Wittgenstein's argumentative purposes. If so, the relationship ought to make itself manifest somewhere. If dogmatic application of Augustine's picture is somehow at the root of the 'idea', the 'idea' should eventually make an appearance. In this chapter, I continue to trace Wittgenstein's diagnosis of the influence of Augustine's picture. By the end of this chapter, it should be clear how the 'idea' can have its roots in Augustine's picture.

Explicit critical investigation of the *Tractarian* notions of 'object' and 'name' runs roughly from §37 through to §59 of the *Investigations*. The climax seems to be in §50:

> Let us imagine samples of colour preserved in Paris like the standard metre. We define: "sepia" means the colour of the standard sepia which is kept hermetically sealed. Then it will make no sense to say of this sample either that it is of this colour or that it is not.
>
> We can put it like this: this sample is an instrument of the language used in ascriptions of colour. In this language-game it is not something that is represented, but is a means of representation .... And to say "If it did not *exist*, it could have no name" is as much and as little as: if this thing did

> not exist, we could not use it in our language-game.—What looks as if it *had* to exist, is part of the language. (*PI* §50)

This passage, and especially the last sentence, will be the focal point around which the discussion in the present chapter revolves. Here Wittgenstein is drawing an analogy between certain features he had once attributed to *Tractarian* objects, and certain features of our use of samples (e.g., a sample's use in the employment of a colour word). The focus is on two interdependent and jointly paradoxical features of *Tractarian* objects:

(1) it is impossible to attribute either existence or non-existence to 'objects' (*TLP* 3.221)

(2) despite (1), these 'objects' necessarily 'exist' (*TLP* 2.022f.).[1]

And as we will see, this distinction is reflected in Wittgenstein's 'analogous case', i.e., in the use of canonical samples employed as standards of comparison.

'What looks as if it *had* to exist, is part of the language' (*PI* §50). I suggest that this sentence is a conclusion Wittgenstein is drawing, in particular a conclusion about why *Tractarian* objects were postulated. It is 'objects' which look as if they have to exist. Wittgenstein is telling us that they are actually part of the language, i.e., 'objects' are samples. More precisely, he is saying that reflection on sample use played a part in the postulation of 'objects'. The postulation of 'objects' was partially due to promoting features of our 'means of representation' (samples) to the level of 'that which is represented' ('objects'). If this is right, Wittgenstein is clearly making a diagnostic claim.

One might object straight away to this characterization of §50, perhaps with questions like the following. Is this section engaged in anything more than a comparison? Is Wittgenstein really making a diagnostic claim? On Baker's and Hacker's reading, Wittgenstein is not saying that the features of samples themselves play a role in the tendency to postulate 'objects'. Rather, it is only that some of the needs *Tractarian* objects were intended to satisfy are actually satisfied by samples.[2] That is to say, Wittgenstein is appealing to the use of samples to *undermine* the rationale to postulate 'objects'. He is saying that it is unnecessary to postulate 'objects', because samples actually do the work which the *Tractatus* had assigned to 'objects'. (This is not to deny the existence of a battery of arguments against the existence of 'objects'.) Thus Baker and Hacker read this section as if, for Wittgenstein, an appeal to samples was in competition with an appeal to 'objects' as the correct account of the matter. (Of course, other concerns may also play a part in rejecting *Tractarian* objects. For example, that the idea is incoherent, or that 'objects' are just plain bizarre.)

Certainly Wittgenstein is engaged in a comparison here, for he is asking us to 'consider an analogous case' (ibid.). I will argue that this comparison is also intended to throw light on how reflection on the features of samples *themselves* can play a role in motivating the postulation of *Tractarian* objects. I will argue that Wittgenstein is appealing to certain features of our use of samples in an attempt to diagnose the motivation to postulate *Tractarian* objects. It is a distorted picture of *explanations of words* by appeal to samples which itself motivates the tendency to postulate 'objects'.

The general structure of the sections leading up to §50 suggests my reading. §50 is the culmination of an investigation into the idea that 'a name ought really to signify a simple' (*PI* §39). More immediately, it is the culmination of an investigation of the question, 'What *lies behind* the idea that names signify simples?' (*PI* §46). That is to say, it is the culmination of an inquiry into what underlies the *idea* and the *tendency to say* that names signify simples.

Moreover, §50 immediately follows an investigation of Plato's claims regarding 'primary elements', which Wittgenstein likens to *Tractarian* objects (ibid.). Hence the natural way to read the conclusion, 'What looks as if it *had* to exist, is part of the language', is: "*Tractarian* objects, which look as if they have to exist, are really samples, which are in a sense part of the language". Wittgenstein seems to be saying that 'a *Tractarian* object was in fact a sample ... seen through a glass darkly'.[3]

There is only one feasible alternative to my understanding of the wording in the last sentence quoted above from §50. Wittgenstein is surely referring to something as looking as if it had to exist. If not 'objects', what else could he be referring to? The only feasible alternative is that Wittgenstein is claiming *samples* look as if they have to exist. That is to say, there is at best an allusion to the idea of *Tractarian* objects. Primarily he is referring to samples. And his remark is that, although samples look as if they have to exist, they are really part of the language. This construal of the wording in the last sentence quoted above from §50 coheres nicely with Baker's and Hacker's characterization of the whole section. For on their reading, Wittgenstein's point is that samples fulfil the role which 'objects' were intended to fulfil. The only diagnostic role of the statement is that samples might, under the influence of a misconception, also look as if they have to exist.

'What looks as if it *had* to exist, is part of the language.' I want to emphasize the difference between these two alternate readings of this sentence. The difference lies precisely in what we take Wittgenstein to be referring to as having to exist. Is it samples, *Tractarian* objects, or perhaps both? I will argue that the reference is *not* to samples. And moreover, there is not merely an allusion to (the idea of) *Tractarian* objects. Rather, the primary reference is to *Tractarian* objects. Samples do not (of course) look at all as if they have to exist.

For the purposes of argument, suppose Wittgenstein is suggesting that samples look as though they must exist. Even when read only in the context of the one section, this supposition is highly problematic. Wittgenstein compares the standard metre with Plato's 'primary elements'. (He has already likened Plato's elements to *Tractarian* objects.) He appeals to the *obvious* fact that the analogy holds not because the sample shares any of the *extraordinary* properties attributed to *Tractarian* objects: 'this is, *of course*, not to ascribe any extraordinary property to it [viz., the sample], but only to mark its peculiar role in the language-game' (*PI* §50, my emphasis). Appeal to the role of the sample in the language-game is presented in *opposition* to an appeal to 'extraordinary properties' as an explanation of those features of the sample which *are* analogous to *Tractarian* objects.

Thus Wittgenstein virtually contradicts the claim that samples look as if they have to exist. Would it not be awfully muddled on his part to immediately go on and remark that the canonical sample 'looks as if it *had* to exist' (ibid.)? Surely this is (the appearance of) an extraordinary property! Indeed, this is surely the very extraordinary property which Wittgenstein is discussing. If the *sample* itself looks as though it has to exist, then at the very least it would be an illegitimate shift in the burden of proof for Wittgenstein to say that it is *obvious* that the sample does not have this (or any other) extraordinary property. If the sample actually did look as if it must exist, then surely it is not *obvious* that it does not have to exist.[4] If Wittgenstein is discussing motivations underlying the postulation of *Tractarian* objects, an appeal to the ordinary usage of 'sample' is justified. In a context where the word 'sample' itself is re-employed in a metaphysical discussion, Wittgenstein's appeal to ordinary usage would be question-begging. This is not the situation in §50 of the *Investigations*.

I will detail an interpretation of §50 which does not have the unwelcome (and implausible) conclusion that Wittgenstein is engaged in a completely illegitimate shift in the burden of proof (or even virtually contradicting himself in the span of one paragraph). Moreover, my reading fits neatly into the structure of argumentation leading up to §50. I suggest that Wittgenstein discerns the *motivation* to postulate 'objects' in a misrepresentation of word explanations by means of samples. If this interpretation is correct, there is more truth in Hacker's claim, that *Tractarian* objects are samples seen through a glass darkly, than is captured in the idea that *Tractarian* objects were postulated to satisfy the needs that are actually satisfied by samples. Rather, a misunderstanding about—and hence a (perhaps fuzzy) awareness of—explanations by means of samples has a hand in the tendency to postulate 'simples' like the 'objects' of the *Tractatus*.

The sample of sepia, as it operates in this (imaginary) language-game, shares certain important features with a *Tractarian* object. We are asked to imagine that appeal to this sample is the sole criterion for distinguishing correct from incorrect applications of 'sepia'. Something is sepia if and only if its colour matches the colour of the sample. (Let's never mind about what 'matching' consists in here: one problem at a time.) It follows trivially that its existence is presupposed by the language-game. This is not to say that another criterion could not be devised; or that, if this imaginary language-game were actual, this word would necessarily cease to have meaning if someone dyed the sample purple. Rather, *if* we imagine that appeal to this canonical sample is a defining characteristic of the language-game, *then* (trivially) the existence of that sample is a presupposition of the language-game. Analogously, the existence of *Tractarian* objects is a presupposition (or requirement) of language. For 'If the world had no substance ... we could not sketch any picture of the world (true or false)' (*TLP* 2.0211f. see below).

Furthermore, it is a feature of a *Tractarian* object that one cannot *say* it exists. This too is comparable with the canonical sample of sepia as it is used in this imaginary language-game. For it is being assumed that the sample is *the* standard of comparison justifying ascription of that colour to objects (or surfaces of objects, or two dimensional squares, as the case may be). To claim that the sample itself is that colour is to say, as it were, that "it is the colour that it is". This is as if we had compared the sample with itself and noticed that it is the same colour. This is patent nonsense, for obviously one cannot compare something with itself.

Under normal circumstances, of course, it does indeed sound strange to say that one cannot *say* that the standard metre is one metre long. But this is because we do not really employ any sample 'absolutely canonically'. In actual fact, there are various criteria for saying that the standard metre has changed its size. If we decided that the standard metre grew, this could be said to be tantamount to ceasing to regard it *as* a sample (of what it was a sample of). As Wittgenstein would put it, we are no longer playing that particular language-game with it.

So far, then, the similarity between a *Tractarian* object and the sample of sepia is noteworthy. However, there are certain features of a *Tractarian* object not shared by the sample of sepia. 'Absolute' simplicity is one which I will leave aside for the moment. Two further features are conspicuously absent in the sample. (1) The sample is not the bearer of a (logically) proper name in the language; and (2) the sample is not the meaning of a name (*TLP* 3.203). For one would not ordinarily say of a sample of some colour that it is the bearer of the name of that colour. Neither would one say that the sample *is* the meaning of 'red', even if one was inclined to say the *colour* of the sample is the meaning of 'red' (*infra*).

Consider these differences together with my argument that §50 makes diagnostic claims. I argued that §50 is intended to throw light on *why Tractarian* objects were postulated in the form that they were. If this is the correct interpretation of §50, two questions need answering. (1) What might motivate mistaking features of (our use of) samples as features of the bearers of such (logically) proper names? And (2) how does (1) relate, if it does, to the 'idea' that the bearer of a logically proper name is the meaning of the name which stands for it?

One possibility is the anti-thesis in this chapter. It is the 'idea' which causes misunderstanding about samples. That answers (1). The answer to (2) is then obvious: the relationship between misunderstandings about samples and the 'idea' is that the 'idea' causes this misunderstanding. That is, we invoke a prior commitment to the 'idea' to explain the temptation to think of these names as (logically) proper names. *Pace* Chapter Three (*supra*), Wittgenstein is not engaged in tracing the route from Augustine's picture to the picture theory. Rather, he is examining the consequences of a theory of meaning which, *inter alia*, identifies the meaning of a word with the object it refers to. If so, the 'idea' plays a critical role in the early Wittgenstein's temptation to postulate *Tractarian* objects. I will argue that this is not Wittgenstein's diagnosis. But this is the anti-thesis, so let us work it out in more detail:

According to the 'idea', the meaning of 'red' is *the* object to which 'red' refers. We often point at a sample when explaining the meaning of 'red'. According to Wittgenstein, features of the object pointed at qua sample somehow get construed as features of some 'object' which is the bearer of 'red'. On the anti-thetical reading, how exactly would this conjure up *Tractarian* objects?

Obviously one can imagine the destruction of samples. Moreover, unlike the canonical colour sample in §50, in reality there are many things that play the role of a sample of 'red'. Hence, someone under the influence of the 'idea' would probably be inclined to deny that it is the *sample* (ordinarily understood) which we point *out*, even if we do point *at* the sample. One could not reasonably say that the *sample* is the meaning: more likely one would say that the meaning of the word is the *colour* of the sample. If so, then 'Red', on this model, seems to operate like a proper name of a (kind of) object, viz., *Redness*, or *Red*. For even if there are different samples of *red*, there are not different *reds* (unless one is considering different shades of red, which just pushes these questions back a step).

The 'idea' might engender this misconception of what is done when one explains a word by reference to a sample. The function of such an explanation is really to point out the colour of the sample, which is *the* meaning of 'red'. This conception seems to give the colour *red* a kind of substantive existence. Thus conceived, *redness* bears a striking resemblance to a *Tractarian* object. 'Red', it seems, although unlike an ordinary proper name (*infra*), is nevertheless a kind of proper name of *red*.

According to the anti-thesis, then, the 'idea' as it were projects language onto reality. It projects features of samples onto mythical objects. Thus the anti-thesis contends that, at the *foundation* of the picture theory lies a conception of meaning which distorts reflection on how language 'connects up with the world'. That is, a referential theory of word meaning is the *primitive* error underlying the postulation of 'objects'.[5] Moreover, this conception of the relationship between *Tractarian* objects and the 'idea' coheres with the anti-thetical interpretation of both (1) Wittgenstein's conception of metaphysics and (2) the nature of Wittgenstein's transition. I discussed (1) and (2) in my introductory chapter. Let me briefly remind the reader of this discussion.

(1) A misconception about *meaning* lies at the bottom of Wittgenstein's picture theory in the *Tractatus*. This misconception is itself a manifestation of the general metaphysical tendency to project language, or

grammar, onto reality. In the particular case of concern in this chapter, this tendency is to construe certain features of our use of samples as though they were features of objects in reality. It is in this sense that metaphysics is the shadow of grammar.

(2) This picture of metaphysics itself goes hand in hand with the anti-thetical conception of Wittgenstein's transition from the *Tractatus* to the *Investigations*. The transition arises primarily out of a rejection of the *Tractarian* conception of the relationship between language, or grammar, and reality. And a foundational tenet of this reorientation is a new conception of meaning: the meaning of a word is its use.

I discuss these generalizations in more detail in the following chapter. But I entreat the reader to bear them closely in mind while reading the remainder of this chapter. For although the following discussion may at times seem exotic, it bears crucially on these more general issues.

I will argue against the anti-thetical reading of Wittgenstein's diagnostic strategy in the sections leading up to *Philosophical Investigations* §50. Like the previous chapter, I will argue that Wittgenstein is not criticizing a theory of meaning which leads to philosophical problems. I will argue that the 'idea' is not a commitment, an assumption or even a 'picture' which informs the philosophical problems Wittgenstein is (thus far) investigating. Neither is Wittgenstein directly criticizing the 'idea'. The 'idea' is not the result of some metaphysical urge or tendency to project language onto reality. On the contrary, it has deeper roots in the purification of the concept of a *name*, this purification itself being the result of an attempt to represent our concept of a name in terms of *one* incomparable essence.

The conception of *meaning* in the *Tractatus* is, I will argue, virtually necessitated by the failure to notice some (not all!) *differences* between ways in which we employ the word 'name'. One might put it this way: in the *Tractatus* the 'idea' is the result of a failure to initially notice some differences, then to notice them, and then to assimilate these differences to a simplistic picture harvested from the initially hasty reflection on the usage of 'name'. (Thus the 'idea' is in this sense comparable to the claim, discussed in the last chapter, that teaching is 'inadequate': the meaning of a genuine *name* '*must*' be the object to which it corresponds). If I can argue this persuasively, then it would seem that, according to Wittgenstein, at the root of the tendency to say, "There *must* be a connection between language *and* reality", is a primitive picture of the working of (aspects of) *language*.

I will argue that, according to Wittgenstein, at the root of these confusions regarding certain features of samples is a dogmatism about the applicability of the model of *proper* names. Proper names are sometimes explained by reference to their bearers, and this model of explanations of proper names is dogmatically applied to names explained by reference to samples. That is to say, the description of explanations by reference to samples is assimilated to, or cast in the mould of, or represented by the model of explanations of proper names. It is this more fundamental tendency that underlies the tendency to equate the meaning of a name with its bearer. Hence Wittgenstein engages in a diagnosis of an important source *underlying* the tendency in philosophy to even frame certain questions about word meaning problematically, e.g., questions like "How can language be connected to the world?", or "How is meaning possible?".

Finally, I will further argue that Wittgenstein also has a diagnosis of this more fundamental tendency (i.e., the tendency to apply the model of proper names to names explained by reference to samples). The motivation lies in Augustine's picture. On my reading, consequently, the first 50 sections of *Philosophical Investigations* contain a detailed, if compressed elucidation of Wittgenstein's initial suggestion that 'in this picture we find the roots of the ... idea' (*PI* §1).

I argue my interpretation in Sections 4.4 and 4.5. In Section 4.3, I argue against the anti-thesis, viz., that the 'idea' informs, rather than results from this misconception about names explained by reference to samples. First, however, I must address an important objection which threatens to undercut my arguments before they get started. Once again things are going to turn on an obscure issue in the *Tractatus*.

4.2 Simples and Determinacy of Sense

If we disregard Wittgenstein's claims in *Philosophical Investigations* §50, is there any reason to believe that a misunderstanding about the employment of samples had anything at all to do with *Tractarian* objects? It is certainly not obvious, for the early Wittgenstein appears to justify his postulation of 'objects' on unrelated grounds, viz., to satisfy the demand for what he calls 'determinacy of sense' (3.23). This seems entirely unrelated to samples, let alone any misunderstanding about their employment. Yet in §50, Wittgenstein is certainly comparing *Tractarian* objects with samples. Are we not forced to reject my interpretation that §50 makes *diagnostic* claims? How could the later Wittgenstein contend that samples had something to do with the postulation of 'objects', if his rationale in the *Tractatus* is the demand for determinacy of sense? This might be seen to lend credence to Baker's and Hacker's interpretation, viz., that Wittgenstein's appeal to sample use is intended to *supplant* his earlier appeal to 'objects'.

I will argue that Wittgenstein's demand for determinacy of sense is not a demand for 'objects' *per se*. Rather, the demand *per se* is for the possibility of simple *signs*. 'The requirement that simple signs be possible is the requirement that sense be determinate' (*TLP* 3.23). *Assuming* the 'idea', this demand for simple *signs* entails a demand for simple objects, for 'If the world had no substance [i.e., 'objects'], then whether a proposition had sense would depend on whether another proposition was true' (*TLP* 2.0211). Thus, 'What lies behind the idea that names really signify simples' (*PI* §45), is not just the demand for determinacy of sense. Rather, it is this demand in conjunction with a commitment to the 'idea'.

This reading of Wittgenstein's 'demand' is crucial to my thesis in the following sections of this chapter. I must first reconcile the *Tractatus'* appeal to determinacy of sense with my interpretation of §50. For my thesis is that, according to (the later) Wittgenstein, it was ultimately misunderstandings about samples which played a role in the postulation of 'objects'. My reading of Wittgenstein's 'demand' is also crucial to my polemic against the anti-thesis (*infra*). Recall that the anti-thesis is not merely Baker's and Hacker's interpretation of §50, viz., that Wittgenstein appeals to samples to do the work which the author of the *Tractatus* intended for 'objects'. I argued that this reading does not do justice to, *inter alia*, Wittgenstein's *diagnostic* claim that 'What looks as if it *had* to exist, is part of the language'. If the anti-thesis is to do justice to this remark, we must supplement Baker's and Hacker's reading of §50: the 'idea' is the primitive motivation underlying the postulation of 'objects'. For an adherent to the anti-thesis, the postulation of 'objects' is the result of reflection on sample use under the influence of a commitment to the 'idea'.

My contention with the anti-thesis is not over the question, Is the 'idea' related to the postulation of 'objects'? Rather, my contention is over the question, *How* is the 'idea' related to 'objects'? Both the anti-thesis and the thesis in this chapter are committed to the 'idea' playing an important role in the postulation of 'objects' in the *Tractatus*. The difference between these two readings lies in how that role is understood. But if the *Tractarian* demand for determinacy of sense is altogether unrelated both to Wittgenstein's later discussion of samples, and the 'idea', then *both* the thesis and the anti-thesis are untenable. And if both the thesis and anti-thesis are untenable, a substantial chunk of my argumentation in the following sections is just plain irrelevant. Thus as a preliminary, I really need to show that the 'idea' does *somehow* underpin the early Wittgenstein's postulation of 'objects'. The rest of this section is dedicated to examining Wittgenstein's 'demand for determinacy of sense' in more detail. I will show how the postulation of 'objects' in the *Tractatus* is grounded crucially on a commitment to the 'idea'.

'The requirement that simple signs be possible is the requirement that sense be determinate' (*TLP* 3.23). This demand for determinacy of sense has an historical precursor in Frege. For Frege, every concept must be such that it is completely determined, for any object, whether or not that object falls under it (*infra*). *Frege's* demand for determinacy of sense, at any rate, is perhaps formulated altogether independently of any confusion about the ordinary practices of word explanation. For this demand was imposed on Frege's "Conceptual Notation", not on natural languages.

Not so for Wittgenstein. In the *Tractatus*, this is a demand which must be satisfied by *any* language. It is not a stipulation for particular purposes. All genuine propositions must be analyzable into truth-functions of elementary propositions. And although molecular propositions may be indeterminate, elementary propositions must be determinate. For instance, *p* v *q* is molecular and is, in a sense, indeterminate. For there is more than one way in which it could be true. Moreover, *p* & *q* is in a sense indeterminate, because there is more than one way in which it could be false. This sort of indeterminacy is not problematic, so long as it terminates at the level of elementary propositions. Although there may be some indeterminacy about which circumstances make a molecular proposition true or false, it must be absolutely precise just what this indeterminacy is (*TLP* 3.24f.). The proposition *p* & *q* is false if and only if either *p* is false, *q* is false, or both *p* and *q* are false. And it is true if and only if both *p* and *q* are true. This determinate specification of the truth conditions of *p* & *q* is only possible if the elementary propositions are determinately true or false. (Let us suppose *p* and *q* are elementary.) Otherwise the question *whether* a proposition is true or false would not always have a determinate answer. (We shall see why this is so presently.)

To this extent there is a correspondence between Frege's and Wittgenstein's demand for determinacy of sense. For Frege conceived the signs for logical connectives as designating functions of a particular sort, viz., as functions mapping their arguments onto truth-values. If these functions are undefined for certain arguments then, in these cases, the value of the function is undetermined. Frege came to insist that they be defined for all arguments. For both Frege and the early Wittgenstein, therefore, the failure to meet this demand results in there being cases where the question, whether a proposition is true or false, may have no answer.

In other respects Frege and Wittgenstein see the demand differently. For Frege, 'A definition of a concept ... must be complete; it must unambiguously determine, as regards any object, whether or not it falls under the concept'.[6] And a concept is a function whose value is a truth value.[7] *Somewhat* analogously, in the *Tractatus* elementary propositions are *written* as functions of names (*TLP* 4.24). If 'Fa' is the expression of a proposition, then the usage of the propositional function F*x* is to map expressions (which are perhaps simple names) onto (not necessarily elementary) propositions.[8]

I want to consider two claims Wittgenstein makes about propositional functions and (free) variables:

(1) *All* variables can be construed as propositional variables, even variable names (*TLP* 3.314). So if we suppose F*x* to be a propositional function (*not* the *name* of a propositional function) where F is a constant expression and *x* is a variable ranging over simples names, it follows (*prima facie* paradoxically) that *x* itself can be construed as a propositional variable, i.e., as an expression which ranges over propositions.

Prima facie this is wrong-headed. Wittgenstein seems to be confusing the argument for a propositional function with its value. But 3.314 shows clearly that the conflation is deliberate. And it is entirely consonant with his conception of the relationship between meaning and well-formedness (see Chapter Two). A name has meaning only if its logical syntax is presupposed, i.e., only if the propositions for which it can be a constituent are given in advance. 'Only propositions have sense; only in the nexus of a proposition does a name have meaning' (*TLP* 3.3). It follows from this that even a name variable, if it does abbreviate its stipulated values, thereby determines a set of propositions. It determines the set of propositions which names of that logical type may enter into as constituents.

For Wittgenstein the range of a propositional variable is not necessarily (nor, one would think, usually) the entire set of well-formed sentences in the language. For propositional variables are type heterogeneous. Wittgenstein's propositional variables are close to what we think of as well-formed formulae with free variables, e.g., F*x*, *X*a, or even *Xx*, except that we must think of them as being generated from propositions by 'turning a constituent [expression] of a proposition into a variable' *TLP* 3.315).[9] These 'propositional variables' each determine a class of propositions. Let F*x*, *X*a, *Xx* be three propositional variables, each constructed from the proposition Fa by turning certain constituent expressions into variables. F*x* determines the class Fa, Fb, Fc, . . . , where a, b, c, . . . , enumerates all expressions of the same form as a; *X*a determines the class Fa, Ga, Ha, . . . , where F, G, H, . . . enumerates all expressions with the same form as F; and *Xx* determines the union of the first two classes.

(2) 'What values a propositional variable may take is something that is stipulated', and furthermore, the propositional variable itself is to be *identified* with its set of stipulated values (*TLP* 3.316). 'To stipulate values for a propositional variable is *to give the propositions* whose common characteristic the variable is' (*TLP* 3.317).

Consider the propositional function (henceforth I will use Wittgenstein's terminology: propositional variable) F*x*. If this propositional variable is constructed from Fa, then it 'gives' a set of propositions with a common characteristic (*TLP* 3.317). If a, b, c, . . . is an enumeration of all the expressions of the same form as 'a', then the propositional variable 'F*x*' 'gives', is even identical with, or is a kind of abbreviation for Fa, Fb, Fc, . . .

Two features of Wittgenstein's conception of a propositional variable distinguish it from Frege's notion of a concept. For my purposes, the first feature is of minor, but noteworthy importance.

(i) For the proposition Fa, it would be incoherent to construe the expression F*x* as *designating* anything. For instance, F*x* is not an object or a concept (*infra*). In this notation, the propositional variable is an (essential) feature in an abbreviation for a set of propositions—an abbreviation which shows what the members of this set of propositions have in common. This is altogether unlike Frege's conception of a concept. Frege's concepts are (unsaturated) 'entities', viz., *functions*. In his notation, the sign for the material conditional is—or at any rate came to be seen as—a designating expression.

(ii) The second feature of Wittgenstein's conception of a propositional variable does more than distinguish itself from Frege's conception of a concept. This second feature distinguishes Wittgenstein's and Frege's conceptions of determinacy of sense. To be sure, it is for Wittgenstein *determinate* what propositions are indicated by the propositional variable. However, it would be misleading to say the propositional variable *determines*, for every argument, what propositions are the values of that function for certain arguments. For the propositional variable is an *abbreviation* for a description of those propositions. So obviously the propositional variable is not in need of a *definition* that unambiguously determines a course of values. Wittgenstein's demand for determinacy of sense is not a requirement imposed on our definitions for specific purposes. It is, as it were, a requirement of sense.

We can express Wittgenstein's reformulation of Frege's demand in the following way. For every propositional variable it must be completely determinate, for any permissible[10] argument (e.g., simple names), what proposition results. And this follows from the definitions in the *Tractatus*: 'To stipulate values for a propositional variable is *to give the propositions* whose common characteristic the variable is' (*TLP* 3.317). If a propositional variable is an abbreviation for a set of propositions, it would be *incoherent* to say of a propositional variable that it is *not* determinate, for every permissible argument, what proposition that argument is mapped onto.

But now a puzzle arises. If it is incoherent to deny that a propositional variable is determinate in this way, then why would Wittgenstein need to *demand* that it is determinate in this way?

The demand is directed at the level of simple signs. Determinacy of sense is guaranteed only by the existence of simple signs (*TLP* 3.23). To see the connection we need to look at Wittgenstein's conception of analysis. For although determinacy of sense is an *a priori* demand in the *Tractatus*, that this determinacy of sense is actually present in ordinary language is only evident upon the analysis of ordinary language. As we can see from the following quotation, Wittgenstein's conception of analysis is closely connected with Russell's theory of descriptions (*infra*):

> A complex can be given only by its description, which will be right or wrong. A proposition that mentions a complex

> will not be nonsensical, if the complex does not exist, but simply false.
>
> When a propositional element signifies a complex, this can be seen from an indeterminateness in the propositions in which it occurs, In such cases we *know* that the proposition leaves something undetermined .... (*TLP* 3.24)
>
> A proposition has one and only one complete analysis (*TLP* 3.25)

For some reason, the demand for determinacy of sense requires the possibility of simple signs, viz., signs which do not signify complexes. So if it is not possible to analyze a proposition down to simple signs, this must somehow undermine determinacy of sense.

It is not immediately obvious why this should be so. For example, suppose 'red' is not a simple sign, and is analyzable indefinitely into sets of names for simple shades (limited perceptual capacities notwithstanding). In this example, it is not completely obvious that it is indeterminate for any object whether or not that object falls under the concept *being red.* (Wittgenstein would use different terminology. He calls the arguments of propositional function 'expressions'.) A stronger example is the concept, 'rational number between one and two'. This concept seems a good candidate for indefinite analyzability, viz., into a disjunctive formula with one free variable and an infinite number of disjuncts (e.g., '*x* is 1 1/2 or *x* is 1 1/3 or *x* is 1 1/4 or *x* is 1 2/3 ...'). Yet surely it is determinate, for any rational number, whether it falls under the concept 'between one and two'.

So again, how is the demand for *simple signs* a demand for determinacy of sense? The Fregean distinction between concept and object does not find any other expression in the *Tractatus* than in this distinction between a propositional function and its arguments. The logical constants were precisely *not* functions of any sort, but rather operations (*TLP* 5.2341). And if it makes sense to say that something like a concept-word occurs as a *simple constituent* of an elementary proposition then, for the *Tractarian* conception of 'object', *concepts* (and relations) are objects too (cf. *NB* p. 61). What could the demand for determinacy of sense mean within the parameters of the elementary proposition?

Consider the proposition that the object *this apple* falls under the concept *red*. Suppose this object and this concept were simple. If the apple is simple, 'apple' does not designate a complex. It must designate an 'object'. If the sign 'red' or 'is red' is simple, then the only *Tractarian* category for its referent is a simple 'object'. And the claim that this apple is red would amount to something like the assertion that these two (*Tractarian*) objects stand in a certain determinate relation to one another. Such a relation is one that cannot and need not be named: the objects fit together 'like links in a chain' (*TLP* 2.03). According to the *Tractarian* conception of objects, there is no such thing as an indeterminate relation between simple objects (*TLP* 2.031f.); and presumably it is a correlate of this conception that there is no such thing as an elementary proposition with an (even determinately) indeterminate sense.

This clarifies things somewhat. It is clear why the possibility of simple signs *satisfies* the demand for determinacy of sense. It is written right into it, by virtue of the notion of '*determinate* relation'. But why would the *impossibility* of simple signs vitiate the demand for determinacy of sense? It is still unclear why the acknowledgment of there being signs that were not simple, and not capable of being defined by means of simple signs, implies that sense is indeterminate.

The answer is discernable by examining how Wittgenstein worked out the consequences of Russell's theory of descriptions within the parameters of the picture theory. Wittgenstein expands on his assertion that 'Objects are simple' (*TLP* 2.02) with the following remark. 'If the world had no substance, then whether a proposition had sense would depend on whether another proposition was true. In that case we could not sketch any picture of the world (true or false)' (*TLP* 2.0211f.). Closely connected is Russell's analysis of definite descriptions such as 'The king of France' in the sentence 'The king of France is bald'.[11] Suppose there is no king of France. Are we to say the proposition 'The king of France is bald' is false? If we do, it is clear that this falsehood has not the same sense as the case where there is a king of France and he has a full head of hair. This might lead one to say that the sentence 'The king of France is bald', in the event that there is no king of France, is neither true nor false.

Russell's theory of descriptions allegedly undermines the need, in the case of definite descriptions, to acknowledge such truth-value gaps. It is well known that Russell suggested an analysis analogous to the analysis, previously devised by Frege, for indefinite descriptions such as 'A man'. The apparent form of 'The king of France is bald' is not its real form, and is to be replaced with the following. '*There is some x such that x is king of France, and for all y, if y is king of France then y is identical with x. And x is bald*'. In the event that there is no king of France, the analyzed form of expression is clearly false. For this sentence explicitly asserts the existence of one (and only one) king of France.

Notoriously, the early Wittgenstein took an existentially quantified sentence to be an abbreviation for a disjunction of all its instantiations. Thus at least for Wittgenstein, a presupposition of this analysis is that we have asserted a proposition of the *form* 'b is the king of France' ('b' here being a dummy proper name).[12] It has been asserted that there is something that satisfies the propositional function '*x* is king of France'. We call this something 'b', and for short, schematize this assertion like so: 'Fb'. If the analysis is to be successful in circumventing the apparent need to countenance truth-value gaps, then the 'b' (in 'Fb'), whatever it signifies, cannot itself be analyzable like 'The king of France' in 'The king of France is bald'. If it can be so analyzed, one has the same problem as before the analysis, viz., two ways in which that proposition might be false. In this case the analyzed expression would also be in need of an analysis into a definite description.

The sign 'b' must designate only by being a proper name of its bearer. As Anscombe notes, this difficulty *by itself* 'does not lead us to 'simples'.':

> [F]or the theory in its logical aspect has nothing to do with any theory of reduction to simples. It only demands that such simple symbols as [b] shall be possible if such propo-

> sitions as 'The [king of France is bald]' are to make sense. The type of name that is postulated here is the type: *name of [a king of France]*. A truth-condition for 'The [king of France is bald]' is 'There is an x such that x [is a king of France]'. The variable 'x' here ranges over [(present) kings of France].[13]

But (as Anscombe notes further on) one immediately wants to object that any use of an ordinary proper name is going to run into difficulties similar to those motivating Russell's theory of descriptions. Let us revert back to the example in the *Investigations*. Following Russell, we might say that the sentence 'Excalibur has a sharp blade', if it is false, could be false in more than one way. It could be false because Excalibur's blade is dull (i.e. not sharp); or it could be false because Excalibur does not exist. If all sentences which predicate something of the bearer of an ('apparent') proper name allow for more than one possible way of being false,[14] it appears as though we could always ask, when presented with the denial of such a sentence, "What do you mean? Do you mean ... or ... ". If this process of clarification could proceed without end then sense would be indeterminate. The denial of 'Excalibur has a sharp blade' would be essentially (and systematically) ambiguous. Hence 'The requirement that simple signs be possible is the requirement that sense be determinate' (*TLP* 3.23). And at this stage of the argument, 'simple signs' would be proper names whose occurrence in a sentence cannot be replaced by a definite description.[15]

Here we come to the crux of our examination of Wittgenstein's demand for determinacy of sense. Recall the wording of Wittgenstein's 'demand' at 3.23 of the *Tractatus*. There the demand for simple *signs* is the demand for *determinacy* of sense. This is not quite the way the argument is represented in the *Investigations*. First, the argument represented in the *Investigations* is not merely for the claim that certain *signs* must be simple. The conclusion is that a name ought to signify a *simple*. Second, the argument in the *Investigations* is premised not merely on the demand for *determinacy* of sense. Wittgenstein appeals to the demand for sense *simpliciter*: 'But then the sentence "Excalibur has a sharp blade" would contain a word that had no meaning, and hence the sentence would be *nonsense*' (*PI* §39, my emphasis).[16]

Within the parameters of the picture theory, this difference is only apparent, and for the following reason. *Wittgenstein assumes that the meaning of a name is its bearer.* Then the significance of that name is entirely a matter of it standing for something. *On this assumption*, the demand for determinacy of sense, apparently undermined by virtue of the indefinite possibility of analysis by means of definite description, *amounts to* the demand for sense.

This is indeed the way this matter is conceived in the *Tractatus*: 'If the world had no substance, then whether a proposition *had* sense would depend on whether another proposition was true' (*TLP* 2.0211, my emphasis). That 'simple signs' = 'signs that signify simples' is the obvious consequence to draw from the argument for determinacy of sense, but only on the assumption that the meaning of a simple sign is identical with its bearer. Without this assumption, the demand for determinacy of sense is merely: the demand for simple *signs* is the demand for *determinacy* of sense. This is different from: the demand for *simples* is the demand for *sense*.

This distinction is important for the purposes of this chapter: it is indeed true that, in the *Tractatus*, the demand for simple objects proceeded via an attempt to satisfy the demand for determinacy of sense. However, a tacit presupposition underlying Wittgenstein's argument was a commitment (at the level of simple signs) to the 'idea'. Only on this assumption does the demand for determinacy of sense require the postulation of simple objects.

In *Philosophical Investigations*, Wittgenstein is cognizant of where the 'idea' is positioned in the *Tractatus'* argument for the existence of simple 'objects'. Indeed, it is '*this* point of the argument' that Wittgenstein discusses in §§40–58 of *Philosophical Investigations*: 'that the [*das*] word [i.e. the *proper* name 'Excalibur'] has no meaning if nothing corresponds to it' (*PI* §40).[17] Furthermore, it is this point in the argument (i.e., the premise identifying meaning and bearer) that I propose Wittgenstein diagnoses as motivated by viewing our use of names explained by reference to samples under the influence of the model of proper names explained by reference to their bearers.[18]

To summarize: In the *Tractatus*, the demand for determinacy of sense is satisfied only by the postulation of simple *objects*. This is because simple *signs* require these objects as their bearers. The assumption here is that meaning is to be equated with bearer. It is this assumption, I will argue, which Wittgenstein was later to diagnose as motivated by distorted reflection on words explained by reference to samples. Consequently, I will argue that it is by virtue of this assumption that the *Tractarian* formulation of the demand for determinacy of sense and postuation of 'objects' is indeed rooted in a fuzzy awareness of features of our use of samples. (I have still to provide an account of the connection between the 'idea' and samples.)

Moreover, we shall see that, on my interpretation, it is misleading to call the 'idea' a thesis about, or theory of, meaning. Even my (provisional) use of the word 'assumption' is misleading. Rather, it is a superstition, or a false grammatical attitude, that one can be forced into, on pain of contradiction, in the face of a particular dogmatic application of Augustine's picture of the functioning of *words*.

4.3 Situating the Meaning Thesis

At the close of the first section in this chapter I promised to argue against the anti-thesis. I promised to argue that, according to Wittgenstein, it is not the 'idea' which underlies the tendency to project features of samples onto reality. This section eventually fulfils that obligation. But let me first detail how the 'idea' *might* motivate such a projection of these features of samples onto mythical objects. That is, let us work out the anti-thesis in more detail.

On the face of it, invoking a prior commitment to the 'idea' goes a long way toward explaining the relations between remarks made in §50, regarding certain uses of samples, and certain important characteristics attributed to *Tractarian* objects. On the face of it, that is to say, the anti-thesis does a good job of explaining *why* one might be inclined to project these features of (certain uses of) samples onto reality.

First, the 'idea' seems to explain how the needs in our language which are actually satisfied by samples seem to be satisfied by simple 'objects'. Samples are important for the business of explaining the meaning of some words in our language. This is also the need which 'simples' seem to satisfy: they give meaning to the words which stand for them. They satisfy this need, however, only together with the 'idea'. It is only together with the 'idea' that we can make sense of the notion that the existence of *Tractarian* objects is a requirement of *Tractarian* names having a meaning. For 'objects' give meaning to those names precisely because they *are* the meaning of those names.

Second, the 'idea' also seems to explain the projection of features of samples onto reality. For, as noted in the first section of the present chapter, a commitment to the 'idea' naturally inclines us to conceive of words like 'red' as though they were proper names of the colour *red*. Consequently, and in general, the anti-thesis seems at first to go a long way in making intelligible Wittgenstein's comparison between canonical samples and sempiternal simples.

Despite all this, it embodies a misinterpretation of Wittgenstein's intentions in comparing *Tractarian* objects and canonical samples. I will first scrutinize this interpretation internally, i.e., without reference to Wittgenstein's writings. My criticism turns on the question, Just how much explanatory value does this reading have? That is to say, just how far does the anti-thesis go in explaining this projection of samples onto mythical simples? I will argue that it goes *too* far, that it as it were explains too much, for it explains everything, and leaves nothing to misunderstandings about samples.

For an adherent to the anti-thesis, Wittgenstein invokes the 'idea' to explain the tendency to mistake features of our use of samples for features belonging to that which is represented. The *point* of invoking the 'idea' at this stage is to make sense of this relationship between samples and 'objects'. But are we not in danger of losing precisely that relationship? For the 'idea' *alone* entails just those characteristics of *Tractarian* objects that are analogous to (certain uses of) samples. The actual features of canonical samples detailed by Wittgenstein in §50 become entirely superfluous from an explanatory perspective, and for two reasons.

(1) Most obviously, if the meaning of a word is the object to which it refers, then similar to the sample used in connection with the language-game (*PI* §50), the existence of that object is (trivially) constitutive of that word having the meaning that it does. This is a consequence of the 'idea' altogether *independently* of (though perhaps consistently with) any characteristics of sample usage that might get projected onto reality. Furthermore, (2) if the meaning of a word (e.g. 'red') is the object (*red*) to which it corresponds it is, again analogous with a canonical sample of red,[19] obvious nonsense to deny that 'it (i.e., the object *red*) is red'; and dubious what it could mean to assert that 'it (i.e., the object *red*) is *red*'. These statements would be like saying "It is (or is not) what it is". This also is a consequence of the 'idea' entirely independently of any features of samples which might get projected onto reality. On the anti-thetical reading, the 'idea' alone does *all* the work Wittgenstein partially attributes to misunderstandings regarding our use of samples. Why then would Wittgenstein appeal to features of *samples* as a (perhaps partial) explanation of the tendency to postulate simples? Why would he suggest that 'What looks as if it *had* to exist [simples], is part of the language [samples]' (*PI* §50)?

This can be elucidated differently: according to Wittgenstein, the postulation of simple objects in the *Tractatus* was partly motivated by mistaking features of our means of representation as features of that which is represented. But what underlies the tendency to mistake explanations by reference to samples as though they operated analogously with proper names explained by reference to their bearers? To explain this, the antithesis invokes the 'idea': Wittgenstein is claiming that this mistake is due to adherence to the 'idea'. Without this supposition the relationship between 'objects' and samples is mysterious. Without this supposition, it is a mystery why Wittgenstein appeals to features of samples as playing a role in the motivation to postulate simples.

My objection is as follows. If we invoke the 'idea' to play this mediating role underlying the tendency to project features of samples onto mythical objects, then the job that these features of samples, projected into the form of extraordinary properties of strange objects, are intended to perform is *already* performed by the 'idea'. The 'idea' alone entails these features. The comparison between samples and *Tractarian* objects would throw no *more* light on *why* the author of the *Tractatus* conceived of 'objects' as he did than the 'idea' explains in isolation. This suggests the possibility that Wittgenstein saw this relationship between the 'idea' and samples differently.

I must acknowledge that my objection here teeters on one foundation block, however firmly placed that block may be. For suppose, in spite of my arguments in Section 4.1, that someone still insists that Wittgenstein is *not* making a diagnostic claim in §50. I argued in Section 4.1 that Wittgenstein appeals to features of *samples* (in §50) to partially explain the tendency to postulate simples. Suppose my reading of §50 is rejected. If rejected, the anti-thesis is still up for grabs, though it would need reformulation. How would the anti-thesis be reformulated so as not to be committed to a diagnostic reading of §50? The story might go as follows.

"Even when in league with the 'idea', misunderstanding explanations by means of samples does not motivate the postulation of 'objects'. For an adherent to this revised anti-thesis, it is *only* the (unexamined) commitment to the 'idea' that lies behind *Tractarian* objects. The 'idea' is the root of all evil, so to speak. The 'idea' does indeed do all the work. Samples are irrelevant from a diagnostic perspective."

Although inconsistent with my discussion of §50 in Section 4.1 above, this revised anti-thesis is consistent with my examination of 'determinacy of sense' in Section 4.2. For there I argued that the 'idea' is an essential element of Wittgenstein's demand for determinacy of sense, and Wittgenstein explicitly cites the demand for determinacy of sense as requiring the postulation of 'objects'. The revised anti-thesis also, of course, works with my argument in the present section that the 'idea' does *all* the work which I suggest Wittgenstein partially attributes to samples. For that is just what the revised anti-thesis contends. Moreover, the revised anti-thesis fits in nicely with the interpretation of §50 that I rejected in Section 4.1, viz., that there Wittgenstein is not engaged in a diagnosis. On the interpretation which I rejected in Section 4.1, Wittgenstein is giving us an alternative account of what (explanations of) meaning consists in for words ordinarily explained by reference to samples. That is, he is claiming that samples actually do the work which 'objects' were intended to do.

The revised anti-thesis also easily accommodates certain critical passages prior to §50. I refer the reader back to the beginning of Wittgenstein's discussion of simple 'objects'. Wittgenstein's claims that the temptation 'to make an objection against what is ordinarily called a name ... can be put like this: *a name ought really to signify a simple*' (*PI* §39). He notes the reasoning involved in this objection:

> The word "Excalibur", say, is a proper name in the ordinary sense. The sword Excalibur consists of parts combined in a particular way. If they are combined differently Excalibur does not exist. But it is clear that the sentence "Excalibur has a sharp blade" makes *sense* whether Excalibur is whole or broken up. But if "Excalibur" is the name of an object, this object no longer exists when Excalibur is broken in pieces; and as no object would then correspond to the name it would have no meaning. But it does make sense; so there must always be something corresponding to the words of which it consists. So the word "Excalibur" must disappear when the sense is analyzed and its place be taken by words which name simples. It will be reasonable to call these words the real names. (Ibid.)

As should be obvious, and as Wittgenstein explicitly notes in the following section, this reasoning invokes the 'idea'. According to the revised anti-thesis, the 'idea' lies behind the claim that 'a name ought really to signify a simple', i.e., an 'object'. And according to Wittgenstein in the above passage, the demand for simples ('objects') is argued by appeal to the 'idea'. Wittgenstein then appears to *criticize* the 'idea': 'It is important to note that the word "meaning" is being used illicitly if it is used to signify the thing that 'corresponds' to the word. That is to confound the meaning of a name with the *bearer* of the name' (*PI* §40).

This (anti-thetical: *infra.*) reading of §40 harmonizes with the revised anti-thetical reading of §50. For, one might contend, Wittgenstein first (1) criticizes the 'idea' as an account of meaning for proper names (*PI* §40). And he then (2) proffers an alternate account of common nouns explained by reference to samples (*PI* §50). For short, let's just call (1) and (2) the (capital 'A') Anti-thesis.

For an adherent to the Anti-thesis, Wittgenstein's war on the 'idea' is two-fold. One strategic manoeuvre is the claim that samples belong to the means of representation; another is the claim 'that the word "meaning" is being used illicitly if it is used to signify the thing that 'corresponds' to the word' (*PI* §40). To accept these claims is to reject two crucial fronts defending the claim that the meaning of a name is the object to which it corresponds.[20] For these two sorts of words (proper names and many common nouns) are the most obvious cases *prima facie* subsumable under the 'idea'. Yet Wittgenstein has shown that they do not actually fit this conception of meaning. The allied forces seem strong indeed.

But *are* they? For the moment, let's never mind about whether the Anti-thesis correctly captures Wittgenstein's intentions. Rather, let us ask whether the Anti-thesis is a persuasive criticism of the 'idea'. I suggest that, on the contrary, it begs the question against the 'idea'.

On the Anti-thetical reading, the 'idea' projects features of certain uses of samples onto imaginary bearers—the imaginary bearers of the names explained by reference to those samples. Obviously, then, it is the 'idea' which interferes with a clear understanding of the status of samples and the words explained by means of them. Does Wittgenstein's relegation of samples to 'the means of representation' carry any weight against someone committed to the 'idea'?

Without supplementation, certainly it does not. First, even if it were accepted that a sample belongs to the means of representation, what does this prove if the meaning of 'red' is *red*? *Red* is not a sample, at any rate not as we ordinarily understand the word 'sample', and certainly not a sample in any sense like that which Wittgenstein relegates to the means of representation in §50. Of course, *red* is a colour.

Second, and more generally, if §50 is taken in isolation, Wittgenstein begs the question against a proponent of the 'idea'. On the Anti-thetical reading, Wittgenstein's claim that samples belong to the means of representation is interpreted as a criticism of the 'idea', a criticism because, in this case, the meaning of the word is not the object or bearer to which it corresponds. The Anti-thesis begs the question against the 'idea' because it is *precisely* those features of samples, which Wittgenstein relegates to the means of representation, that one committed to the 'idea' promotes to the realm of that which is represented. Obviously, then, no appeal to these features themselves can carry any argumentative weight—the interpretation of these facts of our language is itself what is in question. Hence (and this is important), *the 'idea' must be repudiated first.*

Accordingly, an adherent to the Anti-thesis might revert to Wittgenstein's criticism of the argument for simples ('objects'). 'It is important to note that the word "meaning" is being used illicitly if it is used to signify the thing that 'corresponds' to the word. That is to confound the meaning of a name with the *bearer* of the name' (*PI* §40). One might argue that Wittgenstein has already persuasively criticized the 'idea'. This is the way that Baker and Hacker seem to understand the argument of §40. They suggest that,

> One point of §40 is to undermine the doctrine . . . by showing that the worry which led to the erection of this metaphysical edifice [i.e., the postulation of 'objects'] is groundless. The argument was that a proper name has a meaning only if there exists an object for which it stands. But this is absurd. The meaning of a name is not its bearer, and a name may have a meaning even though its bearer no longer exists.

> So the supposition that 'Excalibur' cannot be a real name was groundless and the postulation of sempiternal simples [i.e., 'objects'] needless.[21]

For paradigmatic examples of proper names, it is nonsense to claim that the meaning of the word is identical with its bearer. So, one might argue that Wittgenstein's criticism of the 'idea' by appeal to samples in §50 is not *so* question begging. The criticism of the 'idea' in §40 paves the way for a less dogmatic investigation of those sorts of words characteristically explained by reference to samples. The meaning of a word is clearly not *always* to be identified with what the word stands for. Wittgenstein has, at any rate, already undermined the universal applicability of the 'idea'.[22]

Or has he? Does Wittgenstein's argument in §40 come anywhere close to undermining the 'idea'? On the contrary, it as a question-begging argument against the 'idea'. Wittgenstein's 'criticism' in §40 is effective in undermining only a very weak (perhaps even silly) formulation of the 'idea'. On Baker's and Hacker's reading, the need to postulate 'objects' is a symptom of a commitment to the 'idea'. If an appeal to our ordinary usage of 'meaning', *as it applies to (ordinary) proper names*,[23] was sufficient to undermine the 'idea' (i.e., by way of counterexample), then the *Tractatus* would never have been written. The appeal to ordinary usage is no counter-example. For, as formulated in the picture theory, the 'idea' *itself* embodies an '*objection* against what is ordinarily called a name' (*PI* §39, my emphasis). Conceived as a *criticism* of the *Tractarian* formulation of the 'idea', the appeal at this stage to (an example of) what is ordinarily called a proper name is palpably question-begging. It begs the question against the *Tractatus* because no ordinary proper name was a real *Tractarian* name.

But this is not the worst of it. This interpretation of §40 is inconsistent with the text, for it is question-begging by Wittgenstein's own lights in the *Investigations* (let alone the *Tractatus*). In the *Investigations*, the 'idea' under examination is characterized as *constituting* an objection to what is ordinarily called a name (*PI* §39). (No wonder, too, since it is the picture theory that Wittgenstein is investigating.)

On Baker's and Hacker's reading, the only "idea" that Wittgenstein's argument in §40 would refute, or even contradict, is the notion that *ordinary* proper names like 'Excalibur' have no meaning if their (ordinary) bearer is destroyed. Who says this?

I suggest a different reading of §40. Wittgenstein's appeal to ordinary usage is a step in his *diagnosis* of motivations underlying this tendency to object to ordinary usage. In §40 Wittgenstein is doing no more than reminding us that the concept of 'name' in the *Tractatus* constitutes an objection to its ordinary use.[24] As the later Wittgenstein understood it, the relationship between *Tractarian* objects and samples is altogether different from the Anti-thetical interpretation I have criticized so far. I will argue that 'objects' are what one can get when the use of those names, ostensively explained by reference to samples, is approached on the model of proper names ostensively explained by pointing to their bearers. The 'idea' is the confusion that can *result* from a dogmatic assimilation of (1) word explanations by reference to samples to (2) the model of proper names explained by reference to their bearers. Moreover, I will argue that Wittgenstein traces *this* dogmatic assimilation to its root in the attempt to bring out *the* relation between name and thing named, to discover *the* essence of a 'name' (cf. *PI* §38).

I will summarize my whole argument in this chapter. I have argued that, in §50 of *Philosophical Investigations*, Wittgenstein is claiming that a fuzzy awareness of the role of samples in language partly underlies the tendency to postulate 'objects' as the meanings of logically proper names. However, this interpretation is *prima facie* inconsistent with the claim, in the *Tractatus*, that the demand for simple objects is the demand for determinacy of sense. For a demand for determinacy of sense seems unconnected with samples. My first step in drawing a connection was an examination of the *Tractarian* demand for determinacy of sense. I argued that, as formulated in the *Tractatus*, underlying the demand for 'objects' is a commitment to the 'idea'.

The 'idea' does motivate the *Tractarian* formulation of the demand for determinacy of sense (and hence for simple objects). Nonetheless, I have argued that Wittgenstein does not contend that a prior commitment to the 'idea' underpins the tendency to misconstrue the role of words explained by reference to samples. Rather, as I *will* argue, Wittgenstein characterizes the 'idea' itself as being the result of a tendency to impose order upon the concept of a name.

This summary can itself be encapsulated metaphorically. The 'idea' is not the *route* to a misconception of the nature of words like 'red' and 'sweet'. In a certain sense, the route is the demand for determinacy of sense. For one might think that these are the sorts of names that will result from analysis, as opposed to the objectionable names like 'Excalibur'. Nor is the 'idea' the *origin*. The origin I will argue is an assimilation of these sorts of names to the concept of a proper name. On the contrary, I will argue that the 'idea' is best conceived as the *destination* of this diagnostic journey. (And the diagnosis *is* the cure.)

It should be asked in what sense my interpretation of these sections relates to my general thesis spanning both the present and the previous chapter. My general thesis is that Wittgenstein is engaged in a diagnosis of philosophical problems arising from the dogmatic application of Augustine's *picture* of language. In the sections of the *Investigations* under consideration in this chapter, Wittgenstein is diagnosing the tendency to project features of samples onto reality. That tendency can be motivated by a dogmatic application of the model of proper names of objects—often explained by reference to their bearers—to words actually explained by reference to samples. How does my thesis in this chapter relate to Augustine's picture of the incomparable essence of a name? At this stage of my discussion it is not altogether clear. For what is it which underlies the tendency to apply the model of paradigmatic proper names (e.g., 'Excalibur') to names explained by reference to samples in the *first* place? Although Augustine's picture does state that the words of language are names of objects, this does not—one would think—necessarily mean that these names are *proper* names of objects. Indeed, when Wittgenstein applies Augustine's description to the simple language-game in §2, the names are *not* proper names of objects. Rather, they are names of *sorts* of objects (viz., sorts of building-stones).

In the next section I tie all this together. I explain the relationship between (1) Augustine's picture, and (2) the tendency to apply the model of explanations of proper names (of objects) to explanations of names by reference to samples. In the last section (4.5), I explain how (2) can force the 'idea' on us.

4.4 Where our language suggests a body

Whence the temptation to conceive of colour names as proper names of the colours? Wittgenstein's answer to this question is discernable by reverting back to the end of the last chapter. Recall from Chapter Three how Wittgenstein suggests one might react to the idea that ostensive definitions are essentially ambiguous. Wittgenstein suggests that 'because we cannot specify any *one* bodily action which we call pointing to the shape (as opposed, for example, to the colour), we say that a *spiritual* ... activity corresponds to these words' (*PI* §36). Clearly Wittgenstein is remarking here on the 'purification' of our concept of 'pointing' (see Chapter Three *supra*). He then appears to *expand* on this remark: 'Where our language suggests a body and there is none: there, we should like to say, is a *spirit*' (ibid.). The first remark appears to be about bodily and spiritual actions; the second remark about bodies and spirits *simpliciter*. Is this apparent expansion really an expansion, or is Wittgenstein merely reiterating? If it is intended as an expansion, §36 provides us with an important link between Augustine's picture and the 'idea'. That is to say, it throws considerable light on how the picture can be the root of the 'idea' (*PI* §1).

I will argue that the second remark is not just a reformulation of the first. The second remark expands on the first, and develops the diagnosis from Augustine's picture to the 'idea'. In the first quoted remark, Wittgenstein is suggesting that we may be tempted to purify our concept of 'pointing'. In the second quoted remark, Wittgenstein is discussing the purification of our concept of 'object', viz., that which the purified 'pointing' points to.

It must be granted that Wittgenstein does not explicitly distinguish the two remarks, saying e.g. something like "*And furthermore* 'Where our language suggests a body and there is none ...'". On the other hand, there is obviously a difference between a body and a bodily action. From the passage itself it is perhaps difficult to argue cogently one way or the other. It is not impossible that Wittgenstein was summarizing somewhat aphoristically.

Yet textual evidence from other primary sources does not favour reading Wittgenstein as merely reformulating (1) the claim about bodily and spiritual *actions*. Evidence suggests that he is (2) expanding on (1) and referring to bodies and spirits *simpliciter*. A persuasive case can be made for (2) by consulting a couple of Wittgenstein's other writings:

Some fairly direct support for (2) comes from Wittgenstein's own English translation of this section in an earlier version of *Philosophical Investigations* (TS 226, §42). Where Anscombe renders *Körper* as 'body', Wittgenstein renders it as 'physical thing'. It is unlikely that Wittgenstein would use this translation if he was just reformulating the first remark (quoted above). Surely it is even more of a stretch to equate a 'bodily *process*' with a 'physical *thing*', than it is to equate a bodily process with a body. Moreover, the word 'body' is gone, and thus so is any good reason for thinking that Wittgenstein was reformulating aphoristically.

Stronger, though oblique evidence is available by comparing §36 with a closely related discussion in the early parts of the *Blue Book*. The *Blue Book* begins with a discussion of the question, 'What is the meaning of a word' (*BB*, p. 1). The treatment of this question in the *Blue Book*, just like its treatment in the *Investigations*, quickly moves into a discussion of the appearance of essential ambiguity in ostensive definitions. This ambiguity, he suggests, might lead to the idea that we must always '*interpret*' (cf. 'guess' in *PI* §32) ostensive explanations before we can understand them. Wittgenstein then begins a discussion of the notion that meaning is a mental process. 'It seems', he says, 'that there are *certain definite* mental processes bound up with the working of language'.

> I mean the processes of meaning and understanding .... [I]f you are asked what is the relation between name and the *thing it names*, you will be inclined to answer that the relation is a psychological one .... (ibid., p. 4, my emphasis)

This sounds a lot like the purified 'pointing' discussed above. Wittgenstein then suggests, as a way of partly avoiding the occult appearance of such mental processes, that we should 'replace in these processes any working of the imagination by acts of looking at *real objects*' (ibid., my emphasis). For,

> The mistake we are liable to make could be expressed thus: We are looking for the use of a sign, but we look for it as though it were an *object co-existing* with the sign. (One of the reasons for this mistake is again that we are looking for a "*thing* corresponding to a substantive.") (ibid., p. 5, my emphasis, except on 'co-existing')

Clearly Wittgenstein is here suggesting that these occult processes of meaning and understanding are precisely the occult processes of directing ones attention toward occult objects. It is highly plausible that Wittgenstein is saying exactly this in §36 of the *Investigations*. For, like the *Investigations*, the *Blue Book* begins its examination of the 'idea' by investigating the concept of ostensive definition. Again like the *Investigations*, it is suggested in the *Blue Book* that confusion about the concept of ostensive definition may lead one to think that there is a definite mental process of meaning. The parallel is striking so far. The notion of a mental process of meaning is then, in the *Blue Book*, connected with the idea that the thing pointed to is an 'object' co-existing with the sign, and that this 'object' is the meaning. There is every reason to believe that Wittgenstein, with the last sentence of *Philosophical Investigations* §36, also makes this last move.

In §36 Wittgenstein is surely drawing attention to an intimate relation between a conception of meaning qua occult process and, in a different sense of 'meaning', a conception of meaning qua occult object. In the case of an explanation of a colour word, e.g. 'red', the suggestion is that there is a tendency to distinguish an explanation of the colour (as opposed, e.g., to the shape) in virtue of some kind of mental pointing. Now what, on this account, would this mental pointing mechanism be pointing at? What are you directing your attention to when explaining a colour word by reference to a sample? Is it not the colour red? If you point to one sample of red, and I point to another sample of red, we are, if it is the colour we are pointing out, pointing out the *same* colour. (I am ignoring here that there are shades of red.) The 'body' who's existence our language suggests is *this colour.*

But of course there is no *physical* body, yet one might feel forced to say there is a *kind* of body, a (mental? abstract?) *spirit.* So if *this colour* is a (kind of) body, and we both point to *this colour*, then we both point to the *same* body, viz., the *bearer* of the (proper) name 'red'. Construing the colour as a kind of 'body', we cannot say that we are each pointing to a different *example* of red. Undoubtedly one can (on this model) say the two *samples* are different examples of something that is red. But this is the 'is' of predication, not the 'is' of identity. The *red* that each of us points to is the *same* red. The *body-red* is as it were a (weird) 'particular'. Hence, if 'red' is explained by (mentally) pointing to this (weird) particular, 'red' must be a proper name of the colour.

To summarize, the appearance of essential ambiguity in an ostensive definition may result from dogmatism regarding the applicability of the ostensive teaching appropriate to Augustine's picture. That is, the ostensive teaching typified in §2 is dogmatically applied to the more complicated language-game at §8. This dogmatic application seems to undermine the distinction between ostensively explaining, e.g., (1) 'round' by pointing to an orange ball and (2) 'orange' by pointing to that same ball. Wittgenstein suggests that one might react to this problem by postulating some sort of '*spiritual* activity', a kind of mental pointing mechanism. In §36 Wittgenstein makes one further move. He suggests that it is this notion of a 'mental pointing mechanism' that can incline one to mistake explanations by reference to samples on the model of explanations for proper names by reference to their bearers, and as a result, postulate a kind of *spirit*.

Furthermore, as I will show, Wittgenstein traces the 'idea' to this confusion about explanations by appeal to samples. The 'idea' is the result of mistaking explanations by means of samples for explanations of proper names by references to their bearers. Wittgenstein is already quite clear about this relationship in the *Blue Book*:

> There is a tendency rooted in our usual forms of expression, to think that the man who has learnt to understand a *general* term, say, the term "leaf", has thereby come to possess a kind of general picture of a leaf .... We say that he sees what is in common to all these leaves; and this is true if we mean that he can on being asked tell us certain features or properties which they have in common. But we are inclined to think that the general idea of a leaf is something like a visual image, but one which only contains what is common to all leaves .... This again is connected with the idea that the meaning of a word is an image, *or a thing correlated to the word*. (This roughly means, *we are looking at words as though they are all proper names, and we then confuse the bearer of a name with the meaning of the name.*) (*BB* p. 17f., my emphasis)

Ultimately, then, it is in Augustine's 'picture of language [which] we find the roots of the following idea: Every word has a meaning. This meaning is correlated with the word. It is the object for which the word stands' (*PI* §1). In the following and final section of this chapter, I explain how the connection indicated in the above passage from the *Blue Book* is explained in the *Investigations*. This will complete my retracing of Wittgenstein's journey from Augustine's picture to the 'idea'.

4.5 Bearers and Samples: the diagnosis

In §38 of the *Investigations*, Wittgenstein begins to explicitly discuss the 'idea'. The identification of meaning and bearer is very closely connected with the notion that 'this' is the only genuine name (*PI* §38). And this 'conception springs from a tendency to sublime the logic of our language' (ibid.). We get a hint as to what Wittgenstein might mean by 'subliming' when he remarks that a proper response to this tendency is to say that 'we call very different things "names"' (ibid.); and also when he continues that 'you really get such a queer connexion when the philosopher tries to bring out *the* relation between name and thing named . . . ' (ibid). These two remarks suggest that this 'subliming', manifested in the tendency to call 'this' the only genuine name, is the result of an attempt to distil *the* essence of a name: a kind of purification of our concept of a name. Yet (1) why, when trying to give the essence of 'name', do we have the tendency to say that 'this' typifies that essence? And (2) how does this tendency relate to the 'idea'?

Wittgenstein takes up the first question in a passage I have already quoted, and will re-quote. The inclination to say 'this' is the only genuine name—itself an inclination to *object* to what is ordinarily called a name—

> can be put like this: *a name ought really to signify a simple*. And for this one might perhaps give the following reasons: The word "Excalibur", say, is a proper name in the ordinary sense. The sword Excalibur consists of parts combined in a particular way. If they are combined differently Excalibur does not exist. But it is clear that the sentence "Excalibur has a sharp blade" makes *sense* whether Excalibur is still whole or is broken up. But *if* "Excalibur" is the name of an object, this object no longer exists when Excalibur is broken in pieces; and as no object would then correspond to the name it would have no meaning. (*PI* §39, my emphasis on 'if')

This chain of argument implies that Excalibur is not *really* a name (of an object). For of course the sentence does make sense whether Excalibur is whole or broken up (ibid.). Yet as Wittgenstein points out in the following section, a premise in this argument is that the word 'Excalibur', if it is a name, has no meaning if there exists no object to which it corresponds (i.e., if its bearer does not exist). Wittgenstein notes that this conflicts with our ordinary use of 'meaning' with respect to proper names of objects (and people too). 'It is important to note that the word "meaning" is being used ungrammatically [*sprachwidrig*] if it is used to signify the thing that 'corresponds' to the word' (*PI* §40). This is evident from the fact that, when the bearer of a proper name dies (e.g., the infamous N.N.), we do not say the meaning dies (*PI* §40). This is just not the way we employ ordinary proper names. Although it is imaginable that we should use words otherwise akin to proper names only in the presence of their bearers (*PI* §41, cf. TS 220 §42), to imagine such a use is to imagine a use different from our own.

Wittgenstein's initial reaction here is, therefore, comparable to his initial reaction to Augustine's description of language learning. We seem to have, at this point of the investigation (into the idea that 'this' is the only genuine proper name in *our* language), the uncovering of an *erroneous* account of 'proper name'. It is just plain false—and *obviously* so—that a proper name is used (or has meaning) only in the presence of its bearer.

Thus the question still remains, Why might we be inclined to say that "a name ought really to signify a simple"? For certainly it is not the result of a failure to realize that an ordinary proper name does not lose its meaning when its bearer ceases to exist. So where is the *philosophical* problem? Why do we *object* to what is obviously our employment of 'proper name'? 'What *lies behind* the idea that names really signify simples?' (*PI* §46, my emphasis)

Wittgenstein digs deeper with a quote from Plato's *Theaetetus*:

> [T]here is no definition of the primary elements . . . out of which we and everything else are composed; for everything

> that exists in its own right can only be *named*, no other determination is possible, neither that it *is* or that it *is not* .... (ibid.)

Wittgenstein immediately takes Plato to task: is it legitimate to *completely* de-contextualize the concepts of simplicity and complexity? That is, is it legitimate to talk of simple, i.e., 'primary' elements outside a context where the criteria for something being simple (or not) have been fixed (*PI* §47)? Wittgenstein thinks this is confused. The *language-game* plays an important role in judgments concerning whether something is simple or not. Suppose it has been laid down that a tree is what is called 'composite', and its simple parts are branches. The question as to whether a particular component of the tree is simple is a matter of determining whether that component is a branch (ibid.). At this level the empirical question is whether or not the component of the tree under consideration is in fact a branch. Once it is settled whether such-and-such a component is a branch, it *follows* (in this language-game) that it is what we call 'a simple component part'. Hence whether branches are simple component parts is not, in this language-game, an empirical question, but a grammatical one (ibid.). And hence the question "What is a simple component part?" is potentially ambiguous; for it may be a grammatical question, or an empirical one.

It is a truism that whether something in particular is simple depends in part on what we *call* 'simple' (and in part on whether that something is in fact an example of what we call 'simple'). Wittgenstein is really arguing against the idea that there are absolute criteria for simplicity. Only by softening his interlocutor to the idea that there are *various* criteria for something being 'simple' or not, can Wittgenstein legitimately introduce a language-game to which Plato's remarks actually apply. For he wishes to use the elements of the coloured square language-game, described in §48, as a *model* for Plato's 'primary elements' (*infra.*).

Wittgenstein seems to be satisfied with his argument against absolute criteria for simplicity. For in §48, Plato's 'primary elements' are indeed compared with a language-game for describing coloured squares.

The coloured square language-game is a context in which Plato's claims about primary elements have *some* sort of conceivable application. This imagined language consists of the words 'R', 'G', 'W' and 'B'. Combinations of these words into sentences describe arrangements of squares, each of which is coloured either red, green, white, or black. These squares are arranged in an indefinite number of rows each consisting of three squares. The words are the names of the coloured squares, and naturally Wittgenstein considers them to be the elements, the 'simples' (although he is certainly not dogmatic about it).

How might Plato's claims about primary elements find expression in the coloured square language-game? Plato claims that the primary elements can only be named, not described. Moreover, he conceives of these 'names' as *proper* names of the primary elements. (Or at any rate, *Tractarian* names were (logically) proper names. In §46, Wittgenstein likens Plato's primary elements to his 'objects'.)

Wittgenstein searches for an application of Plato's claims to the coloured square language-game. Of course, how we apply those claims is going to depend on what we are going to call the 'elements' in this language-game, and what should be so-called is not altogether clear. For there are two senses that we might naturally give to 'element'. Both 'name' and 'element' are potentially ambiguous in the coloured square language-game. Wittgenstein has us consider the sentence 'RRBGGGRWW':

> But I do not know whether to say that the figure described by our sentence consists of four or of nine elements! Well, does the sentence consist of four letters or of nine? [note that in this language-game the letters are the names]—And which are *its* elements, the types of letter, or the letters? Does it matter which we say, so long as we avoid misunderstandings in any particular case? (*PI* §48)

If 'the elements of the sentence' are supposed to be the names of *kinds* of coloured squares, we will say there are four elements, viz., the types of letters. If we understand 'the elements of the sentence' to be the names of the individual, particular coloured squares we will say there are nine elements.

Suppose that, by 'name', we mean a name of a *particular* coloured square. If Plato's names are *proper* names of the primary elements, they correspond in this respect to *particular* letters. In the coloured square language-game, the identification of such a name requires answers to two questions: (1) what type of word is it? (2) what position has that word relative to the other words in the sentence? Moreover, this proper name functions as part of the description. That is, this name asserts that a certain position, in the combination of squares being described, is such-and-such a colour. For example, in the sentence 'RGR', the function of the first 'R' is to assert that the first square in the combination is red.

In this sense, 'R' is the name of a particular element of that which is being described. This is so not only by virtue of the shape of the letter, but also by virtue of the position of that letter in the sentence. Otherwise there would be no distinction between the first and the second occurrence of 'R'. Yet obviously, qua names of the individual coloured squares, they stand for different 'elements'.[25] In this language-game, therefore, the type/token distinction can be mapped onto the distinction between a name of a *kind* of thing (e.g., red squares) and the name of a *particular* thing (e.g., a certain red square). This is certainly comparable to, yet a massive simplification of,[26] the distinction in our language between a common noun and a proper name. (Perhaps it is even an example of what Wittgenstein calls a 'perspicuous representation' (*PI* §121)—viz., a perspicuous representation of our use of the word 'name'. See Chapter Six.)

I noted at the beginning of this section that §38 inaugurates Wittgenstein's explicit treatment of the 'idea'. Prior to the introduction of Plato's 'primary elements', and Wittgenstein's representation of these elements in the coloured square language-game, the discussion starting at §38 revolves around *proper* names. Proper names are names which are sometimes explained by pointing to their bearer, but nevertheless are not essentially used only in the presence of their bearer (*PI* §§43f.). In the coloured square language-game, it is possible to view the token words, together with their position in the description, as proper names of 'elements' (an importantly ambiguous word).

Is *this* the kind of element Plato has in mind when he says that 'we cannot define (that is, describe) these elements, but only name them' (*PI* §49)? If so, 'This might mean, for instance, that when in a limiting case a complex consists of only *one* square, its description is simply the name of the coloured square.' (ibid.).

Or is he referring to something more closely resembling the 'elements' named by the *types* of word? If so, then is this not comparable to the case where one 'is teaching someone else the use of the words and uttering them in the course of ostensive teaching' (ibid.)? If the point of *this* exercise is to name an element, i.e., if we are going to call this exercise 'naming an element', this is not the same as explaining the meaning of a proper name by pointing to its bearer. For here 'the use of the signs in the language-game would be taught in a *different* way, in particular by pointing to *paradigms*', as opposed to pointing to *bearers* (*PI* §51, my emphasis).

But suppose, as Wittgenstein suggested in the *Blue Book* (pp. 17f., quoted above), that this explanation of the colour words is viewed on the model of the explanation of a proper name. (In the previous section I explained why, according to Wittgenstein, one might do this.) If the explanations of the colour words in §48 are conceived on the model of explanations of the meaning of a name by pointing to its bearer, the strange features originally attributed to Plato's primary elements (and *Tractarian* objects) seem to immediately apply to the colours. The names are names of the *colours*, and not the samples. Though it is true that, if samples of red did not exist, we could not use them in the language-game for describing coloured squares (*PI* §50), this is re-interpreted as the claim that the proper name 'R' has meaning if, and only if, its bearer exists. *Red* is the meaning of 'red'. (This is the 'idea'.) Consequently, to attribute non-existence to the colour would be nonsense, and to attribute existence to it very odd indeed; for 'if there were no red it could not be spoken of at all' (*PI* §58). This is a reflection of the claim that the sample cannot be described as having the property for which it serves as the paradigm. (Of course, we can describe it in other terms.) But this is not a necessary truth. Rather, this is merely a remark contingent on the role these samples play in this language-game. That *red* can only be named is the conclusion one is inexorably led to when the practice, described in §49, of explaining the meaning of simple signs, is conceived on the model of explanations of proper names by means of pointing to their bearers (cf. *PI* §46).

On the other hand, if 'R' is a *description*, viz., the assertion of the existence of one coloured square, there is nothing paradoxical about the idea that R does or does not exist. This is precisely the function of 'R' qua description. 'R' qua description asserts (truely or falsely) that there exists a particular square of a certain colour. Wittgenstein's diagnosis of this philosophical problem about 'elements' is that it is the result of a failure to notice *different* uses of 'name'. He contributes to the dissolution of this problem by representing Plato's claims in the coloured square language game, where he represents the use of 'name' so as to decompose it into two parts. And for neither of these 'parts' do Plato's *puzzling* claims apply, although certain non-puzzling, analogous claims apply to each 'part'. Each 'part' captures aspects of Plato's claims about elements which, when considered by themselves, are not puzzling.

According to Wittgenstein, the tendency to call 'this' the only genuine name is a typical manifestation of the subliming of 'name'. And this tendency is itself a manifestation of the objection to what is ordinarily called a name, on the grounds that 'a name ought really to signify a simple'. Recall that between the discussion concerning (1) proper names and (2) common names, Wittgenstein interpolates a discussion of the concepts of simplicity and complexity, tying these notions to criteria, and arguing that there are various criteria for complexity (and hence simplicity) (*PI* §47). In the language-game for describing coloured squares, the 'words "R", "B", etc. corresponded to the colours of the squares' (*PI* §51). And the coloured squares are the elements of the language-game: they are simple.

Following Wittgenstein, I will generalize these observations about the coloured square language-game. When explanations of meaning of these kinds of common names are misconceived as explanations of proper names (by reference to their bearers), it looks as though they are the proper names of 'simples'. What plays the role of a simple *sign* in the language-game gets interpreted as a proper name of a simple. (Recall in this connection the way in which the 'idea' transformed the early Wittgenstein's demand for simple *signs* into a demand for *simples*. See section 4.2 above.) Moreover, it is a simple whose existence is essential if that proper name is to have a meaning. It is this which 'lies behind the idea that names really signify simples' (*PI* §46), and hence lies behind the objection to what is ordinarily called a proper name (*PI* §39). Wittgenstein illuminates the confusion by juxtaposing these two uses of 'name':

> "What the names in language signify must be indestructible; for it must be possible to describe the state of affairs in which everything destructible is destroyed. And this description will contain words; and what corresponds to these cannot then be destroyed, for otherwise the words would have no meaning." .... In a sense, however, this man is surely what corresponds to his name. But he is destructible, and his name does not lose its meaning when the bearer is destroyed.—An example of something corresponding to the name, and without which it would have no meaning, is a paradigm that is used in connexion with the name in the language-game. (*PI* §55)

If we take the name of a colour for a (kind of) proper name of a (kind of) object, the proposition 'Red exists' looks as though it were saying something about the colour qua 'meaning-body'. For the claim that 'Excalibur exists' *does* say something about Excalibur. The puzzling difference, however, is that 'Red exists' seems to be essentially true; for 'Red does not exist' seems to be a kind of contradiction. 'Whereas the only contradiction lies in something like this: the proposition looks as if it were about the colour, while it is supposed to be saying something about the use of the word "red"' (*PI* §58).

Thus it is Plato's primary elements which, in §50, Wittgenstein claims look as though they have to exist. When Plato's remarks are represented in the coloured-square language-game, 'primary elements' no longer look as though they have to exist. For the primary elements are the samples. 'What looks as if it *had* to exist, is part of the language. It is a paradigm in our language-game; something with which comparison is made' (*PI* §50).

The reader might, at this point, object to Wittgenstein's conclusion at the end of §50. For it sounds as though he is drawing conclusions about our actual use of language by reflecting on *imaginary* uses of language. Is this not as if one imagined an experiment and then took the result of this imagined experiment as empirically verified? Why would one proceed in this way?

These questions deserve a fair amount of consideration, but for now let us take note: Wittgenstein is perfectly aware of this. Indeed, he makes the appropriate qualification to his conclusion in §50, viz. that 'this may be an important observation; but it is none the less an observation concerning our language-game' (*PI* §50). That is, this observation concerns the coloured square language-game introduced in §48. This is not a dissolution of the problem of simples unless it provides a correct, if simplified, picture of the reasoning which led to the problem. This is not a dissolution of the problem unless Wittgenstein's method of representing Plato's claims is accepted as an appropriate model of the reasoning that led to those philosophical problems.

The question still remains, however, why Wittgenstein would employ such an indirect route to dissolving philosophical problems. Why not investigate *actual* language? These questions will occupy us in Chapter 6 below.

I have made little mention of Wittgenstein's dictum that the meaning of a word is its use in the language (*PI* §43). Wittgenstein is perhaps most famous for this alternative account of 'meaning'. Yet in what relationship does this dictum stand to the 'idea'? Surely Wittgenstein's alternative is not in *competition* with the 'idea'. For, as we have seen, a commitment to the 'idea' is a commitment one can be *inexorably* led to in an attempt to assimilate the facts of our language to Augustine's picture. If it is in competition with anything, one would have to say that this dictum is in competition with Augustine's picture. But, for a philosophical context, the competition is a bit peculiar. For the two are not *essentially* incompatible. One can imagine a language in which the meaning—the use—of *every* word is to *designate an object* (*PI* §3). In this case they would not contradict.

The point of Wittgenstein's claim that the meaning of a word is its use should, really, be seen as an attempt to widen our possible forms of description. Wittgenstein is recommending the adoption of a different form of representation. The adoption of this form of representation is part of Wittgenstein's attempt to dislodge the prejudice that every word *must* designate an object *in some sense*. It is not a different theory: it is a different picture.

Notes

1. These two features are interdependent because the 'claim' that the necessary existence of *Tractarian* objects is ineffable (i.e., that one cannot consistently *say* they exist) is partly constitutive of the saying/showing doctrine (see Chapter Two). Neither is this an isolated incident. To a considerable degree, necessity and inexpressibility go hand in hand in the *Tractatus*. Nor, from the point of view of the later Wittgenstein, is the connection completely lacking reasonable motivation. The intimate connection between the saying/showing distinction and the essential bipolarity of meaningful propositions is a distorted reflection of a distinction which Wittgenstein later came to see, in a large number of cases, as usefully decomposed into 'rules' and 'empirical propositions'. (Though Wittgenstein's reflections in *On Certainty* suggest that one should not be dogmatic about this decomposition.) Wittgenstein's discussion of samples is intended to throw light on one formulation of this marriage of necessity and inexpressibility.
2. Baker and Hacker, *Wittgenstein: Understanding and Meaning* (Blackwell, 1980) 2.1ff.
3. Hacker, *Insight and Illusion*, p. 113.
4. Incidentally, we need not take Wittgenstein to be contending that it is impossible for someone, under certain circumstances, to claim that 'samples' (in some sense of 'sample') 'have to exist'.

Wittgenstein, however, is referring to ordinary samples, and are there any circumstances in which one could reasonably maintain that the standard metre, the one actually kept hermetically sealed at the Louvre, *necessarily* exists—*cannot* be destroyed? This claim could be refuted by experience. Suppose I sneak into the Louvre, bust the standard metre in two, and present the pieces.

5. Cf. Baker and Hacker, *Understanding and Meaning* (op. cit.) p. 204, §viii.
6. Frege, *Translations from the Philosophical Writings of Gottlob Frege*, Peter Geach and Max Black (eds.) (Blackwell, 1952), p. 159.
7. This is in any event his conception in 'Function and Concept', in ibid., p. 31.
8. The use of a function expression is not, in the *Tractatus*, confined to the mapping of simple names onto elementary propositions. Generally speaking, the usage of an (elementary or non-elementary) propositional function would be to map 'expressions', in the technical sense of this term (*TLP* 3.31-3.314), onto propositions. The immediately following discussion will, for simplicity's sake, stick to a general discussion of propositional functions whose arguments are expressions of any sort. Since 'elementary' propositional functions (as one might call them), viz., propositional functions which map names onto elementary propositions, are a species of propositional function, anything said regarding propositional functions in general, will *mutatis mutandis* apply to 'elementary' propositional functions.
9. Cf. Frege's notion of concept formation in 'Conceptual Notation'. See T.W. Bynum (tr.), *Conceptual Notation and related articles* (Clarendon, 1972), p. 107.
10. The comparison between the *Tractarian* notion of a propositional function, and Frege's formulation of the requirement for determinacy of sense, breaks down here. For the propositional function does not determine a value (i.e., a proposition) for *every* argument, but only for the stipulated values for the propositional variable. Any other argument would presumably generate nonsense.
11. Russell's classic discussion of this is in 'On denoting', repr. in *Logic and Knowledge* (Unwin Hyman, 1956), pp. 41-56.
12. In this paragraph I am in part following G. E. M. Anscombe's illuminating discussion in *An Introduction to Wittgenstein's* Tractatus (Hutchinson & CO., 1959), Chapter 2.
13. Ibid., p. 48. For continuity, I have substituted the standard 'king of France' example for Anscombe's.
14. For the sake of brevity, I am discussing only the ambiguities inherent in the *denial* of such sentences. A similar account could, however, be given for the assertion of such sentences. Wittgenstein's reflections, in the *Notebooks 1914-1916*, on how many differentiable situations would make 'My watch is on the table' true, is a good example.
15. Here, it seems, we are forced to distinguish between an unending analysis and an analysis that ends at infinity. For, if sense is to be determinate, it must be *possible* for the analysis to terminate at the level of simple signs. Yet Wittgenstein does not deny that there might be an infinite number of 'objects': 'Even if the world is infinitely complex, so that every fact consists of infinitely many states of affairs and every state of affairs is composed of infinitely many objects, there would still have to be objects and states of affairs' (*TLP* 4.2211).
16. Cf. Russell (op. cit.), p. 46.
17. It is rather odd that Anscombe translates 'das' as 'a' in 'daß das Wort keine Bedeutung hat...'. Because of the implied generality, and because Wittgenstein is rejecting this 'point of the argument', the translation has the consequence that Wittgenstein contradicts himself fifteen sections later: 'An example of something corresponding to the name, and without which it would have no meaning, is a paradigm that is used in connexion with the name in the language-game' (*PI* §55).

18. Discussion of the demand for determinacy of sense, shorn from its relationship with the thesis identifying meaning and bearer, and from its relationship with 'simples', is forestalled until *Philosophical Investigations* §66, and explicitly discussed in §79. See Chapter 5 *infra*.
19. I say 'analogous' here because, unlike a *Tractarian* object, it is possible to imagine a use for the claim that a canonical sample of red is not red. To repeat, this would be tantamount to no longer employing it as a canonical sample. There is no such liberty with respect to a *Tractarian* object.
20. Cf. Norman Malcolm, *Nothing is Hidden* (Blackwell, 1986), p. 46.
21. Baker and Hacker (op. cit.) p. 247f. Baker and Hacker also note that this argument does not directly bear on the doctrines of the *Tractatus*, for the 'sublimed names and mythological objects were *expressly designed* to meet this anxiety', i.e., the anxiety about a name losing its meaning in the event that its bearer ceases to exist. Now presumably they were expressly designed to meet this anxiety precisely because ordinary proper names do not. Consequently, and as is obvious in the first place, the *Tractarian* concepts of 'object' and 'name' were explicated in *full awareness* of the fact that they conflicted with ordinary usage. And if they were indeed explicated in full awareness of this fact, it is difficult to see how Baker's and Hacker's suggestion—that an appeal to the *ordinary* usage of 'meaning', as it applies to *ordinary* proper names—could undermine the worry that lead to the postulation of simple objects. Unless, perhaps, what we must accept *ab initio* is that "words must be brought back from their metaphysical to their everyday use". But why? Perhaps "because grammar (e.g. the grammar of 'name') is autonomous, not responsible to reality". But how *can* it be? Perhaps "because the meaning of a word is its *use*!" (*PI* §43). But how *can* it be, if the meaning of a word MUST be the object to which it corresponds?
22. This tends to be the general strategy employed by scholars who wish to use Wittgenstein's remarks, in the *Investigations*, to attack referential theories of meaning. Wittgenstein is seen to be refuting a referential, or 'bi-planar', conception of meaning, and replacing it with his own conception of the meaning of a word as its use. For example, see Harris, *The Language Myth* (Duckworth, 1981).
23. It is important to note that Wittgenstein, in §40, is not arguing that *in general* the word 'meaning' is being used illicitly if it is identified with what corresponds to the word. Nor is he appealing to the general usage of 'meaning', and then applying this to the particular case of proper names. If this were his aim, then his explicit *justification* for the claim (the claim that 'the word "meaning" is being used illicitly if it is used to signify the thing that 'corresponds' to the word') would be obviously inadequate—a very crude *non sequitur*. For the justification is that it is nonsense to equate the meaning of a name with the bearer of the name, and *this* claim is justified by appeal to the actual usage of ordinary *proper* names; viz., that we do not say the meaning dies when the bearer dies. This justification, since it appeals to the use of a paradigmatic case of proper names, does not licence any conclusions about either (1) other sorts of proper names, (2) other sorts of names, (3) names in general, or most importantly, (4) the logically proper names of the *Tractatus*. On the other hand, it would, of course, be invalid to conclude from this that in other cases he argues that the meaning of a word *is* the object to which it corresponds. Rather, nothing has so far been said in this connection.
24. In §40, Anscombe translates *sprachwidrig* as 'illicit': 'the word "meaning" is being used illicitly [*sprachwidrig*] if it is used to signify the thing that 'corresponds' to the word'. This is potentially misleading. Note that 'ungrammatical' would be a more literal rendering.
25. This is at any rate how the different proper names would be distinguished in the language-game; this method of differentiation could certainly be replaced by another. The *real* distinction, one might say, is that I *mean* a different coloured square by each token word in the sentence. More on this to come.

26. For instance, how is 'Sunday' or 'Christmas day', 'War and Peace' or 'Crime and Punishment' to be fitted into this scheme? (I am indebted to Peter Hacker for this important point.)

5

From the Everyday to the Metaphysical Use[1]

> We predicate of the thing what lies in the method of representing it. Impressed by the possibility of a comparison, we think we are perceiving a state of affairs of the highest generality.
>
> *PI*, §104

5.1 From Augustine's picture to the Picture Theory

In the previous two chapters I examined Wittgenstein's investigation into the roots of the 'idea'. Those roots lie in Augustine's picture of language. The 'idea' is rooted in the claim that all words name objects. Of course, as these ideas were worked out in the *Tractatus*, Wittgenstein could point to nothing which would satisfy the demands set for his notions of 'object' and 'logically proper name'. But much discussion in the later writings points to the sort of thing he (vaguely) had in mind. If not for the demand that elementary propositions be logically independent, the sorts of thing Wittgenstein seemed to have in mind were common nouns like 'red', 'circularity' and (perhaps) proper names of points in the visual field.[2] And if not for the further requirement of 'absolute simplicity', seemingly required by the conjunction of (1) the demand for determinacy of sense and (2) the possibility of analysis, one could just boil things down to confusion surrounding the early Wittgenstein's attempt to construe all names as proper names (cf. *BB* p. 18). It was partly because of this attempt that Wittgenstein could point to nothing that would satisfy the demands he imposed on his concept of a name.

The claim that words name objects is only the first strand of Augustine's picture. So far I have ignored the second strand, viz., that sentences are combinations of such names (*PI* §1). It is possible that this second strand also bears on the picture theory. If every sentence is a *combination* of names that name objects, the re-employment of 'name' and 'object' discussed in previous chapters might carry along with it a corresponding transformation in the use of 'combination'. If, in addition to slabs and bricks, *red* and *circular* are also 'objects', this might strain our ordinary concept of 'a combination of objects'.

In the *Tractatus*, this purification of 'name' and 'object' did require a transformation of the concept of 'a combination of names (and objects)'. In the picture theory all 'names' are (logically) proper names, and a sentence is a 'combination' of 'names'. The names are the 'constituents' of *facts*, as opposed to complexes: 'Instead of 'The complex sign "aRb" says that *a* stands to *b* in the relation R', we ought to put, '*That* "a" stands to "b" in a certain relation says *that* *a*R*b*." (*TLP* 3.1432). This twist on the word 'combination' runs hand in hand with the claim that the elements of the sentence 'aRb' are elements of a fact.

Moreover, this 'combination' of 'names' represents a possible 'combination' of 'objects', these 'objects' also being constituents of *facts*. The concept of an 'object' almost looks as though it is supposed to be a symbol for everything that can be named. The concept of a 'combination' contributes to this picture by symbolizing any sort of relationship which these 'objects' might stand in. From the vantage point of the later Wittgenstein, the picture theory looks like a monstrous metaphor. He might even have called it a 'full-blown pictorial representation of the grammar of our language' (*PI* §295).

There is some discussion in *Philosophical Investigations* of 'The general form of a proposition' that so captivated the author of the *Tractatus* (see *TLP* 4.5, *passim*). However, explicit discussion of the proposition conceived as a concatenation of names does not find its way into the final and published form of the *Investigations*. Fortunately, there is a (concise) discussion of the issue in its immediate ancestor, the unpublished typescript TS 220. The theme which I have been tracing in these chapters is Wittgenstein's diagnosis of the misunderstandings surrounding the picture theory. Thus it will facilitate closure to examine briefly this treatment in TS 220. After all, we are tracing Wittgenstein's diagnosis from Augustine's picture to the picture theory.

There is, however, another and perhaps more important reason for scrutinizing this typescript. At the end of his treatment of the picture theory in TS 220, Wittgenstein gives us a hint as to his conception of 'metaphysics'. He says some illuminating things about his conception of 'the metaphysical use of words' (TS 220, §110). And he makes a remark about the proper treatment of the metaphysical use of words. He remarks that one role of the philosopher is to 'bring words back from their metaphysical to their everyday use' (ibid., *PI* §116). I want to address two questions regarding this methodological pronouncement. First, *what is* a 'metaphysical use of words', and how is it related to the everyday use? Second, with what *right* does the philosopher bring these words back 'to their everyday use'? While examining the context of this remark in TS 220, I suggest answers to these questions. Examining these questions is the counterpoint to my main theme in this chapter, i.e., Wittgenstein's later treatment of the notion of a sentence as a 'combination' of 'names'.

Wittgenstein recalls some of the reasoning that lay behind his early conception of the (elementary) proposition:

> I at one time said (in the *Tractatus Logico-Philosophicus*), that the 'elementary proposition' is a concatenation of names. For, to the names correspond objects, and to the sentence corresponds a complex of them. The sentence "The bottle is to the right of the glass", if it is true, corresponds to the complex consisting of the bottle, the glass, and the relation to-the-right-of .... What a misuse of the words "object" and "complex"!! .... To say a red circle '*consists of*' redness

and circularity, is a complex of these constituents, is a misuse of these words, and is misleading. (TS 220, §108)[3]

Wittgenstein blames this 'misuse', at least partially, on certain possibilities of transformation which lay in our language. He was held captive by certain possibilities for transforming expressions in language. Wittgenstein elaborates: (1) he notes certain possibilities for transforming *sentences*. For example, one might rephrase "the bottle is to the right of the glass" as "the bottle stands to the glass in the relation to-the-right-of". Transforming sentences into a fixed mode of expression can make many sentences appear to be, in essence, merely combinations of names. This can lead one to say that every word with a quasi-material meaning is distributed in a pure network of logical relations (ibid., §109). Searching for a unity underlying all propositions, the author of the *Tractatus* became a prisoner of a fixed form of expression. That is, he became a prisoner to the idea that the *possibility* of expressing an enormous number of sentences with this fixed form shows something about the essence of the proposition. *Every* proposition, one might say, is *really* a combination of 'names'. Every proposition is really a distribution of names into a network of logical relations.

(2) Wittgenstein also notes the possibility of being misled by another sort of fixed form of expression. One can express an enormous number of explanations of word meaning with the form 'the word ... signifies ...'. This may induce one into saying that all 'real' names signify an object. (1) and (2) work together, and may make it appear that to a 'combination' of 'names' there corresponds a 'combination' of 'objects'.

Immediately following the discussion of these possibilities of transformation, Wittgenstein considers the sentence, 'Every sentence says: This is how things stand'. In the *Tractatus*, Wittgenstein calls this the 'general form of the proposition' (*TLP* 4.5). In TS 220, he remarks that it is a form that can (and for him did) mislead (TS 220, §110). This conception of the essence of description consisely expresses (1) and (2) above, i.e., it concisely expresses the essence of the proposition as a concatenation of names and the essence of the word as naming an object.

When the early Wittgenstein says that the general form of the proposition is 'This is how things stand', he is saying that every (elementary) proposition is a combination of names describing a combination of objects. (Molecular propositions are truth functions of elementary propositions.) The 'general form of the proposition' is itself a portrait of the picture theory.

In the midst of his remarks on the misleading character of 'This is how things stand', Wittgenstein says something especially enigmatic (even for him). The sentence expressing the general form of the proposition, viz., the sentence "This is how things stand", 'is the kind of sentence one repeats to oneself countless times. One thinks that one is tracing the outline of the thing's nature over and over again, and one is merely tracing round the frame through which we look at it' (ibid., see *PI* §114).

How should we interpret this simile? What is the 'frame' and what is it we are looking at through it? Wittgenstein immediately elucidates by making his point again with another simile:

> Suppose people used always to point to objects in the following way: they describe as it were a circle round the object with their finger in the air. One could then imagine that a philosopher might say: "Everything is surely circular; for the table looks like *this*, the stove like *this*, the lamp like *this*", etc., drawing a circle round the thing each time. (TS 220, §110)[4]

On a first reading, both these similes are obscure. As we shall see, however, upon reflection they are not so much obscure as ambiguous. Since the second simile is a bit more worked out, let us first consider how it might be intended to apply to Wittgenstein's misleading form: 'Every sentence says: this is how things stand'.

The 'fixed form of expression' in the simile is the drawing of circles around things when pointing to them. So this might stand for the 'misleading form', 'Every sentence says: this is how things are'. Of what, then, does one say that "everything is surely like this"? In this simile, the philosopher uniformly predicates circularity of things such as household furniture. What would these *things* represent in the early Wittgenstein's misleading form of expression 'Every sentence says: this is how things are'? Surely the natural answer is sentences, for every *sentence* says: this is how things stand.

Although this reading seems to be natural, and I believe it is correct, another reading has been proposed in favour of this one. Baker and Hacker argue that the 'things' which, in Wittgenstein's simile, the philosopher uniformly predicates circularity of are intended to stand not for sentences, but rather are intended to stand for that which the sentences describe, viz., facts.[5] Baker's and Hacker's interpretation of Wittgenstein's simile fits in well with the general conception of Wittgenstein's method that I have been criticizing in this book. For, on that conception, the cardinal error of metaphysics is to project language onto reality. On Baker's and Hacker's interpretation, the 'misleading form' in Wittgenstein's simile is intended to represent something like 'Every fact is a combination of objects'.

To repeat, this is *prima facie* an unnatural reading. There is no sentence like 'Every fact is a combination of objects' in §110. The only comparable sentence is the one which occurs immediately before Wittgenstein makes this simile: 'Every *sentence* says: this is how things stand'. And it is impossible to apply *this* 'misleading form' to facts—what is manifestly at issue is sentences. It seems obvious, rather, that the philosopher's claim that 'Every*thing* is surely circular' is intended to illuminate the 'misleading form', 'Every *sentence* says: This is how things stand'.

Moreover, Wittgenstein tells us in the previous passage that he was 'searching frantically after a *UNITY* underlying all *sentences*' (TS 220, §109, my emphasis on 'sentences').[6] In the *Tractatus*, the general form of the proposition is that unity (*TLP* 4.5). *Every* sentence says, this is how things are.

There is, however, another sentence which Wittgenstein quotes. He cites Plato as saying: 'When we mean something, we mean something existent'. (Both these 'misleading forms' occur one after the other in §110, and are then followed by the simile.) Perhaps the simile of drawing circles is, or is also, intended to characterize Plato's expression.

Plato's 'misleading form' is surely an expression of the 'idea', the point being that to mean something, there must be something actual that we mean. But here again this idea has its roots in a fixed form of expression. Here again the primitive error is not the projection of language onto reality. Rather, it is the possibility of casting explanations of the meaning of words (e.g., colour words, shape words, and so on) in the form "The word .... signifies ....", which can make it look as though every word stands for an object (cf. *PI* §10, TS 220 §109). My arguments in the previous chapter lead precisely to this conclusion:

In the previous chapter, I argued that the tendency to project features of our use of samples onto mythical objects resulted in the 'idea'. And this tendency itself has deeper roots. As Wittgenstein presents it, such tendencies manifest superstitions we can *inexorably* be drawn to in an attempt to give *the* essence of a name, when that attempt is informed by Augustine's primitive picture of the essence of human language. This superstition is fed by reflections informed by a conception of the essence of *language* (viz., 'name'). So if my arguments in the previous chapter are sound; and if we apply the above quoted metaphor to this feature of the picture theory, here too we arrive at the idea that Wittgenstein is referring to the tendency to predicate features of a picture of language onto language itself. He is not referring to the projection of language onto reality. Of course, languages are themselves 'realities' of a sort. But even so, the 'projection' is still of a *picture* of reality onto reality.

Although sometimes a mouthful, assertions and explanations of word meaning can often be transformed into these 'fixed forms of expression'. And these transformations seem legitimate enough in themselves. For they are not *essentially* misleading (whatever it might mean to say that they are). They merely happened to exercise a tyranny over the author of the *Tractatus* (among many others, to be sure). These fixed forms of expressing (1) word explanations and (2) sentences dovetail in the idea that the general form of the proposition is captured by the form of expression, 'This is how things stand'. Although this proposition is often employed as a propositional variable in ordinary usage, the form of expression tantalized the author of the *Tractatus*. One could even imagine the early Wittgenstein arguing similarly to the philosopher in the later Wittgenstein's simile:

"Every proposition says 'this is how things are'. For example, I may leave a message for you by leaving my penholder on my table. This might represent me being upstairs. How things are with these *things* (i.e., the penholder and the table) will say how things are with *these* things, i.e., that I am upstairs, i.e., *on* the second floor. Or again: 'the table is red' says 'this (i.e., 'the table' and 'red/is red') is how things (i.e., the table, and *red*(!)) are'. Or yet again, 'the penholder is on the table' says 'this (i.e., 'the penholder', 'the table', 'is on') is how things (i.e., the penholder, the table, *is on*(!!) are'. And so on."

One looks at every proposition through the form 'this is how things are', and this can make it look as though every sentence describes a combination of objects. (Certainly some sentences may do precisely this. Compare the coloured square language-game.) The form of expression is taken quasi literally, and it becomes the frame through which we look at our *concept* of a proposition. 'Impressed by the possibility of a comparison, we think we are perceiving a state of affairs of the highest generality' (TS 220, §110, *PI* §104). It is, Wittgenstein tells us, only when we dispel this 'optical' illusion—an illusion produced by looking at our concept of the proposition through this simplistic 'picture' of the proposition—that we can see language (and specifically, the sentence) simply as it is (TS 220, §110). The 'optical illusion' results from taking what lies in a fixed form of expressing sentences as a discovery about the essence of the sentence itself.

Wittgenstein's first simile should be interpreted analogously. The 'frame' is the fixed form of expression. And it is *language* that we are looking at through this frame. One fancies that they are 'tracing the outline of the things nature over and over again, and one is merely tracing round the frame through which we look at it' (TS 220, §110).

Certainly this optical illusion did produce that strange and fascinating conception of 'the world' in the *Tractatus*. As early as 1916 Wittgenstein remarked that his 'work ... extended from the foundations of logic to the nature of the world' (*NB* p. 79). Yet according to the later Wittgenstein, the author of the *Tractatus* fell victim to a primitive picture of the concept of a *proposition*. The conception of 'the world' in the *Tractatus* is an implication of that metaphysics of *symbolism*.[7]

I wish to generalize this account of 'metaphysics'. Clearly the picture theory is about language. But language is not the only subject the metaphysician might concern herself with. Regardless, I suggest there is something misleading about saying that metaphysics, as Wittgenstein uses this word, is a metaphysics of 'reality'. That is, there is something misleading about saying that metaphysics is the result of projecting features of grammar onto reality, even a linguistic reality. And this is so not only in those cases we have been considering in this book, cases explicitly concerned with the nature of language. Clearly I cannot argue comprehensively, but with an example I may clarify my point. Let us look at a case which is less obviously a metaphysics of symbolism.

Wittgenstein also elucidates his conception of the metaphysical use of words in the *Blue Book*. I must note straight away that, in the *Blue Book*, Wittgenstein equates 'form of expression' with 'notation' (*BB* p. 57).[8] We have seen that, in TS 220 §109, he is discussing the fascination which can be exercised by reflection on the possibility of transforming sentences into a fixed form. This fascination can restrict freedom and, as Wittgenstein expresses it, can lead to being held prisoner by a fixed *form of expression*. In the *Blue Book*, Wittgenstein seems to be using this phrase, 'form of expression' in the same way. Thus, other things being equal, I take his remarks about 'notations', which are more numerous, as applicable to what in TS 220 he is calling 'forms of expression'.

In the *Blue Book*, a new form of expression, or notation, is a new way of expressing distinctions which find (a different, and often more or less obvious) expression in our language:

> He [i.e., the metaphysician] sees a way of dividing the country different from the one used on the ordinary map. He feels tempted say, to use the name "Devonshire" not for the county with its conventional boundary, but for a region differently bounded. He could express this by saying: "Isn't it absurd to make *this* a county, to draw the boundaries *here*?" But what he says is: "The *real* Devonshire is this". We could answer: "What you want is only a new notation, and by a new notation no facts of geography are changed" (*BB* p. 57)[9]

According to Wittgenstein the metaphysician is, unconsciously, objecting to a convention, viz., the 'notation which of all possible notations is the one which pervades all our life' (*BB* p. 59). The objection is to our ordinary language (ibid.). Yet the metaphysician characteristically employs the same *signs* in a different way. This is one reason for the metaphysician's unclarity about her own pronouncements. For although the use of 'an assertion which the metaphysician makes expresses discontentment with our grammar ... the words of this assertion can also be used to state a fact of experience' (*BB* p. 57). Indeed, the everyday use of these expressions employed in such metaphysical assertions *is* to state a fact of experience. 'Thus when he says "only my pain is real pain", this sentence might mean that the other people are only pretending ....' (ibid.). This is not the metaphysician's use. Rather,

> The man who says "only my pain is real", doesn't mean to say that he has found out by common criteria—the criteria, i.e., which give our words their common meanings—that the others who said they had pains were cheating. But what he rebels against is the use of *this* expression in connection with *these* criteria. That is, he objects to using this word in the particular way in which it is commonly used. (ibid.)

It is both illuminating and misleading to characterize this 'rebellion' as predicating of reality what lies in grammar—as projecting grammar onto reality. At one level it is illuminating. From the vantage point of the later Wittgenstein, the claim 'Only my pain is real' can result from a dogmatic comparison between having a pain and having a physical object, say, a penny. (I am forced here to make a long story extremely short.[10]) If a pain is like a physical object, except 'private' in some sense, then 'pain' can be given meaning by (private) ostensive definition. But undoubtedly, there is no *comparable* ostensive definition of 'pain' by appeal to a pain that is not mine. (This lack of comparison may get expressed by saying that there is *no such thing* as ostensively defining another's pain.) Features of the use of 'pain' dis-analogous to 'penny' force this conclusion. Therefore, the string of words, 'Pain that is not mine' has at best a different sense. One might claim that, at best, 'So-and-so has pain' could only mean something more comparable to 'So-and-so behaves like I do when I have pain' (cf. *PR* §64). One might express this by saying that "Only my pain is real", and this is a distorted reflection of grammatical conventions in ordinary language. That is to say, understood in a *peculiar* way, it is nonsense to say "You have pain". If it is real pain, then it is my pain.

Consider a closely related example, but one which is easier to work with. Suppose the metaphysician says 'I don't feel your pain'. Just as Wittgenstein noted with 'Only my pain is real', 'I don't feel your pain' might have a legitimate use to state a fact of experience. For instance, suppose you are engaged in a dangerous activity of which I disapprove, and despite my warning. In exasperation, I might say "I don't feel your pain". This would mean something like "Do as you please then, for I don't hurt when you injure yourself" or "Suit yourself: I don't feel pain as a result of you feeling pain". Both these assertions deny significant propositions. Of course, I do not feel physical pain when you physically injure yourself. But I might. Perhaps it is even imaginable that I feel pain in *your* arm when it is injured. (Wittgenstein employs virtually identical examples, see *BB* p. 54.) This is not, however, a metaphysical use of these expressions. The claim "I *can't* feel your pain", as spoken by the metaphysician, is an assertion without a *conceivable* negation (as opposed to, in this case, a significant yet as a matter of fact impossible negation). If I can feel it, then it is my pain—even if it is in your arm.

The metaphysician *conceives* of these assertions as essential truths about *pain* (or experience). It is the way in which the metaphysician *conceives* them that, from the perspective of the later Wittgenstein, it is illuminating to characterize as a projection of language (or grammar) onto reality. For these words, as spoken by the metaphysician, actually manifest a decision to attach no sense to the expression, 'I feel your pain'. And yet the metaphysician *conceives* them as remarks on the essence of pain, not as remarks on her use of the word.

On the other hand, this characterization is misleading. What underlies the temptation to think that such metaphysical pronouncements are 'about reality'? If the metaphysician conceives of it as a necessary truth that 'I can't have your pain', Wittgenstein's argument is that this is a disguised grammatical rule. But there is a good reason why it is disguised. For this expression is conceived on analogy with 'I can't have your penny'. This is why it is *puzzling*. *Why* can't I have your pain?—this is a fact which *needs explaining*. There is nothing analogous to this in the grammar of 'physical object', and therefore the claim seems startling. (For remember that it is precisely the comparison with 'physical object' that motivates the objection to ordinary usage.) It appears to be a fact about pain that requires explanation in terms of the strange *nature* or extraordinary *properties* of these mental objects. At the bottom of this tendency to project grammar onto reality is a bad comparison. And this (bad) picture is a (bad) picture of *the use of our words*.

This is what the tendency to project language onto reality amounts to. If we are mislead by such a comparison between the grammar of (i) 'pain' and the grammar of (ii) 'physical object', features of the *grammar* of (i) may be *assimilated* to—i.e., find a different expression in—(ii), viz., in terms of the strange and extraordinary properties that they *must* have. To fall victim to the comparison in this way *forces* these explanations on us, or forces explanations akin to them on us, in an attempt to come to terms with the *linguistic* facts. The misleading comparison, in these cases, *forces* a projection of language onto reality.

It is no accident that idealism and solipsism are not propounded alongside claims such as "One cannot be a married bachelor"[11], "One cannot fire C sharp out of a cannon", or "One cannot put an event in a hole". Underlying the *appearance* of substantive significance in these metaphysical pronouncements is a re-employment of words from ordinary language, this re-employment itself resulting from a dogmatic comparison between sectors of language.

Let us get back to Wittgenstein's example of 'Only my pain is real'. As this expression might be used by the metaphysician, it is obviously contrary to ordinary word usage. (This is not so obvious with 'I can't feel your pain'.) To be sure, Wittgenstein also claims that the metaphysician 'is not aware that he is objecting to a convention' (*BB* p. 57). Certainly it is conceived as a (kind of) discovery. However, it is of paramount importance for understanding Wittgenstein's conception of 'the metaphysical use of words' that we do not confuse an objection to *this* convention— i.e., 'our *notation*'—with an objection to what I will differentiate by calling 'our concepts'.[12]

To clarify this distinction, suppose there was a culture that did not distinguish, in their language, between 'red' and 'blue' (as we use these words). Perhaps this is because where they come from the two colours always appear together (or whatever). Their *concept* of colour would be different from ours. There would, in this language, be no counterpart (not even a confused one) for our distinction between red and blue. Suppose our concepts of red and blue were introduced to this tribe, and suppose their perceptual capacities are such that they recognize the distinction. It is imaginable that they would *object* to our colour concepts, perhaps on practical or aesthetic grounds (cf. Wittgenstein's discussion of the French tricolour in §64 of *Philosophical Investigations*).

This is most certainly not the sort of objection to word usage that Wittgenstein has in mind as the characteristic mistake of metaphysics. But neither is it like the following: Suppose that a philosopher comes to learn the language of this tribe. Noticing that their language has no counterpart for our distinction between blue and red, this philosopher *objects* to their grammar on the grounds that it is not *true to the facts*. Undoubtedly Wittgenstein considered this kind of objection confused: grammar is not, in this sense, responsible to reality (cf. *PI* §230). Nonetheless, this kind of objection is also not Wittgenstein's understanding of the objection of the metaphysician.

On the contrary, the metaphysical use of words is not (or does not embody) an objection to our concepts (as I am here using 'concept'). Rather, it is precisely certain important grammatical distinctions inherent in our language, perhaps even distinctions that *do* find *expression* in 'the notation' of our ordinary language, that the metaphysician attempts to assimilate *to a* (different) *notation*.

For example, 'I can't feel your pain' is itself the expression of certain features of the grammar of our language of immediate experience. According to Wittgenstein, this metaphysical claim is an attempt to find expression for differences between the everyday use of first- and third-person attributions of pain (*PI* §§303-4). This is comparable to the assimilation of our concept of ostensive definition (*simpliciter*) to our concept of ostensive definitions of ordinary objects. The grammatical distinctions between names of shapes, colours, and numbers are *sublimated* to the paradigm case of ostensive explanations of ordinary objects; but they are not thereby obliterated! Rather, they find confused expression in the claim that shapes, colours, and numbers are (as it were *very*) different sorts of objects.

In the picture theory there is an intimate relation between (1) a picture of the proposition (viz., 'this is how things are'), and (2) a picture of 'name' (looked at in previous chapters). Put them together and you have the basic ingredients of that conception of representation: the elementary proposition is a combination of names, each name standing for an object and the whole combination of names representing a (possible) combination of objects. Both these sublimed or purified uses of words (i.e., 'name' and 'proposition'), although not entirely separable in the picture theory, have their roots in separable simplistic pictures. The formal relationship between the everyday use, and the metaphysical use of the words resulting from these simplistic pictures can be characterized with the simile of a developmental hypothesis. In cases such as these, it is as if the ordinary use of these words is 'transformed' in the 'process' of assimilating recalcitrant cases (i.e., names that are not names of objects ordinarily understood, propositions that do not describe configurations of objects ordinarily understood).

This is certainly a misnomer. According to Wittgenstein, the correct method of diagnosis is to trace the physiognomy of error (see below). The success of the diagnosis would not depend upon a precisely correct description of the processes of thought that went on, e.g., in the formulation of the picture theory. Rather, Wittgenstein seems to determine the correctness of the diagnosis by appeal to the acknowledgment of the 'patient'.

In whatever terms it is best to characterize the source of error, its *expression*, according to Wittgenstein, is singular. 'The expression of this illusion is the metaphysical use of our words. For one predicates of the thing what lies it our method of representing it' (TS 220, §110).[13] Applying this generalization to the subject of this thesis: we predicate of language what lies in Augustine's picture of it.

5.2 Im Anfang war das Bild

According to Wittgenstein, the primitive error underlying the metaphysical use of words is not a projection of features of language 'onto reality'. Underlying this projection of language onto reality is a primitive picture of the functioning of language. I have argued that this was his conception of the confusions embodied in the picture theory. In the context of the discussion in TS 220, the tendency to impose the misleading form of expression 'this is how things are' onto our concept of a proposition typifies the errors characteristic of metaphysics: 'We predicate of the thing what lies in our method of representing it'. The early Wittgenstein predicated of language what lay in a primitive picture of it.

If this is Wittgenstein's conception of metaphysics, what justifies his notorious call to ordinary usage? With what right does the philosopher bring words back from their metaphysical to their everyday use? Firstly, it cannot be an appeal to the autonomy of 'grammar', i.e., the idea that our *concepts* are neither correct nor incorrect 'to the facts'. For as we have seen, (Wittgenstein's characterization of) the mistake of the metaphysician is not in this sense an objection to *concepts*, though to be sure the metaphysician may partially conceive of it as such. The metaphysician does not in effect object to an established set of concepts, and set up new ones on the grounds that the old concepts are incorrect to the (non-linguistic) facts. If an objection to concepts was the characteristic mistake of the metaphysician, then one might appeal to the (putative) autonomy of grammar as grounds for indicting the whole enterprise as misconceived. But on the contrary, the metaphysician's objection is, as Wittgenstein explained in the *Blue Book*, an objection to the conventional notation(s) in which the use of our ordinary language is embodied. (Wittgenstein later came to see his use of the word 'notation' as itself misleading, in so far as it suggests a comparison between natural languages and calculi. See Chapter Six below.)

Still, one might retort, if the metaphysician's objection amounts to an objection to a notation, nonetheless a notation is *itself* conventional. Wittgenstein thought so (*BB* p. 57). Can we not complain that the metaphysician's objection is the result of (*inter alia*) the confused idea that one notation—viz., the metaphysician's—is in some sense correct to the facts? This complaint does not turn on whether it is the facts of 'reality' *or* 'language' that the metaphysician objects to. And if this complaint is justified, can we not further object that the metaphysician's construction of a new notation, in addition to having a confused rationale, is also highly misleading? In the cases I have been considering in this book, the new notation constantly gets conflated with the notation of our ordinary language. It is this conflation that results in the postulation of mythical pointing mechanisms, abstract objects and their abstract realms, logical spaces and logical places, and so on and so forth. Moreover, if Wittgenstein is right, the metaphysician does not even clearly understand the activity they are engaging in.

I think that, yes, we can object in this way to such metaphysical activities. *However*, the validity of such an objection, i.e., to the metaphysician's dissatisfaction with the ordinary use of words, presupposes the establishment of the fact that such dissatisfaction is unjustified in these aforementioned respects. (I.e., one must determine that (1) this objection to ordinary usage lacks legitimate rationale, (2) the activity itself is misunderstood, and (3) it can mislead, or has misled).

How is one to establish these claims about the activity of the metaphysician? Well, this is precisely what is established by a *diagnosis* of the temptation to use words 'metaphysically':

> One of the most important tasks is to express all false thought processes so characteristically that the reader says, "Yes, that's exactly the way I meant it". To make a tracing of the physiognomy of every error.
>
> Indeed we can only convict someone else of a mistake ... if he ... acknowledges this expression as the correct expression of his feeling ...
>
> What the other person acknowledges is the analogy I am proposing to him as the source of his thought.[14]

The therapeutic role of the philosopher is not only to show *that* the metaphysician's use of words conflicts with ordinary usage.[15] In many cases this is, or at least can easily be made to be all too obvious to any parties concerned (e.g., "a number is an object", "the world consists of facts, not things"). On the other hand, in many cases it is not obvious (e.g., "I can't feel your pain", and perhaps sometimes even "the external world does not exist"). Where such conflict is not obvious, showing *that* the metaphysician's use of words conflicts with ordinary use is an important *preliminary*. (Cf. Wittgenstein's argument in *PI* §40, discussed in the previous chapter.)

Suppose the problems treated by Wittgenstein in the first 50 sections of the *Investigations* are characteristic of 'metaphysics'. If so, showing *that* the metaphysician's use of words is in conflict with ordinary usage may be insufficient treatment. Moreover, as we saw at the end of Chapter Three, it may even be insufficient to demonstrate that the metaphysician's usage is at some level inconsistent or incoherent. In Chapter Three we noted an inconsistency between 'object' qua what is pointed at in an ostensive definition, and 'object' qua what is designated by a word in the language. The inconsistency in the use of 'object' was at best useful in showing that there *is* a problem here (one should be puzzled if there is reason to be puzzled). As it turned out, it was met by making the form of representation, i.e. the application of Augustine's picture, more sophisticated.

Over and above these certainly important goals, the philosopher must show that such a dissatisfaction with the ordinary use of words is a dissatisfaction grounded in the fact that one is held captive by a picture. This dissatisfaction with ordinary usage has its source in a picture which was 'not a *result of investigation* [of our language]: it was a requirement' (*PI* §107). To ignore this is to deny the *internal* connection between diagnosis and dissolution.

By 'internal connection' I wish to point out that the connection between diagnosis and dissolution is not merely of rhetorical importance. It is not merely a matter of whether or not, in abstraction from diagnosis, a careful description of the ordinary uses of words will actually *convince* the person under the influence of the primitive picture. Suppose I cogently argue *that* the metaphysician's use of words conflicts with their ordinary use, i.e., that from the standpoint of ordinary language the metaphysician is talking nonsense. This only constitutes a valid objection on the assumption that the *metaphysician's* objection to ordinary usage is unjustified. This, it seems to me, can only be achieved by a diagnosis of the tendency to misuse these expressions. Consequently, the diagnosis of a philosophical problem can be, from an argumentative and not merely rhetorical point of view, essential to its dissolution. Hence, and as we have seen in previous chapters, diagnosis is an important part of Wittgenstein's method of treating the confusions embodied in the picture theory. Wittgenstein reveals the root of these objections to ordinary usage. They are grounded in the dogmatic assimilation of the facts of our language to the shackles of a primitive form of representation. A first and important step in the attempt to bring words back from the metaphysical to the everyday use is, it seems, to trace the converse. The philosopher must first trace the route from the everyday to the metaphysical use.

5.3 Language-games are Methods of Representation

In the previous chapter I presented my interpretation of Wittgenstein's diagnosis of the root underlying the tendency to project features of samples onto reality. That tendency resulted from the dogmatic application of our concept of a proper name (of an object) to names characteristically explained by reference to samples. One could say that the error consists in predicating of our concept of a name what lies in Augustine's picture of it. Wittgenstein clarified this confusion with a comparison between the *Tractarian* notion of an 'object' and a simplified version of our concept of a sample. That is to say, he invented a language-game—the coloured square language-game—where the samples are employed in teaching.

Certainly the use of samples in this imaginary language-game *is* dramatically simplified in comparison with the uses of colour samples in ordinary life. This must be acknowledged. For the comparability between a *Tractarian* object and the canonical sample of sepia described in *Philosophical Investigations* §50 only goes through in so far as that sample is used, as it were, 'absolutely canonically'. That is to say, the adequacy of the analogy depends upon the fact that the sample is an essential presupposition of the language-game, and hence in this sense has to exist if that language-game is to exist. Of course, this is not the way we use any colour samples in ordinary life. No actual sample is, as far as I know, used in such a way that it is essentially presupposed by the language-game in which it is employed. The practice of metric measurement, for instance, does not come to a screeching halt in the event of the destruction of the standard metre.

Wittgenstein is aware that this language-game is a highly simplified representation of the actual use of samples in the practice of colour ascriptions. I noted in the previous chapter that he qualifies his claim about the canonical colour sample, i.e., he qualifies the claim that the sample is a *paradigm*, that it belongs to the *means* of representation. Wittgenstein's qualification is that 'this may be an important observation; but it is none the less an observation concerning our *language-game*—our *method of representation*' (*PI* §50, my emphasis). Wittgenstein is careful *not* to predicate of the multifarious facets of our uses of samples what lies in his immensely simplified representation of that use. On the contrary, he acknowledges various possible alterations to, and twists on this language-game. He acknowledges that there might be various criteria, perhaps an indefinite number.

> Our language-game (48) has *various* possibilities; there is a variety of cases in which we should say that a sign in the game was the name of a square of such-and-such a colour. We should say so if, for instance, we knew that the people who used the language were taught the use of the signs in such-and-such a way. Or if it were set down in writing, say in the form of a table, that this element corresponded to this sign, and if the table were used in teaching the language and were appealed to in certain disputed cases. (*PI* §53)

Moreover, 'what if no such sample is part of our language' (*PI* §56), as might very well be the case? In mine or, I conjecture, your practice of colour ascription, there is no sample comparable in this respect to the 'absolutely canonical' sample of sepia introduced in §50.

Wittgenstein's method for treating the puzzles surrounding the *Tractarian* conception of 'object' is a comparison with an *imaginary* language-game. Moreover, he imagines a language-game which conflicts in important ways with the parallel usage of samples in ordinary language. This, put in just this way, sounds *prima facie* puzzling. If the errors of metaphysics consist primarily in the tendency to misuse the words of ordinary language, should not the treatment at least primarily consist in an appeal to the *actual* use of words, rather than to an imaginary use? To be sure, there is an all-important difference between the coloured square language-game and the picture theory. The coloured square language-game (like Augustine's picture!) has an imaginable *application*. We have no idea what the 'objects' or 'names' of the *Tractatus* are. But again, why this *prima facie* indirect route in diagnosing the philosophical problems surrounding the 'naming relation'? Why does Wittgenstein employ this *intermediate case* between a *Tractarian* object and our actual use of samples (cf. *PI* §122)?

I think some light can be thrown on Wittgenstein's language-game method if we explore some of the reasons why Wittgenstein may have dropped the term 'notation' when referring to the 'grammar' of our language. This is the subject of the following and final chapter in this book.

Notes

1. In this chapter there will be a lot of talk about metaphysics and the activity of the metaphysician. The terms 'metaphysics' and 'metaphysician' are employed for the sake of convenience and because these are the terms Wittgenstein used. It will not be argued to what extent Wittgenstein's characterization of metaphysics accords with the practice of that subject by other philosophers.
2. See Wittgenstein's 'Some Remarks on Logical Form', in *Philosophical Occasions* (op. cit.), pp. 29-35.
3. 'Ich habe seinerzeit (in der *Log. Phil. Abh.*) gesagt, der 'Elementarsatz' sei eine Verkettung von Namen. Denn den Namen entsprächen Gegenstände und dem Satz entspreche ein Komplex aus ihnen. Dem Satz, "Die Flasche steht rechts vom Glas", wenn er wahr ist, entspricht der Komplex bestehend aus der Flasche, dem Glase und der Relation Rechts-Links[...] Die Sprachwidrige Verwendung des Wortes "Gegenstand" und "Konplex"!! [...] Zu sagen, ein roter Kreis '*bestehe aus*' Röte und Kreisförmigkeit, sei ein Komplex aus diesen Bestandteilen, ist ein Missbraüch dieser Wörter, und irreführend.' It has been noted (by Baker and Hacker, *Understanding and Meaning* (op. cit.), Exg. §104), that in the *Tractatus* it is not said that a *complex* of objects corresponds to the concatenation of names. Rather, he uses the terms 'combination' [*Verbindung*] or 'configuration', and reserves 'complex' for a different use. This *might* be sloppiness and, if so, nothing turns on it. But it might also be an affirmation of the claim that, with respect to the *Tractatus'* use of 'combination' (or configuration),

   > . . . where concepts are lacking,
   >
   > We shall always find a word in good time.
   >
   > (Quoted by Wittgenstein from Goethe's *Faust* in 'Cause and Effect: Intuitive Awareness', repr. in *Philosophical Occasions (op. cit)*, p. 393.)

4. This paragraph from §110 of the typescript corresponds very closely to *Z* §443, and I have for the most part, i.e., except for slight deviations in the German between the two passages, used the translation from *Zettel.*
5. *Understanding and Meaning* (op. cit.). See their discussion on *Philosophical Investigations*, §104. I should say here that my interpretation of these sections in TS 220 owes much to Baker's article

'Section 122: Neglected Aspects' (op. cit.). Baker evidently rejects his and Hacker's reading of §104 in *Understanding and Meaning*. However, it is unclear to me in many other instances whether Baker would draw the same implications as I do in this chapter. Nonetheless, anyone who reads the article will see the extent to which it informs this chapter.

6. 'suche krampfhaft, nach einen ... *EINHEIT* aller Sätze'
7. I owe my usage of 'metaphysics of symbolism' to Gordon Baker's *Wittgenstein, Frege, and the Vienna Circle*. See especially the Preface and Chapter Two of Baker's book.
8. Viz., in the following parenthetical remark: 'We easily forget how much a notation, a form of expression, may mean to us, and that changing it isn't always as easy as it often is in mathematics or in the sciences.'
9. If one is puzzled by the idea that it is *language* (as opposed to 'reality') which Wittgenstein is likening to the country, and that it is this country (i.e., language) which the metaphysician wants to divide up differently, one should remember that in *Philosophical Investigations* it is *language* which he compared to an ancient city. (And not to a *map* of an ancient city, or even the division of the city into municipalities or districts.)
10. For a detailed account of the Wittgenstein's reflections on solipsism, see Hacker, *Insight and Illusion* (op. cit.) ch. 4.
11. This is not to deny that an expression such as this could, under certain circumstances, cause puzzlement. For instance, if one reflects on the claim that concept words 'designate' concepts, one might be tempted to conceive of these concepts, e.g., as in some sense abstract entities inhabiting abstract realms. Under these circumstances one might be puzzled about why it is that we cannot *conceive* of a married bachelor. Do the concepts as it were not fit together?
12. Cf. Hacker, *Insight and Illusion* (op. cit.) p. 201.
13. 'Der Ausduck dieser Tauschung aber ist die Metaphysische Verwendung unsrer Wörter. Denn man prädiziert nun von der Sache, was in der Darstellungweise liegt.' (cf. *PI* §104).
14. From the chapter "Philosophie" in TS 213, translated in *Philosophical Occasions* (op. cit.), 165. cf. TS 220 §106.
15. Cf. Hacker (op. cit.), pp. 154f.

6

The Chapter 'On Philosophy'

> If I give you the light and shadow on a body in a picture I can thereby give you the shape of it. But if I give you the highlights in a picture you don't know what the shape is.
>
> L. Wittgenstein, *Lectures and Conversations on Aesthetics, Psychology and Religious Belief* (University of California Press), p. 5.

6.1 No Chapter 'On Philosophy'?

E. Von Savigny contends that there is 'No Chapter "On Philosophy" in *Philosophical Investigations*'.[1] On the face of it, this contention is counter-intuitive. The 'chapter' to which he refers is §§89–133 and, surely the reader will agree, §89 *looks* like the introduction to a kind of 'chapter' on philosophy:

> These considerations bring us up to the problem: In what sense is logic something sublime?
>
> For there seemed to pertain to logic a peculiar depth—a universal significance. Logic lay, it seemed, at the bottom of all the sciences.—For logical investigation explores the nature of all things. It seeks to see to the bottom of things

> and is not meant to concern itself whether what actually happens is this or that.—It takes its rise, not from an interest in the facts of nature, nor from a need to grasp causal connexions: but from an urge to understand the basis, or essence, of everything empirical.

Appearances can be deceiving, however, so we should not reject Von Savigny's thesis out of hand. I believe he is on to something very important. Nonetheless, I will argue that there *is* a kind of 'chapter' on philosophy in *Philosophical Investigations.*

Although prima facie counterintuitive, Von Savigny's argument is not absurd. For he does not go so far as to deny that Wittgenstein draws methodological morals from the discussion of particular philosophical problems. To deny this is quite impossible (see, at the very least, *PI* §§109, 111, 116, 118, 119, 121–128, 133). Be this as it may, according to Von Savigny there is not 'even one hint at something like an enterprise designed to convince the reader that such-and-such is how philosophy must necessarily be'.[2]

Von Savigny is probably correct that Wittgenstein has no desire to entirely close discussion on the nature of philosophy (cf. *PI* §92). Yet Von Savigny is leading up to a thesis significantly stronger than this. He argues that the primary subject matter in these sections is not Wittgenstein's conception of philosophy at all. There is no *sustained* methodological discussion. This 'chapter' is not, for the most part, *on* philosophy.

Von Savigny's argument begins with some general scepticism: it is not *prima facie* plausible that these sections are, even loosely speaking, Wittgenstein's 'metaphilosophical chapter'. For

> no reader, lead by his experience of customary ways of compiling books, would expect something on the character of the author's enterprise at this very place, lost and lonely between discussions of names, sentences, ostensive definitions and pointing, primary elements, games and Moses on one side, and on understanding, reading, meaning, and following rules on the other. Any reader accustomed to usual

> conventions would expect the author to collect his methodological insights in the introduction ...[3]

So far the argument is not convincing. First, Wittgenstein was no ordinary compiler of books. Second, there is a good reason to put a 'chapter' on philosophy in this very place, after the investigation and treatment of one set of philosophical problems, and before the treatment of another set. For, one might suggest, the foregoing sections are supposed to give substance to his remarks on the nature of philosophy; and these remarks on the nature of philosophy are in turn intended to illumine subsequent discussion. In fact, this is precisely the way things do proceed in TS 213 (the 'Big Typescript'). There a chapter *entitled* 'Philosophy' occurs not at the beginning, but after the treatment of a set of philosophical problems (and before the treatment of another set). What is more, many of Wittgenstein's remarks in this 'chapter' from *Philosophical Investigations* actually originate from that chapter 'Philosophy' in TS 213!

But it would be unfair to let too much ride on the remark from Von Savigny quoted above. For it expresses only his initial scepticism, and not the crux of the argument. The bulk of Von Savigny's article concerns his interpretation of the first part of this 'chapter', viz., §§89-115. And in his defence, none of the remarks in §§89-115 are derived from that chapter 'Philosophy' in TS 213. (It is in §§116-133 where we see a number of passages from TS 213.)

If restricted to §§89-115, Von Savigny's initial scepticism can be reformulated much more persuasively: §§89-115 in the *Investigations* follow Wittgenstein's sections on issues surrounding family resemblance and vagueness. Is there any reason to expect a methodological discussion (§§89-115) to be placed immediately after a discussion of family resemblance and vague concepts (§§65-88)? Even if Wittgenstein was no ordinary compiler of books, is this not a rather abrupt change of subject?

Admittedly, for a text such as *Philosophical Investigations*, abrupt changes of subject are almost inevitable. After all, it is a medium sized book with neither chapter nor section headings. Wittgenstein himself notes that he would 'sometimes make a sudden change, jumping from one topic to another' (*PI Preface*). But even so, §89 is still very puzzling if considered to be Wittgenstein's introduction to his 'chapter' on philosophy. For the opening sentence in §89 actually harks back to previous discussion: 'These considerations [viz., the discussion prior to §89] bring us up to the problem: In what sense is logic something sublime?' It is not so much *that* we seem to have an abrupt change of subject. Rather, it is this together with the fact that *Wittgenstein* suggests we do not.[4]

Von Savigny sets out to explain this. On his interpretation, there is no abrupt change of subject here, for Wittgenstein is not even introducing a methodological issue, let alone a whole 'chapter' on philosophy. To be sure, the question—'In what sense is logic something sublime?'—can be viewed as a kind of 'introduction' to a kind of 'chapter' (*PI* §§89-133). But according to Von Savigny, it is not regarding the stature, importance, or depth of Wittgenstein's philosophical investigations (nor the depth of the problems he investigates). On his view, this is a doubly mistaken interpretation. For by 'sublime' Wittgenstein does not mean 'deep', and with the word 'logic', Wittgenstein is not referring to his philosophical investigations. Rather, this question ought to be paraphrased, In what sense are the *rules* (the 'logic') governing word use in ordinary language *pure* ('sublime')?[5] It is not at all the sublimity qua importance (or depth) of philosophy/logical investigation that is in question here.

According to Von Savigny, therefore, there is no puzzle about the fact that §§89ff. follow Wittgenstein's discussion of family resemblance and vagueness. For the two sets of sections are closely related. There is no abrupt change of subject, but in fact substantial continuity. For obviously it is precisely the 'purity' of the rules governing our use of words (e.g., 'game', 'number', even 'chair') that is under consideration prior to §89. Indeed, the *main* issue in §§65-88 is whether ordinary word usage is generally governed by precise rules.

This argument of Von Savigny's *is* convincing. He notes that (1) §89 immediately follows the sections on family resemblance and vagueness; that (2) discussion of family resemblance and vagueness concerns the 'purity' of the rules governing word usage; and that (3) §89 harks back to this and reflects on it. On the face of it, these facts about the text cast reasonable doubt on the idea that §89 is about the nature of philosophy. Surely Wittgenstein would not first make an abrupt change of subject and then wrongly suggest that the foregoing is related to this new subject, viz., 'the nature of philosophy'. At best this would be extremely sloppy.

Von Savigny's point is sharpened by his scrutiny of the English translation for the opening sentence in §89. The translation is, 'These considerations *bring us up to* the problem ...' (my emphasis), which suggests a potentially new, though related topic is being introduced in §89. But Von Savigny proposes that a more natural rendering into English is 'These considerations *got us involved in* the problem'. (I am not going to argue with Von Savigny about nuances of the German language.) If §89 introduces a discussion of the nature of philosophy, how is it that this discussion *already began* in the sections on family resemblance and vagueness?

For myself, this is the interesting part of what Von Savigny means when he says that this 'chapter' is not about the nature of philosophy. I am persuaded that these sections are, in any event, not in any simple or obvious way 'on philosophy'. However, I also believe Von Savigny's interpretation is not quite right. For (to give a bit of my own initial scepticism) it is difficult to reconcile the bulk of §89 with the connotations on 'sublime' which Von Savigny underlines. Why does Wittgenstein respond to this question, about the sublimity of logic, in the way he does? ('For there seemed to pertain to logic a peculiar depth—a universal significance', etc. (*PI* §89)). This is the puzzling part of *Von Savigny's* reading of the opening sentence in §89, and I will come back to it in more detail later. To fix ideas, let me first outline generally my objection to Von Savigny's argument that §89 does not open a methodological discussion.

Von Savigny concludes that §89 is not the introduction to a discussion about the nature of philosophy. His argument for this is explicitly premised on (1) the (correct) observation of the close connection between this 'introduction' and the previous sections on family resemblance and vagueness. It is explicitly premised on (2) the (correct) observation that the sections on family resemblance and vagueness are about the nature of the rules governing ordinary language. There is an additional premise, this time implicit and, I will argue, incorrect. (3) If family resemblance and vagueness are issues concerning the nature of ordinary language, then Wittgenstein's discussion of them is *not* methodologically significant. Strictly speaking, it is only together with this (standard) reading of family resemblance and vagueness that (1) and (2) strongly suggest Von Savigny's reading of §§89ff. Von Savigny's reluctance to attach methodological significance to §§89ff. relies on the assumption that Wittgenstein's remarks on family resemblance and vagueness are merely remarks on the nature of ordinary language, i.e., that *they* have no direct methodological import.

Even more generally, therefore, my objection is that Von Savigny's argument relies on a false dichotomy. Must §§89ff. be exclusively either (1) a discussion of issues surrounding the nature of philosophy or (2) a discussion of the 'purity' of the rules governing our use of words? Can it not be both? Certainly the rules governing word use is central to Wittgenstein's conception of philosophy (cf. *PI* §124). So the nature, the 'purity' of these rules might bear crucially on the very nature of philosophy.

I will argue that Wittgenstein discusses family resemblance and vague concepts *primarily* for methodological reasons. These sections play an important preliminary role in Wittgenstein's explication of his method for treating philosophical puzzlement. If I am correct here, we are heavily indebted to Von Savigny for unearthing this discontinuity between (1) the standard interpretation of Wittgenstein's sections on resemblance and vagueness, and (2) the subsequent putative 'chapter' on philosophy.

'These considerations bring us up to the problem: In what sense is logic something sublime?' (*PI* §89). My suggestion is that, *even when* read as a question about the nature of philosophy (qua logical investigation), Wittgenstein's query is not a radical and misleading change of subject. The context of §§89-133 does not militate against reading Wittgenstein as proffering an account of the nature of philosophical puzzlement, and of his conception of its proper treatment. On the contrary, I will show that, if placed in a wider context in the *Investigations*, §§89-133 shed much light on Wittgenstein's conception of philosophy. I will argue that §§89-133 are, loosely speaking, *part* of Wittgenstein's metaphilosophical chapter, which is illuminatingly conceived of as encompassing §§*65*-133.

6.2 Family Resemblance and Vagueness

Baker and Hacker have emphasized that §§65-88 are relevant to philosophical problems surrounding the concepts of meaning and understanding a language.[6] For example, no account of understanding can be right when committed to the idea that every concept is understood (somehow) on the basis of properties common to all things that fall under it. With family resemblance concepts there are, by definition, no such properties. Moreover, acknowledgement of vagueness in language sits uncomfortably with the claim that to understand a concept means to be (somehow) familiar with the necessary and sufficient conditions for its application. For it is unclear how there could be any such conditions (*infra*).

I will not argue that §§65-88 have nothing to do with meaning and understanding. Yet at this stage in his argument, this is not the issue occupying Wittgenstein. For his *expressed* motive for introducing family resemblance is methodological. The notion of family resemblance is introduced, in §65, in response to the interlocutor's objection to Wittgenstein's treatment of those philosophical problems in §§1-64: 'You take the easy way out! You talk of all sorts of language-games, but have nowhere said what the essence of a language-game, and hence language, is' (*PI* §65). This is the interlocutor's objection to the *method* employed so far in §§1-64, viz., the method of employing imaginary linguistic settings. The objection is that this method does not bear on the important question of what the essence of language is.

In reply, Wittgenstein does not straightaway positively defend the language-game method. Rather, he explains his refusal to give an account of the essence of language, or even of the essence of some feature of language, such as the meaning of 'name'. The explanation is, quite simply, that 'these phenomena have no one thing in common which makes us use the same word for all' (ibid.).

To repeat, I do not here prejudge the question whether Wittgenstein's remarks in §§65-88 have repercussions for our conception of meaning and understanding, nor do I prejudge whether Wittgenstein explores these repercussions later in the text. I shall (very) briefly touch on these repercussions later in this chapter. My point is that the discussion is explicitly introduced in response to a criticism of the *language-game method.* Wittgenstein responds to his interlocutor's criticism that the language-game method has no point. It is quite as if the interlocutor is asking, What *are* you doing anyway, Wittgenstein? (And this is not an uncommon reader's response.)

As I see it, there is a very strong methodological theme running right from §65 through to the end of this 'chapter on philosophy' at §133. The theme is Wittgenstein's language-game method of treating philosophical problems. Where Von Savigny wants to significantly shrink the number of sections which are standardly conceived to be Wittgenstein's 'chapter on philosophy', I wish to significantly expand that number.

The discussion of family resemblance and vagueness ends in §88, and then §89 introduces a problem. As noted, Wittgenstein tells us that it is '*These* considerations that bring us up to the problem: In what sense is logic something sublime?' (*PI* §89, my emphasis). Since §89 immediately follows discussion of family resemblance and vagueness, surely by '*These* considerations' Wittgenstein is referring to that discussion. Just as he did in §65, Wittgenstein begins §89 by harking back to previous passages. In §89, Wittgenstein is now harking back to those sections on family resemblance and vagueness themselves.

Thus there is every reason to view Wittgenstein's sections on family resemblance and vagueness as interpolated between two methodological remarks. The discussion begins as a reply to criticism of the language-game method. (E.g., the method of imagining language-games which straightforwardly apply to Augustine's description of the workings of language, or Plato's description of the nature of 'elements'). That is to say, Wittgenstein defends his failure, or rather refusal, to inquire after the 'essence of language' (*PI* §§65ff.). For the logic of our language has no essence in this sense, and hence is not in this sense *pure*.

This defence then becomes a backdrop to consideration of the purity of logical *investigation* (*PI* §§89ff.). Moreover, Wittgenstein explicitly relates his discussion of vague concepts to the nature of philosophical puzzlement, remarking on the futility and blinding effect of the attempt to find either a complete or exact system of rules for a vague concept, e.g., 'language' or 'name' (see, e.g., *PI* §105, §107).

But how is the existence of family resemblance concepts methodologically significant? Wittgenstein's initial response to his interlocutor, even if correct, does not *yet* go to the heart of the objection to the language-game method. Let us grant with Wittgenstein's interlocutor—as Wittgenstein does grant in §92—that the 'essence', or function, or structure of language is an important concern for philosophy. Even supposing this, the claim that 'language' (or 'name') is a family resemblance concept does not obviously do much work to justify, or even explain, Wittgenstein's language-game method. So what if nothing is common to all that we call 'name' or 'language'? Does this render these concepts ineffable, so that we must resort to fabrication?

Wittgenstein does, however, draw a clear connection between philosophical puzzlement and family resemblance. Let us reflect back on Wittgenstein's treatment of Augustine's picture. Prior to §65, Wittgenstein often emphasizes that philosophical puzzlement may arise from trying to capture the use of 'name' in terms of *one* paradigm case. For example, in §9 Wittgenstein considers the different sorts of training that would likely accompany the ostensive teaching of different sorts of names (e.g., number, colour, and object words). His intention here is to emphasise different kinds of (use of) 'name'. In §38, Wittgenstein is quite explicit that this 'tendency to sublime the logic of our language' results from imposing uniformity on a family resemblance concept. For he suggests that the proper response to such a tendency is to note that 'we call very different things "names"; the term "name" is used to characterize many different kinds of use of a word ...' (*PI* §38). Since 'name' is a family resemblance concept, Wittgenstein refuses to inquire into it's essential features, for it has none, and the attempt leads to philosophical puzzlement. Instead, Wittgenstein employs imaginary language-games.

But again, why such a radical alternative? Let us grant to Wittgenstein that all the things we call 'name', 'language', or 'game', 'have no one thing in common which makes us use the same word for all' (*PI* §65). Even so, can we not propose, following Wittgenstein's interlocutor, that 'the concept of number is defined . . . as the logical sum of these individual interrelated concepts: cardinal numbers, rational numbers, real numbers, etc.' (*PI* §68), and likewise for concepts such as: name, language, or game? For if the concept of number or of name is a family resemblance concept, this means only that objects falling under it do so not because they share *one* common property (unless we are to call the disjunction of their properties a 'common property', which Wittgenstein rejects as trickery). Can we not still define—give the essence of—'number' by citing necessary and sufficient conditions for application?

'It need not be so', says Wittgenstein, for 'I *can* give the concept 'number' rigid limits in this way . . . . But I can also use it so that the extension of the concept is *not* closed by a frontier. And this is how we do use the word "game"' (ibid.)

Here we have an important transition: Wittgenstein is introducing a *new* complication into the discussion. In addition to being family resemblance, a concept might be vague. Wittgenstein claims that 'game' has vague boundaries, and he is certainly suggesting that this is true for other concepts as well, perhaps even 'number'. (He seems to be exploiting the fact that 'game' is a word not dragging a lot of philosophical baggage with it and, unlike 'name' or 'language', might be looked at without prejudice.) And obviously, vague concepts cannot be defined by a precise and comprehensive list of necessary and sufficient conditions for *correct* application. (Though one might still be inclined to insist that vague concepts *can* be defined by necessary and sufficient conditions for application *simpliciter*. More on this later.)

On my reading, one part of Wittgenstein's reply to his interlocutor is now evident. If a concept has vague boundaries, it makes no sense to inquire after essential characteristics. But the thrust of his interlocutor's objection remains unsolved. Why does this lead Wittgenstein to invoke *imaginary* language-games? What is Wittgenstein doing with this 'talk of all possible [*möglichen*] language games' (*PI* §65)? If there is vagueness in word usage, surely this can be described, and such a description will be a description of *actual* word usage.

A short, but not entirely satisfactory, answer is the importance Wittgenstein attaches to perspicuity. The type of description Wittgenstein sees as useful in philosophy is what he calls a 'perspicuous representation'. For 'A main source of our failure to understand is that we do not *command a clear view* of the use of our words.—Our grammar is lacking in this sort of perspicuity' (*PI* §122). Wittgenstein's method for attaining this sort of perspicuity has so far been to employ *clear and simple* language-games, which can only be fabricated, since the ordinary use of 'name' is neither clear nor simple.

However, this short answer is not satisfying, for it raises problems in its wake. If language is *not* 'clear and simple', then surely it is wrong to describe it in this way. What useful role could a clear and simple (and fabricated) language-game play in the description of the actual use of words? In what sense is the language-game method a 'logical investigation'? For,

> If someone were to draw a sharp boundary I could not acknowledge it as the one that I too always wanted to draw .... For I did not want to draw one at all. His concept can then be said to be not the same as mine, but akin to it. The kinship is that of two pictures, one of which consists of colour patches with vague contours, and the other of patches similarly shaped and distributed, but with clear contours .... Imagine having to sketch a sharply defined picture 'corresponding' to a blurred one. In the latter there is a blurred red rectangle: for it you put down a sharply defined one. Of course—several such sharply defined rect-

angles can be drawn to correspond to the indefinite one. (*PI* §§76ff.)

The goal of logical investigation is perspicuity, and the method of attaining perspicuity is by the employment of clear and simple language-games. Yet our *subject* of investigation is ordinary language, which is neither uniformly clear nor uniformly simple.

So are Wittgenstein's logical investigations even descriptive? Or, as Ramsey emphasized to Wittgenstein, is there after all a sense in which logic is 'a normative science' (*PI* §81)? It is these *methodological* issues which occupy Wittgenstein in §§89-133.

6.3 Logical Investigation

To impose a kind of false or misleading order upon the ordinary use of (e.g.) 'name' is, as Wittgenstein expresses it, to 'sublime the logic of our language' (*PI* §38). We have also seen that this idea of logic being sublime crops up at the close of his discussion of vague and family resemblance concepts: 'These considerations bring us up to the problem: In what sense is logic something sublime?' (*PI* §89). Von Savigny isolates two different connotations for the German word *Sublimes*. It could connote either 'pure' or 'elevated'/'divine'.[7]

In section §38 the connotation is quite clearly 'pure'. For the tendency under consideration there is the tendency to impose order on our concept of a name. Moreover, in §94 Wittgenstein explicitly identifies 'subliming' with 'purification': 'The tendency to assume a pure intermediary between the propositional *signs* and the facts. Or even to try to purify, to sublime, the signs themselves'.

This certainly suggests Savigny's preferred connotation: there is a clear identification of 'sublime' with 'purify' in §38 and §94. But in §89 the surroundings certainly conjure up notions like 'elevated' or 'divine':

> For there seemed to pertain to logic a peculiar depth—a universal significance. Logic lay, it seemed, at the bottom

> of all the sciences.—for logical investigation explores the nature of all things. It seeks to see to the bottom of things and is not meant to concern itself whether what actually happens is this or that.—It takes its rise, not from an interest in the facts of nature, nor from a need to grasp causal connexions: but from an urge to understand the basis, or essence, of everything empirical. (*PI* §89).

In §89 'sublime' is an adjective. In §38 and §94, 'sublime' is used as a verb, and refers to the attempt (or perhaps the result of that attempt) to give an account of the essence of some aspect of language, when that attempt is influenced by a primitive picture. In §38 and §94 the tendency to sublime the logic of language *results* in a kind of purified logical investigation (into the concept 'name') under the influence of one use (the concept of a 'name of an object'). Such an investigation, under the influence of a primitive picture, results in a kind of puri*fication* of the concepts under scrutiny. Such an investigation results in the *imposition* of order upon our concepts.

In §89 the 'problem' is in what sense logic (qua logical investigation) is *itself* something sublime. Wittgenstein seems to mean this question quite literally, i.e., in what sense of 'sublime' is logic (qua logical investigation) sublime? That is, Wittgenstein is cognizant that 'sublime' is an ambiguous word. For immediately following this question he isolates two different senses of 'sublime': (1) It seems more fundamental or elevated, or 'sublime': logic seems to have a peculiar depth, a universal significance. For it lies at the bottom of the sciences, concerning itself with the essence of everything empirical. In short, logical investigation is "deep".

It also seems sublime in a different sense: (2) it is *unclouded* by the dubitations of empirical investigation. Logical investigation is a purely *a priori* activity in that one does not need to hunt out new facts. Everything is, it seems, in *plain view*.

But how can something in plain view be *deep*? Or to put it another way: how can something obvious be profound? It is this which

Wittgenstein is referring to at the opening of §89 as 'the problem'. 'We want to *understand* something that is already in plain view. For *this* is what we seem in some sense not to understand' (*PI* §89). 'We feel as if we had to *penetrate* ["see through"] phenomena', see '[s]omething that lies *beneath* the surface ... which an analysis digs out' (*PI* §90, §92). Although logical investigation seems essentially an attempt to understand something that is already in plain view, when we try to engage in this sort of investigation we 'feel as if we had to *penetrate* phenomena'. In short, the problem is to answer the question, How can something lie beneath the surface (be deep), and yet already be in plain view?

This is a philosophical problem about the nature of logical investigation itself. This problem takes the form of a paradox: the logic of our language is in plain view, but in some sense we cannot see it. One might call this a 'metaphilosophical' problem, for as we will see momentarily, it is a problem which bears on the very methods and subject matter of philosophy itself.

Wittgenstein does not straightaway directly address *the* 'problem' itself. But in §89f. he does illuminate it by revealing his conception of the subject matter which the philosopher handles:

> Something we know when no one asks us, but no longer know when we are supposed to give an account of it, is something that we need to *remind* ourselves of. (And it is obviously something of which for some reason it is difficult to remind oneself.) .... We remind ourselves, that is to say, of the *kind of statement* that we make about phenomena. Thus Augustine recalls to mind the different statements that are made about the duration, past present or future, of events. (These are, of course, not *philosophical* statements about time, the past, the present and the future.)

It is these 'kinds of statement' about phenomena which puzzle us. It is not facts about time (or language) which puzzle us. Rather, puzzlement arises when we reflect on the sorts of things we might (and perhaps often do) say, e.g., claims made about the duration of events (or explanations given of the meaning of 'blue'). When we do this, it can happen that we wonder 'How is that *possible*' or 'How *can* that be'.[8]

Wittgenstein seems to explain his claim, that the subject matter of philosophy is 'kinds of statement', by reference to the character of Augustine's recollections. So apparently the subject matter which *Wittgenstein* handles is no different from traditional philosophy, in so far as Augustine's reflections on time are characteristic. (This is not to say that Wittgenstein handles this subject matter in a traditional way.) And since in this sense the *subject* of investigation is 'kinds of statement'—viz., those that puzzle us—Wittgenstein concludes that,

> Our investigation is *therefore* a grammatical one. Such an investigation sheds light on our *problem* by clearing misunderstandings away. Misunderstandings concerning the use of words, caused, among other things, by certain analogies between the forms of expression in different regions of language.—Some of them can be removed by substituting one form of expression for another; this may be called an "analysis" of our forms of expression, for the process is sometimes like one of taking a thing apart. (*PI* §90, my emphasis)

This is a *conclusion* (viz. that our investigation is a grammatical investigation) from some preceding premise(s). And since §90 is a continuation of a discussion of the 'problem' of the sublimity of logic, the premise(s) should lie somewhere between Wittgenstein's introduction to the 'problem' and his conclusion that he is engaged in a 'grammatical' investigation.

Only three paragraphs lie between the introduction and this conclusion, and if we read §§89-90 carefully it is not easy to overlook the premise that Wittgenstein appeals to here. Wittgenstein first observes that logic seems sublime, for it lay at the bottom of all the sciences, explores the nature of all things, and takes its rise from an urge to understand the essence of everything empirical. But logical investigation is not a process of *discovery*. It is rather a process of recollection, of a sort.

So far there is no obvious connection with the notion of grammatical investigation. But it is immediately forthcoming: what we remind ourselves of is 'kinds of statement'. It is immediately following this (emphasized) claim, viz., that the subject matter which the philosopher handles is 'kinds of statement', that Wittgenstein draws the conclusion that his investigation is grammatical. Wittgenstein's philosophical investigations are grammatical investigations because the subject matter under consideration is 'kinds of statement'.

On one conception of 'grammar', this conclusion is a straightforward consequence to draw from Wittgenstein's premise. On one conception, a 'grammar' is largely a *categorization* of aspects of language use.[9] A 'grammar', on this conception, is largely a categorization *for particular purposes.* (And what other sorts of useful categorizations are there?) A 'grammar' is a *representation*, and a more or less selective one. In this respect, therefore, grammatical inquiry is akin to map making (cf. *PI* §18), and has a normative element (cf. *PI* §81). If I want to make a road map I will probably be largely uninterested in representing elevation or population distribution (or, for that matter, the kind of grass growing in the ditch) and so on. What I want to represent is, among other things, the network of roads between different locales, and for this purpose there are an indefinite number of irrelevant features of geographical terrain.

Let us for the moment grant Wittgenstein's claim that the raw materials for logical investigation are those 'kinds of statement' that we make in non-philosophical contexts, yet puzzle us in philosophical contexts. For if we do, 'grammatical investigation' is a fairly innocuous label for an arrangement of that subject matter. 'Grammatical investigation', on the one hand, characterizes the raw material or subject matter which the philosopher handles: the kinds of things we say. On the other hand, it characterizes what the philosopher—including, as we saw in the previous chapter, the metaphysician (unwittingly)—does with this subject matter, viz., *arranges* it (cf. *PI* §92).

So far so good, perhaps. These considerations about grammatical investigation take some of the heat off the interlocutor's objection at §65. For the goal of Wittgenstein's grammatical investigations are not so much a correct and exhaustive tabulation of some facet of our ordinary language. More than this, Wittgenstein aspires to arrange and order aspects of word usage. Yet there is still no obvious connection with the employment of imaginary language-games. Moreover, so far we seem not to be doing justice to the prominence of *diagnosis* in Wittgenstein's philosophical investigations. Fortunately Wittgenstein continues to clarify his method:

Grammatical investigation is also likened to analysis. Grammatical investigation clears 'misunderstandings away, [sometimes] by substituting one form of expression for another' (*PI* §90). This activity 'may be called an "analysis" of our forms of expression, for the process is sometimes like one of taking a thing apart' (ibid.). So Wittgenstein's treatment of philosophical problems in the *Investigations*, and not just the method of the *Tractatus* (or, say, Russell's method of definite description), is a kind of analysis.

Looking back on Wittgenstein's treatment of 'name' discussed in previous chapters, the word 'analysis' does capture features of Wittgenstein's method. In Chapter Four above, I characterized Wittgenstein's *treatment of* the tendency to sublime 'name' very much like this 'taking apart' alluded to in §90. That is, Wittgenstein's method is to emphasize distinctions between proper names and common nouns blurred by certain forms of expression. Wittgenstein as it were 'takes apart' or 'analyzes' the word 'name'.

Yet in §91 Wittgenstein warns that this might make it 'look as if there were something like a final analysis of our forms of language, and so a *single* completely resolved form of every expression'. The warning continues from §91 to §102. In grammatical investigation we are often engaged in something like making our forms of expression more exact, e.g., marking the distinction between proper names and names explained by reference to samples; or relatedly, underlining different sorts of ostensive explanation. However, we are not striving after an ideal exactness or completeness. (Cf., we do not want a map which represents *every* aspect of some geographical terrain, whatever it might mean to speak of 'every aspect'.)

This whole methodological discussion follows Wittgenstein's consideration of family resemblance and vagueness in ordinary language. And as we have seen in previous chapters, the method demonstrated in the sections preceding considerations of vagueness and family resemblance consisted in diagnosing philosophical problems by means of tracing their roots to a primitive picture. A feature of this method is to highlight distinguishable differences in word usage, differences which Augustine's picture blurs, yet potentially assimilates. For instance, Wittgenstein imagines differences of training between ostensive explanations of object, colour, and number words. This is intended to highlight differences between our uses of these different sorts of names. Or again: the language-game of describing coloured squares in §48 was an attempt to dispel the simple picture of the way 'name' operates. In the coloured-square language-game, differences between a proper name and a colour name are brought into sharp relief.

Certainly there is a sense in which Wittgenstein's method is akin to analysis. It is as though one decomposes a facet of our use of 'name' into parts. And Wittgenstein's general warning in §91 would then be that there is no such thing, in this case, as a 'final analysis'. And 'no final analysis' would here mean that there is no definitive decomposition of our forms of expression—no definitive *arrangement* or categorization of these forms into 'kinds of statement'.

Consider again the coloured square language-game (*PI* §48). The distinction made, in our language, between (1) certain common nouns (i.e., properties we might predicate of objects) and (2) proper names (of objects), *can* be illuminated by comparing it with the type/token distinction in the language-game of §48. Yet clearly the comparison does not go all that far. For one thing, if under normal circumstances I employ a proper name twice in a particular sentence it does not thereby become a common noun. (But in the coloured square language-game, there is no such thing as employing a *proper* name twice in the same sentence.)

Rather, the coloured square language-game is an immensely simplified representation of the multifarious use of our concept 'name'. It is a representation that highlights two aspects of our concept of a name. The rationale for this representation is that it emphasizes differences that are blurred from view when represented with a form of expression derived from Augustine's picture. These differences, however, *do* find expression in the application of Augustine's picture, but in a misleading way. And it is this that can lead to the kinds of claims, about names and what they stand for, that were made in the *Tractatus* and, arguably, in the *Theaetetus*.

Thus 'analysis' is a word which nicely captures features of Wittgenstein's method. However, from the perspective of the problems we are addressing in this chapter, the comparison between Wittgenstein's method and analysis appears puzzling. A task of the philosopher is (1) the categorization and representation (at some level of exactness) of the ordinary use of words. On the other hand, Wittgenstein employs imaginary language-games for the (diagnostic) purpose of (2) analyzing our forms of expression. How are (1) and (2) related? Are they descriptions of the same activity?

On the face of it, it is unclear how they could be descriptions of the same activity. I compared a representation of aspects of ordinary language to making a map of a territory. But it would be unnatural to call either the representation or the activity of representing an *analysis* of that territory. We do not take anything apart, for a representation does not affect or change that which is represented (though certainly it can result in our seeing things differently). And even in the case where, say, I make a more exact 'map' than you, would this be at all comparable to analysis? Do I take apart *your* 'map' *or* the 'territory'? No. So what is an analysis of 'forms of expression', and how does it contribute to a representation of the rules governing the use of words?

The answer can be discerned, I believe, with a more careful look at the sections immediately following §89 (the 'Introduction'). It is here that family resemblance and vagueness connect up with meaning and understanding. It is also here that we shall (finally) find a satisfying answer to the interlocutor's initial puzzle in §65, viz., why Wittgenstein uses imaginary language-games, instead of describing actual word usage.

6.4 Doubt about the Application of a Rule

As Wittgenstein remarks in the *Blue Book*, 'In practice we very rarely use language as ... a calculus' (p. 25). In *Philosophical Investigations*, the discussion of family resemblance and vagueness is part of, or perhaps shades into a critical discussion of this potentially misleading comparison between ordinary languages and calculi. The early Wittgenstein was led to 'think that if anyone utters a sentence and *means* or *understands* it he is operating a calculus according to definite rules' (*PI* §81). As we shall see, the effect of a dogmatic application of the model of calculi to (all of) ordinary language is analogous in its effects to the dogmatic application of Augustine's picture diagnosed in §§1-64. The dogmatic application of the model of calculi results *not* in an erroneous account of the nature of our natural languages. It is not that the early Wittgenstein said that no word, not even 'game' is vague. The effect, rather, once again 'proves to be a superstition (*not* a mistake!), itself produced by grammatical illusions' (*PI* §110). Vagueness is not rejected, it is explained away.

§§65-80 are in large measure concerned with showing *that* ordinary language is unlike a calculus, i.e., that it is just wrong to say that the rules governing ordinary language are uniformly precise. But once again errors are not what fascinates Wittgenstein (cf. Chapter Three and Chapter Four *supra*). §§82-133 is Wittgenstein's diagnosis, and these sections are primarily concerned with two issues. First, *how* the comparison may mislead, and second, how this bears on the nature of logical inquiry itself. These two issues are intimately related for Wittgenstein. For, like the philosophical problems treated in §§1-64, so too is the early Wittgenstein's conception of logical investigation—i.e., his conception of the proper method in philosophy—based on a misunderstanding ultimately arising from a misleading comparison.

Initially, therefore, Wittgenstein draws our attention toward an erroneous though perfectly imaginable account of the rules governing the use of all words (*PI* §§65-80). For it is not that we *never* use language as a calculus, which is absurd, but that we *rarely* do (*BB*, p. 25). This discussion then shades into a diagnosis of how the mistake turns into a superstition (*PI* §§82ff., *passim*). The transition point between these two related discussions is §81:

> F. P. Ramsey once emphasized in conversation with me that logic was a 'normative science'. I do not know exactly what he had in mind, but it was doubtless closely related to what only dawned on me later: namely, that in philosophy we often *compare* the use of words with games and calculi which have fixed rules, but cannot say that someone who is using language *must* be playing such a game...
>
> All this, however, can only appear in the right light when one has attained greater clarity about the concepts of understanding, meaning, and thinking. For it will then also become clear what can lead us (and did lead me) to think that if anyone utters a sentences and *means* or *understands* it he is operating a calculus according to definite rules.

I cannot here give a full account of what it was that lead Wittgenstein to 'think that if anyone utters a sentence ... he is operating a calculus according to definite rules'. I cannot, that is to say, give a full account of what led Wittgenstein, and perhaps others, to dogmatically compare ordinary languages with calculi. This would take us deep into the rule-following discussion, the discussion of 'reading', 'rule-following' by machines, the concept of interpreting, the compulsion of a rule, etc. I will explore only the later Wittgenstein's understanding of how, in the *Tractatus*, vagueness is assimilated to this picture of meaning, thinking, and understanding. This suffices to relate the discussion of family resemblance and vagueness to the methodological remarks about logical investigation in §§89ff. This is sufficient, that is, to explain why there is a kind of 'chapter on philosophy' in *Philosophical Investigations.*

There are two different senses in which a calculus is more 'regulated' than ordinary language. (1) For calculi, the application of the rules are usually more *strictly circumscribed.* (2) For calculi, the rules are usually more *explicitly formulated.* Throughout §§65-88 Wittgenstein constantly flips between these two senses in which calculi are more regulated. But if we may cut up this 'chunk' of the *Investigations* into two pieces we can, I think, say that §§65-80 is concerned primarily with (1), and §§82-88 primarily with (2). (So, significantly, the transition point is again §81.) The difference between these two senses can be brought out more clearly by juxtaposing two of Wittgenstein's remarks about rules.[10]

> [1] I say "there is a chair". What if I go up to it, meaning to fetch it, and it suddenly disappears from sight?—"So it wasn't a chair, but some kind of illusion".—But in a few moments we see it again and are able to touch it and so on.—"So the chair was there after all and its disappearance was some kind of illusion".—But suppose that after a time it disappears again—or seems to disappear. What are we to say now? Have you rules ready for such cases—rules saying whether one may use the word "chair" to include this kind of thing? (*PI* §80)

Compare this with the following.

> [2] A rule stands there like a sign-post.—Does the sign-post leave no doubt open about the way I have to go? Does it shew which direction I am to take when I have passed it; whether along the road or the footpath, or cross-country? But where is it *said* which way I am to follow it ...? (*PI* §85, my emphasis)

With the example in §80, the point is surely that there are *no* rules, in any sense of the word, for the use of 'chair' which we can use to decide whether or not this kind of thing is to be called a chair. The application of 'chair' is not that strictly circumscribed. (However in this case, neither is any calculus *that* regulated. No logic book, e.g., has rules telling us whether a string of symbols that periodically vanishes is a well-formed formula. This does not affect the point.) If one can call this sort of case '*doubt* about the application of a rule', it is doubt of a sort which can only be removed by a decision.

With the example characterized in §85 (and here I am following Von Savigny), while there is certainly no explicitly formulated rule for how I am to follow the sign-post, nevertheless one is probably supposed to go along the road (or in the direction of the finger, or along a line of chalk marks, as the case may be). The sort of doubt here about the rules is something that *can* be removed by further explanation. (Wittgenstein's rule-following discussion later in the *Investigations* is a diagnosis of why one might be inclined, even here, to think that it cannot ever entirely be removed; or at any rate that the removal of doubt here would be a colossal achievement (cf. *PI* §§84, 87)).

Consider the propositional calculus. This is a fair example of a 'game' played according to definite rules. Truth-table computation, e.g., is a method by which we can decide if *any* well-formed sentence is a tautology, a contradiction, or is contingent. The application of the truth-table method is quite strictly circumscribed: there are not, relative to a wide range of normality conditions, any decisions to be made regarding its application. In this sense the rules are relatively fixed and precise. The rules governing the use of 'game' are not so fixed and precise. Is Russian Roulette to be called a game? On one occasion we might say that it is, on another that it is not; and on yet another occasion we might not know what to say.

The propositional calculus is also more regulated than many games in the second sense. It is unlike the game of tennis, for instance, in that most everything which could be called 'a move in the game' is justifiable by appeal to some explicitly formulated rule. This is exemplified by the convention, in derivations, of justifying *each* move in the proof by citing transformation rules and/or axioms. (When one is first taught logic derivations it is often not permitted, at first, even to 'skip' or 'combine' moves in a proof, e.g., to make a move without citing a rule, or which requires more than one rule.) Any move permitted by the rules is justifiable by appeal to *explicitly formulated* rules. This is not to say that a formal logician always cites these rules when she is deriving some proposition. But it is to say that she *can* cite these rules.

As I shall detail in a moment, Wittgenstein traces his earlier conception of logical investigation to the dogmatic assimilation of (1) vagueness in much of ordinary language to (2) how calculi are 'regulated' by rules in the two senses discussed above. This dogmatic assimilation can foster the idea that the 'analysis' which Wittgenstein engages in is really the uncovering of rules (somehow) underlying language use. Logical investigation, though legitimately conceived as an attempt 'to understand the essence of language—its function, its structure', can come to seem like an activity of uncovering something that lies *beneath* the surface (*PI* §92).

Wittgenstein is not rejecting this picture wholesale. This picture of logical investigation may perhaps even be illuminating in certain respects and circumstances. With the sign-post, if we are in doubt about whether we are supposed to follow the road, or the footpath, this is a doubt which can be removed with further explanation (e.g., by drawing chalk marks). This is a doubt which can be removed by a more *explicit formulation* of the rule (though it *might* raise another doubt). To give the rule more explicit formulation is precisely to make a form of expression more *exact*. The degree of exactness required in some particular case is contingent on what it takes to avert a misunderstanding in that particular case. The situation is likewise for many cases of explaining word meaning.

But what about the example of the disappearing chair? Can we make our *forms of expression* (of rules) more exact in this case? Certainly not by replacing our vague *concept* by a more 'perfect' one. To *replace* a (more or less) vague rule with a more exact rule is not to make our *expression* of the former more exact. This would be comparable to replacing a dull knife with a sharp one, and calling this an example of sharpening a knife. Apropos the disappearing chair, Wittgenstein asks, 'Have you rules ready for such cases—rules saying whether one may use the word "chair" to include this kind of thing?' Clearly the answer is "No". We do not have rules saying that we should include such a thing, nor rules saying that we should not include such a thing.

How, then, should this doubt in the face of vagueness be described? For various reasons, one can be tempted to describe this *sort* of 'doubt' such that 'there must be perfect order even in the vaguest sentence' (*PI* §98). The description turns on how we answer the question, What is it that *justifies* our 'doubt' in the face of the disappearing chair? Is it comparable to the case of an ill-formed string of symbols from the propositional calculus, such as '*p q* v'? Here our 'doubt' about the application of the truth-table method is justified by the formation rules. Since this string is not a well-formed formula, it does not fall under the rules of truth-table computation. Here the doubt about the application of a rule is justified by appeal to other rules—the formation rules. We could remove this doubt only by supplementing the rules of formation and (therefore) the rules for truth-table computation so as to include '*p q* v' (though it is unclear off-hand what purpose this new calculus might serve).

Is it on analogous grounds that we deny that we can apply the rules governing 'chair' to this disappearing chair? One might be (and the early Wittgenstein was) inclined to say that it *must* be so. One might be inclined to contend that, what this doubt reveals is that this case does not fall under the purview of the rules. That is to say, one might incline towards the idea that the vagueness here is not vagueness *in the rules.* The vagueness here, if we want to call it that, is merely that the rules governing the conditions under which something is *or is not* a chair do not decide the matter in this case. If we decided we wanted to affirm (or deny) that the disappearing chair really is a chair, this decision is not a decision to apply the rules in a certain way. What this decision amounts to is a decision to *supplement* our rules so that they, i.e., the rules governing 'chair', now apply to this doubtful case. Thus, after all, there is no vagueness in the rules themselves.

This distinction between vagueness *in the rules* and, for lack of a better expression, vagueness *not in the rules* can be elucidated differently. We might say, apropos the case of the disappearing chair, "Sure, our rules for the use of 'chair' may not determine that this is, *or* is not, to be called a 'chair'. But *that* this is not determined *is rule governed too*!" (So there is no vagueness in the rules.) This would then be comparable to the string of symbols '*p q* v' in the propositional calculus. The rules do not determine whether it is a tautology, contradiction, or contingent. Nevertheless, one might be tempted to say, it is only possible to *understand* the rules governing whether some well-formed formula is a tautology and so on, *if* we understand the conditions under which something is a well-formed formula. The rules must determine that it is not a well-formed formula, and hence that the truth-table method does not apply.

Is the situation analogous for the disappearing chair or for Russian Roulette? Does the removal of doubt about the application—and hence, does the application *simpliciter*—of *any* rule require either more explicit formulation (as in the sign-post), or a decision to supplement and/or change the rules (as in '*p q* v')? Is there no other possibility? Does this account of vagueness even do justice to the character of our doubt in the case of the disappearing chair? And even supposing it does, does this account do justice to *all* cases of vagueness, e.g., the vagueness of 'game' and the resulting doubt about whether Russian Roulette is to be called a 'game'? Suppose you call Russian Roulette a game and I object, saying "Russian Roulette, that's definitely *not* a game". If our disagreement is not about definitions, could our disagreement *only* come about as a result of our having a different concept of a game? And even supposing that *this* is still the correct explanation, what are we to say when this lack of agreement manifests itself in a *single* person?—

> What do I call the 'rule by which he proceeds'?—... [T]he one which he gives in reply if we ask him what his rules is?—But what if... the question brings none to light?—For he did indeed give me a definition when I asked him what he understood by "N", but he was prepared to withdraw and alter it.—So how am I to determine the rule according to which he is playing? He does not know it himself.—Or, to ask a better question: What meaning is the expression

> "the rule by which he proceeds" supposed to have left to it here? (*PI* §82)

That is to say, how is 'the rule by which he proceeds' best *described*. Is it a case of someone changing their concept of 'N' from one moment to the next? (Or perhaps discovering the rules which, unbeknownst, one is really following when they use 'N'?) The only thing that can be said at this point regarding these matters, is that the reasons for explaining things thus turn on misleading pictures of thinking, meaning and understanding. In the absence of these pictures (and other things being equal), we have every reason not to explain things thus.

Under the influence of these pictures, one might think that this possibility of introducing order into our knowledge of the word 'chair' is really the discovery of a process operating beneath the surface in ordinary language. That is, one might think that, by noting that we have no rules governing whether the disappearing 'chair' is really to be called a chair, we have done something analogous to what we *did* do when we noted that one is supposed to follow the sign-post in the direction of the finger. Somehow and somewhere this 'operating with signs' is at every step proceeding according to definite rules.[11] There must be rules governing the use of ordinary language which, though hidden, are clearly circumscribed. 'The strict and clear rules of the logical structure of propositions appear to us as something in the background—hidden in the medium of the understanding' (*PI* §102). Vagueness itself is okay but, one might want to say, 'it isn't a game, if there is some vagueness *in the rules*' (*PI* §100). But this conception is dogmatic: it does not arise from the examination of what people do when they employ the rules governing 'chair' or 'game'. Wittgenstein suggests looking at this from the perspective of a different comparison:

> Doesn't the analogy between language and games throw light here? We can easily imagine people amusing themselves in a field by playing with a ball so as to start various existing games, but playing many without finishing them

> and in between throwing the ball aimlessly into the air, chasing one another with the ball and bombarding one another for a joke and so on. And now someone says: The whole time they are playing a ball-game and following definite rules at every throw. (*PI* §83)

A dogmatic comparison between a calculus and ordinary language may make it look as though logical investigation, in so far as it resembles analysis, is a process of discovering the rules underlying our use of language. Wittgenstein contends, rather, that it is a kind of analysis of our *expression* of grammatical distinctions. The coloured square language-game in §48 is an attempt to put some order in our knowledge of the use of 'name'. But that order is one with a particular end in view (cf. *PI* §132), emphasizing—even exaggerating—differences between the employment of, on the one hand words like 'Excalibur', and on the other hand words like 'red'. And the reason that it is *this* order that is established is because it is precisely these aspects of our use of 'name' that were, in the *Tractatus*, sublimated to a primitive picture. The result was to identify the meaning of a name with its bearer (cf. *PI* §129).

Wittgenstein's 'philosophical analysis' is an analysis of the way in which these distinctions are expressed within the confines of a commitment to Augustine's picture. To appropriate the motto which opened this chapter: Wittgenstein aspires to represent our use of 'name' in such a way that, not just the highlights of Augustine's picture, but also its *shadows* are given prominence. The clarity this treatment introduces is the clarity requisite for the dissolution of a particular set of philosophical problems regarding meaning. 'To this end', remarks Wittgenstein, 'we shall constantly be giving prominence to distinctions which our ordinary forms of language easily make us overlook' (*PI* §132).

This analysis of our forms of expression is not a straightforward description of rules. Grammatical investigation is not merely, nor always, a process of discovering the rules governing word usage. Nor is it an activity of introducing order into our *use* of language. Rather, Wittgenstein's language-games introduce order into 'our *knowledge* of the use of language; an order with a particular end in view; one out of many possible orders; not *the* order' (*PI* §132, first emphasis mine). It is even misleading to characterize Wittgenstein's language-games as *descriptions* of language at all. Rather they are *contributions* to a description of the use of words. For 'Our clear and simple language-games . . . are rather set up as *objects of comparison* which are meant to throw light on the facts of our language by way not only of similarities, but also of dissimilarities' (*PI* §130).

Thus there is a sense in which Wittgenstein's language-games stand on the same level as the primitive pictures they are intended to displace. Both are 'methods of representation'; both are often intended to capture the *same* grammatical distinctions. The difference lies in the form in which these distinctions are expressed. Thus the important issue is neither the correctness nor incorrectness of these representations, although obviously at some level correctness is relevant. Wittgenstein does not just pull his language-games out of a hat. But for any of Wittgenstein's language-games as much as for Augustine's picture, the more important question is, 'Is this representation *useful* [*Darstellung brauchbar*] or not' (*PI* §3, my emphasis). Does it 'surround the working of language with a haze'? Has it misled?

There is also a sense in which Wittgenstein's employment of language-games is vitally different from the employment of Augustine's picture diagnosed in *Philosophical Investigations*. The difference is that Wittgenstein's language-games are not dogmatically applied. Wittgenstein does not predicate of ordinary language what lies in his imaginary language-games. Rather, he wants only to impress upon the reader the possibility of a comparison (*PI* §104). 'For we can avoid ineptness or emptiness in our assertions only by presenting the model as what it is, as an object of comparison—as, so to speak, a measuring-rod; not as a preconceived idea to which reality *must* correspond. (The dogmatism into which we fall so easily in doing philosophy.)' (*PI* §131, cf. *PI* §81).

Notes

1. Eike Von Savigny, 'No Chapter "On Philosophy" in the *Philosophical Investigations*' (Metaphilosophy, Vol. 22, No. 4, Oct. 1991).
2. Ibid., p. 319.
3. Ibid., p. 307.
4. It is also possible that it is merely harking back to his discussion of ideal languages: i.e., calculi which have fixed rules (*PI* §§82-88). This however itself builds on the discussion of vagueness. The 'Introduction' at §89 then, is at least indirectly related to the discussion of family resemblance and vagueness. More on this later.
5. Von Savigny, op. cit., p. 309.
6. Baker and Hacker, *Understanding and Meaning*, p. 320.
7. Von Savigny, op. cit., p. 309.
8. Cf. F. Waismann, 'How I see philosophy', in A. J. Ayer, *Logical Positivism* (Macmillan, 1959), especially pp. 348ff.
9. This conception of the activities of the grammarian is illuminatingly discussed in P. H. Matthews' *Generative Grammar and Linguistic Competence* (Allen & Unwin, 1979).
10. I am indebted to Von Savigny's article (op. cit.) for marking these two distinguishable features of Wittgenstein's discussion of rules.
11. Many interesting things could be said regarding Wittgenstein's treatment of this conception of rule-following. The discussion of 'reading' (*PI* 156ff.), for instance, shows how this conception can spring from reflection on the reading of a beginner, and more generally on introspecting the processes that go on *in foro interno* when one follows rules. Or again, how it can arise from a comparison with 'rule-following' as performed by a machine; or dogmatic comparison between the notion of 'following a rule' and the concept of 'interpreting', and so on.

Bibliography

Anscombe, G. E. M., *An Introduction to Wittgenstein's Tractatus* (Hutchinson & CO., 1959).

Arrington, R., and Glock, H.-J., *Philosophical Investigations: Text and Context* (Blackwell, 1991).

Ayer, A. J., *Language Truth and Logic* (Dover, 1952).

Ayer, A. J., *Logical Positivism* (MacMillan, 1959).

Baker, G. P., *Wittgenstein, Frege and the Vienna Circle* (Blackwell, 1988).

Baker, G. P., 'Section 122: neglected aspects', in Arrington and Glock, 1991.

Baker, G. P. and Hacker, P. M. S., *Understanding and Meaning* (Blackwell, 1980).

Baker, G. P. and Hacker, P. M. S., *Language Sense and Nonsense* (Blackwell, 1984).

Baker, G. P. and Hacker, P. M. S., 'Wittgenstein and the Vienna Circle: the exaltation and deposition of ostensive definition', repr. in Shanker, 1986.

Budd, M., *Wittgenstein's Philosophy of Psychology* (Routledge, 1993).

Crary, A., and Read, R., *The New Wittgenstein* (Routledge, 2000).

Diamond, Cora, *The Realistic Spirit: Wittgenstein, Philosophy, and the Mind* (MIT Press, 1991).

Fann, K. T., *Wittgenstein's Conception of Philosophy* (University of California Press, 1969).

Frege, G., *Basic Laws of Arithmetic*, trans. by M. Furth (University of California Press, 1964).

Frege, G., 'Conceptual Notation', in Bynum, T.W. (tr.), *Conceptual Notation and related articles* (Clarendon, 1972).
Frege, G., 'Function and Concept', repr. in Geach, 1952.
Geach, P. and Black, M. (eds.), *Translation from the Philosophical Writings of Gottlob Frege* (Blackwell, 1952).
Glock, H. J., 'Section 128: no theses in philosophy', in Arrington, 1991.
Goldfarb, W. D., 'I want you to bring me a slab: remarks on the opening sections of the *Philosophical Investigations*' (*Synthese* 56, 1983).
Hacker, P. M. S., 'Laying the Ghost of the *Tractatus*', in Shanker, 1986.
Hacker, P. M. S., *Insight and Illusion: themes in the philosophy of Wittgenstein* (Clarendon, 1986).
Hacker, P. M. S., *Wittgenstein: Meaning and Mind* (Blackwell, 1990).
Hacker, P. M. S., *Wittgenstein's Place in Twentieth-Century Analytic Philosophy* (Blackwell, 1996).
Harris, J. F., 'Language, language-games and ostensive definition' in *Synthese* (69, pp. 41-49, 1986).
Harris, R., *The Language-Makers* (Duckworth, 1980).
Harris, R., *The Language Myth* (Duckworth, 1981).
Harris, R. and Taylor, T. J., *Landmarks in Linguistic Thought* (Routledge, 1989).
Johnston, P., *Wittgenstein and Moral Philosophy* (Routledge, 1989).
Kenny, A. J. P., *Wittgenstein* (Harvard University Press, 1973).
Kenny, A. J. P., 'Wittgenstein's early philosophy of mind', in I. Block (ed.), *Perspectives on the Philosophy of Wittgenstein* (Blackwell, 1981).
Kenny, A. J. P., 'The Ghost of the *Tractatus*', in Shanker, 1986.
Matthews, P. H., *Generative Grammar and Linguistic Competence* (Allen & Unwin, 1979).
Malcolm, N., *Nothing is Hidden*, (Blackwell, 1986).
Monk, R., *Ludwig Wittgenstein, The Duty of Genius* (Vintage, 1991).
Ring, M., 'Baker and Hacker on section one of the *Philosophical Investigations*' (*Philosophical Investigations* 8: 3 July 1985).
Russell, B., *The Problems of Philosophy* (Oxford University Press, 1912).
Russell, B., *Logic and Knowledge* (Unwin Hyman, 1956).
Russell, B., 'On Denoting', in Russell, 1956.

Russell, B., *The Philosophy of Logical Atomism*, in Russell, 1956.

Russell, B., *Theory of Knowledge* (Allan and Unwin, 1984).

Shanker, S. (ed.), *Ludwig Wittgenstein: Critical Assessments* (Croon Helm, 1986).

Taylor, T. J., *Mutual Misunderstandings: Skepticism and the theorizing of language and interpretation* (Duke University Press, 1992).

Von Savigny, E., 'No chapter "on philosophy" in *Philosophical Investigations*' (*Metaphilosophy* 22: No. 4, Oct. 1991).

Waismann, F., *Wittgenstein and the Vienna Circle: conversations recorded by Fredrick Waismann*, ed. B. F. McGuinness (Blackwell, 1979).

Waismann, F., *Principles of Linguistic Philosophy*, edited by R. Harre (Macmillan, 1965).

Waismann, F., *How I see Philosophy*, edited by R. Harre (Macmillan, 1968).

Winch, P., *The Idea of a Social Science* (Humanities Press, 1958).

Wittgenstein, L., *Notebooks 1914-1916*, ed. G. H. von Wright and G. E. M. Anscombe (Blackwell, 1979).

Wittgenstein, L, *Tractatus Logico-Philosophicus*, tr. D. F. Pears and B. F. McGuinness (Routledge and Kegan Paul, 1961).

Wittgenstein, L., *Tractatus Logico-Philosophicus*, tr. C. K. Ogden (Routledge, 1990).

Wittgenstein, L., 'Philosophy: Sections 86-93 of the so-called "Big Typescript" (TS 213)' in J. C. Klagge and A. Nordmann, *Ludwig Wittgenstein: Philosophical Occasions* (Hacket, 1993).

Wittgenstein, L., *The Blue and Brown Books* (Blackwell, 1958).

Wittgenstein, L., *Philosophical Remarks* (Blackwell, 1975).

Wittgenstein, L., *Philosophical Grammar* (Blackwell, 1974).

Wittgenstein, L., TS 220, unpublished typescript deposited in the Bodlian Library, Oxford.

Wittgenstein, L., *Philosophical Investigations* (Blackwell, 1958).

Wittgenstein, L., *Remarks on the Foundations of Mathematics*, Third edition (Blackwell, 1978).

Wittgenstein, L., 'Cause and effect: intuitive awareness', repr. in J. C. Klagge and A. Nordmann, *Ludwig Wittgenstein: Philosophical Occasions* (Hacket, 1993).

Wittgenstein, L., *Remarks on the Philosophy of Psychology Vol. I* (Blackwell, 1980).

Wittgenstein, L., *On Certainty* (Blackwell, 1969).

Wittgenstein, L., *Culture and Value* (Blackwell, 1980).

Wittgenstein, L., *Lectures and Conversations*, ed. Cyril Barrett (Blackwell, 1970).

Wittgenstein, L, *Wittgenstein's Lectures, Cambridge, 1932-35* (University of Chicago Press, 1979).

Index

Wittgenstein-Studien

Im Auftrag der Internationalen Ludwig Wittgenstein Gesellschaft
herausgegeben von Wilhelm Lütterfelds, Stefan Majetschak,
Richard Raatzsch und Wilhelm Vossenkuhl

Band 1 Katalin Neumer (Hrsg.): Das Verstehen des Anderen. 2000.

Band 2 Gianluigi Oliveri (ed.): From the *Tractatus* to the *Tractatus* and Other Essays. 2001.

Band 3 Wilhelm Lütterfelds / Djavid Salehi (Hrsg.): „Wir können uns nicht in sie finden". Probleme interkultureller Verständigung und Kooperation. 2001.

Band 4 Sebastian Lalla: Solipsismus bei Ludwig Wittgenstein. Eine Studie zum Früh- und Spätwerk. 2002.

Band 5 Fritz Breithaupt / Richard Raatzsch / Bettina Kremberg (eds.): Goethe and Wittgenstein. Seeing the World's Unity in its Variety. 2003.

Band 6 Jesús Padilla-Gálvez (ed.): Wittgenstein, from a New Point of View. 2003.

Band 7 Wilhelm Lütterfelds (Hrsg.): Erinnerung an Wittgenstein. „*kein* Sehen in die Vergangenheit"? 2004.

Band 8 Wilhelm Lütterfelds / Thomas Mohrs / Djavid Salehi (Hrsg.): *Die Welt ist meine Welt.* Globalisierung als Bedrohung und Bewahrung kultureller Identität? 2004.

Band 9 Mathias Iven: Rand und Wittgenstein. Versuch einer Annäherung. 2004.

Band 10 Katalin Neumer (Hrsg.): Traditionen Wittgensteins. 2004.

Band 11 Wilhelm Lütterfelds / Thomas Mohrs (Hrsg.): Wahr *oder* tolerant? Religiöse Sprachspiele und die Problematik ihrer globalen Koexistenz. 2005.

Band 12 Stefan Majetschak (Hrsg.): Wittgensteins ‚große Maschinenschrift'. Untersuchungen zum philosophischen Ort des *Big Typescripts* (TS 213) im Werk Ludwig Wittgensteins. 2006.

Band 13 Jesús Padilla-Gálvez (Hrsg.): Idealismus und sprachanalytische Philosophie. 2007.

Band 14 Dale Lindskog: Diagnosis and Dissolution. From Augustine's Picture to Wittgenstein's Picture Theory. 2007.

www.peterlang.de